PENGUIN CLASSICS

CATILINE'S WAR, THE JUGURTHINE WAR, HISTORIES

GAIUS SALLUSTIUS CRISPUS (86–?35 BC) was born in the Sabine highlands of central Italy. In 52 he became tribune of the plebs but two years later he was expelled from the senate for alleged immorality. Rehabilitated through the influence of Julius Caesar, whom he served in the civil war which broke out in 49, he became praetor in 46 and was installed by Caesar as governor of Africa Nova. Sallust is said to have enriched himself so blatantly at the expense of the province that it was only through Caesar's protection (possibly secured by an enormous bribe) that he was saved from a second condemnation. He used his wealth to acquire a mansion and parkland at Rome, the famous Horti Sallustiani, later the property of the Roman emperors.

After Caesar's death in 44 Sallust retired from public life and turned to the writing of history. His monographs on the conspiracy of Catiline and the Jugurthine War, written in the late 40s, both survive intact; his *Histories*, covering the post-Sullan period from 78 onwards, survive only in fragments. His literary achievement was such that he became one of the most influential and popular historians in antiquity and beyond.

A. J. WOODMAN is Basil L. Gildersleeve Professor of Classics at the University of Virginia. He has published numerous books on the interpretation of Latin literature, especially in the fields of Augustan poetry and early imperial historical writing: his *Rhetoric in Classical Historiography* helped to transform our understanding of how the ancient historians wrote history. He has co-authored commentaries on Books 3 and 4 of Tacitus' *Annals*, and a monograph *Latin Historians*. Most recently he has produced *Tacitus Reviewed*, co-edited *Traditions and Contexts in the Poetry of Horace* and published an award-winning translation of Tacitus' *Annals*.

SALLUST

Catiline's War, The Jugurthine War, Histories

Translated with an Introduction and Notes by
A. J. WOODMAN

PENGUIN BOOKS

PENGUIN CLASSICS

Published by the Penguin Group
Penguin Books Ltd, 80 Strand, London WC2R 0RL, England
Penguin Group (USA) Inc., 375 Hudson Street, New York, New York 10014, USA
Penguin Group (Canada), 90 Eglinton Avenue East, Suite 700, Toronto, Ontario, Canada M4P 2Y3
(a division of Pearson Penguin Canada Inc.)
Penguin Ireland, 25 St Stephen's Green, Dublin 2, Ireland
(a division of Penguin Books Ltd)
Penguin Group (Australia), 250 Camberwell Road, Camberwell, Victoria 3124, Australia
(a division of Pearson Australia Group Pty Ltd)
Penguin Books India Pvt Ltd, 11 Community Centre, Panchsheel Park, New Delhi – 110 017, India
Penguin Group (NZ), 67 Apollo Drive, Rosedale, North Shore 0632, New Zealand
(a division of Pearson New Zealand Ltd)
Penguin Books (South Africa) (Pty) Ltd, 24 Sturdee Avenue, Rosebank, Johannesburg 2196, South Africa

Penguin Books Ltd, Registered Offices: 80 Strand, London WC2R 0RL, England

www.penguin.com

Published in Penguin Books 2007
8

Translation, Introduction and Notes copyright © A. J. Woodman, 2007
All rights reserved

The moral right of the editor has been asserted

Set in 10.25/12.25 pt PostScript Adobe Sabon
Typeset by Rowland Phototypesetting Ltd, Bury St Edmunds, Suffolk
Printed in England by Clays Ltd, St Ives plc

ISBN: 978-0-140-44948-5

www.greenpenguin.co.uk

Contents

Preface

'Of course there is nothing inherently superior about a translation which is made directly from the original language.' These
words were written very recently by a distinguished Professor
of Classics at Oxford. To illustrate his point he referred to a
celebrated twentieth-century poet whose 'ignorance of their
original languages never inhibited him from translating poets
who wrote in Russian, Czech, Hungarian, Serbo-Croat, German, Spanish or Portuguese'. Some readers may wonder how
one can 'translate' a language without knowing it; but the
answer appears to be that such 'translators' simply rewrite in
their own words one or more of the English translations which
are already available. This is not a doctrine or a practice to
which I subscribe: whatever the resulting product of such a
process may be, it is not a translation, and to pretend otherwise
is simply to collude in the fraudulent misuse of language which
now corrupts every aspect of modern life. Readers of this new
translation of Sallust may like to know from the start that it is
indeed 'made directly from the original language'.

In the middle of the last century, when it was taken for
granted that classical scholars would know Latin and Greek
and that a degree in Classics would involve the study of the
classical languages, the general fashion was to translate classical
texts into a modern and readable English idiom. But times and
fashions change. Contemporary readers of translated classical
texts are more diverse than forty or fifty years ago, and their
requirements are different. In those days it was no doubt acceptable for a translator to memorize half a page of a Greek or
Latin text and then to produce a fluent, if not necessarily exact,

English translation from memory. At least one Penguin Classic was indeed produced in this way. But those who study classical civilization or ancient history at university, and who know no ancient language, constitute a significant proportion of those who now read translated classical texts, and they require a more scholarly and accurate product than is possible by this eccentric method. I have kept these potential readers firmly in mind, while not, I hope, alienating those who simply desire to read about some of the more famous episodes of Roman republican history as narrated by the first Roman historian of whom complete works have survived.

My translation of Sallust keeps closer to the original Latin than do the other translations which are currently available. I have gone some way in attempting to reproduce Sallust's word order and sentence structure, in the hope that readers will get at least some idea of the 'feel' of the original Latin; and as a general rule I have tried to avoid producing an 'edited' translation, relegating explanatory matter to endnotes. Nevertheless, whenever adherence to Sallust's Latin seemed incompatible with readability, I usually decided in favour of the latter.

I am extremely grateful to those whom I have consulted on individual points or who have kindly agreed to offer me comments or suggestions on the Introduction or translation or both: P. J. E. Kershaw, C. S. Kraus, C. B. Krebs, J. F. Lazenby, J. E. Lendon, D. S. Levene, D. P. Nelis, J. J. Paterson, C. B. R. Pelling, Z. Stamatopoulou and T. P. Wiseman. I owe an especial debt of gratitude to Robin Seager, who is certainly not to be blamed for any errors that may remain. But my greatest debt, as usual, is to Ronald Martin, who has subjected the entire book to his critical gaze and provided me with copious corrections and observations.

If readers detect any mistakes or misconceptions, especially in the translation, I hope most sincerely that they will bring them to my attention.

Abbreviations and References

Cat.	Sallust, *Catiline's War*
Hist.	Sallust, *Histories*
Jug.	Sallust, *The Jugurthine War*
OCD	*Oxford Classical Dictionary*, ed. S. Hornblower and A. Spawforth (rev. 3rd edn, 2003)
OCT	Oxford Classical Text(s)
OLD	*Oxford Latin Dictionary*
Summers	W. C. Summers, *C. Sallusti Crispi Iugurtha* (1902)
Syme, *Sallust*	R. Syme, *Sallust* (2nd edn, 2002)

It is conventional to refer to the text of *Catiline's War* and *The Jugurthine War* by chapter number and section number (e.g. *Cat.* 10.1, *Jug.* 41.2–3), and to the text of *Histories* by book number and fragment number (and, where appropriate, section number): e.g. *Hist.* 1.12, *Hist.* 4.69.5–6. Since I have sometimes re-paragraphed or re-punctuated the text, chapter numbers and section numbers do not always coincide with the beginnings of paragraphs or sentences respectively.

My numbering of the fragments of Sallust's *Histories* follows that of L. D. Reynolds in the OCT (1991), who in turn retains that of the standard edition by B. Maurenbrecher (1891–3); but often I have added secondarily the numbering introduced by P. McGushin in his *Sallust: The Histories*, 2 vols. (1992–4).

Roman names are given in full in the Index; forenames (*praenomina*) are often abbreviated in the text and Notes. Unqualified dates are BC.

Introduction

Sallust is the earliest Roman historian of whom complete works survive, although his last and reputedly most significant work, the *Histories*, has survived only in fragments.[1] His narratives disclose archaic words and forms, and the manuscript tradition preserves old-fashioned spellings. From this combination of circumstances one might infer that Sallust is an 'early' author, yet such an inference would be misleading. When Sallust began writing *Catiline's War* in the very late 40s, Pompey, Caesar and Cicero – defining figures of the Roman republic – had already been murdered; Brutus and Cassius, the killers of Caesar, were probably also dead; the poet Catullus, an exact contemporary, had died a dozen or so years before. Within scarcely more than a decade the centuries-old republic would have ended and been replaced by the autocratic system of government which we know as 'the Roman empire'. Sallust is very much an author of the *fin de siècle*.

Sallust

Catiline's War deals with the famous conspiracy which was mounted in 63 by L. Sergius Catilina and thwarted by Cicero, consul in that year.[2] The monograph is assumed to be Sallust's first work from the fact that it begins with an unusually long preface which skilfully incorporates both a defence of the writing of history (*Cat.* 1.1–3.2, 8.2–4) and an account of the author's own political career (3.3–4.2). This account is highly schematized: it includes no details of dates or of offices held but is presented in sweeping, moral terms such as those used to describe contemporary public life (3.3 'instead of propriety, self-denial and prowess, it was daring, bribery and avarice which were thriving'). In particular, Sallust portrays himself implicitly as a second Plato, whose career is described in the so-called *Seventh Letter* which goes under Plato's name. Sallust's entire autobiographical section is structured by and imitated from that letter. Thus, for example, he begins with the statement that 'as a young adolescent (like many others) I was initially swept by enthusiasm towards politics, and there many things were against me' (3.3), which is strikingly reminiscent of Plato's opening: 'As a young man once, I felt the same as many others: I thought that, as soon as I became independent, I would embark immediately on political life in the city. And certain developments in the affairs of the city confronted me, as follows . . .' (324b–c). Since Plato was widely regarded in the ancient world as almost divine,[3] this was a shrewd move on Sallust's part; but it also calls into question the very nature of his apparently veristic writing, since external evidence suggests that his career had been blighted by ignominy and that he turned to historiography only because he had been compelled to leave politics.

St Jerome tells us that Gaius Sallustius Crispus (to give him his full Latin name) was born in the town of Amiternum, now a series of ruins in the western foothills of the Gran Sasso, in 86.[4] The Social War, in which Rome's Italian allies (*socii*) fought against Rome and won Roman citizenship for themselves, had ended in the previous year. It is possible that, when he left his home town for a career in the capital, Sallust as a non-Roman will have encountered a similar kind of condescension as that illustrated by Catiline's jibe against Cicero: 'an immigrant citizen of the City of Rome' (*Cat.* 31.7).[5] It is known that Sallust was tribune of the plebs in 52, having almost certainly held the quaestorship, which brought with it entry to the senate, three years earlier. Since no previous member of his family had entered the senate, Sallust was a 'new man' (*nouus homo*) according to one of the definitions current in the late republic.[6]

Sallust was beginning his career halfway through a decade whose political chaos is impossible to describe with any concision. In a standard account it is summed up as 'the anarchy of the fifties, when violence, compounded by bribery, made the city of Rome at times unmanageable, and basic constitutional functions, such as elections, could not be performed.'[7] Having survived satisfactorily for most of the second century, the relatively orderly system of government headed annually by pairs of consuls had begun to take on a different character when Gaius Marius, an earlier 'new man', held the consulship six times between the years 107 and 100 and thereby inaugurated an age of power-seeking which was dominated by the successive figures of Sulla, Pompey and Caesar. At the same time the radical proposals of the Gracchi brothers during their tribunates towards the end of the second century (133 and 123–122), to say nothing of their violent deaths at the hands of the 'guilty' nobility (*Jug.* 42.1), had brought about a developing polarization in political life between those who supported the status quo (the *optimates*) and those who did not (the *populares*). These combined pressures culminated in the outbreak of civil war in 49 when Julius Caesar crossed the River Rubicon in northern Italy with his army.

Dio Cassius, a historian of Roman affairs who wrote in Greek in the early third century AD, tells us (40.63.4) that in 50 Sallust had been expelled from the senate: whether the opprobrious conduct alleged against him was true is not known. At any rate, after unfortunate experiences of command with Caesarian legions in Illyricum in 49 and in Campania in 47, Sallust returned to the senate as praetor in 46, having presumably regained his status through the influence of Caesar, whose magistracies in the years 49–46 included his second and third consulships (48, 46) and three appointments as dictator (49–46). The anonymous author of *The African War*, which represents itself as a continuation of Caesar's own commentaries on the Gallic War and the Civil War,[8] says that as praetor Sallust performed valuable and successful service in Africa, where Caesar's forces were engaged in fighting the Pompeians (*African War* 8, 34). After the Pompeians were defeated at the battle of Thapsus in that year, one of their leaders, M. Porcius Cato, famously committed suicide in the African town of Utica;

Sallust for his part was rewarded when Caesar appointed him proconsul (governor) of the province of Africa Nova (New Africa) which Caesar had created in the aftermath of his victory (*African War* 97).

We are told by Dio (43.9.2–3) that Sallust capitalized on his appointment by plundering the province to amass a personal fortune. On his return to Rome, presumably in 45, he faced charges of extortion, which, along with the possibility of a second expulsion from the senate, he escaped, perhaps through having bribed Caesar to exert his influence once again (cf. Dio 43.47.4). In March of the following year Caesar was murdered, and it was no doubt round about this time that Sallust, as he tells us himself at the start of *Catiline's War*, 'determined that the remainder of my life must be kept far away from politics' (4.1), another statement indebted to Plato's *Seventh Letter* (325a 'I withdrew myself from the evils of the time').

Catiline's War

Sallust says that he was drawn to the subject of the Catilinarian conspiracy because he thought it 'especially deserving of recollection owing to the newness of the crime and of its danger' (*Cat.* 4.4 *memorabile . . . nouitate*). Such statements are conventional and in line with rhetorical theory, according to which a speaker would have an attentive audience if in his exordium he promised to speak 'about important, novel or unusual matters, or about those which relate to the commonwealth'.[9] Yet despite the novelty of the crime at the time, Cicero, who as consul in 63 was the principal protagonist in the affair apart from Catiline himself, had already ensured that the conspiracy was recollected on as many occasions as possible. He published his four speeches *Against Catiline* (the 'Catilinarians'); he wrote two historical accounts of the episode, one in Latin and one in Greek, and an epic poem as well (Cicero was reputed to be the best poet of his day); his exile in 58 was precipitated by, and therefore revived memories of, decisions he had taken at the time of the conspiracy; and to the end of his life he maintained that he had been the saviour of his country. There was certainly no need for any third party to bring to public attention the definitive event of Cicero's career.

Yet that, characteristically, was precisely what Cicero wanted. In 55 he wrote to Lucius Lucceius, a friend who was also a historian, begging him to write a monograph on the conspiracy (*Letters to Friends* 5.12):

I have often tried to raise the following matter with you in person, only to be prevented by an embarrassment which is uncharacteristic of my metropolitan temperament. However, now that we're apart, I feel bold enough to broach the subject. After all, a letter can't blush.

You won't believe how much I want you to celebrate my name in your writings – a quite justifiable desire, in my opinion. I know you've often indicated that this was your intention, but please excuse my impatience. You see, I always had high hopes of your particular kind of writing, but it has now exceeded my expectations and taken me by storm: I've a burning desire for my achievements to be entrusted to your monumental works as quickly as possible. It's not just that I can hope for immortality by being remembered by posterity: I also want to enjoy while I'm still alive the authority which only your work can provide – your seal of approval coupled with your literary distinction.

It's true that even as I write I am only too well aware of the pressure you're under from the material which you have embarked upon and already arranged. But, as I see that you've almost finished your account of the Italian and Civil Wars, and you told me yourself that you've made a start on the remaining period, I don't want to miss the opportunity of asking you to consider this question. Would you prefer to incorporate my story into that remaining period or ... deal with the Catilinarian conspiracy separately from the wars with foreign enemies? As far as my reputation is concerned, I don't see that it makes much difference either way; but I'm frankly impatient and don't want you to wait till you reach the appropriate point in your continuous narrative: I'd much rather you got down to the period of the *cause célèbre* straight away and on its own terms. In addition, if you give your undivided attention to a single theme and a single personality, I can envisage even now the greater scope for rich elaboration.

Of course I'm well aware how disgracefully I'm behaving: having first landed you with this considerable responsibility (though you can always plead other engagements and turn me down), I'm now demanding elaborate treatment. What if you don't think my achievements deserve elaboration? Still, once the limits of decency have been passed, one should be well and truly shameless. So I repeat – elaborate my activities even against your better judgement, and in the process disregard the laws of historiography: that prejudice, which you discussed quite beautifully in one or other of your prefaces ... well, please don't suppress it if it nudges you strongly in my favour, but simply let your affection for me take a degree of precedence over the truth.

If I can persuade you to take on the responsibility, I'm sure you'll find that the material will bring out the best in your fluent artistry. For it seems to me that a modest volume could be compiled if you start with the beginning of the conspiracy and end with my return from exile . . .[10]

Despite the hilarious brilliance of this letter, there is no evidence that Lucceius ever wrote the monograph for which Cicero asked. Instead it was Sallust who, roughly a dozen or so years later, wrote his own monograph on the Catilinarian conspiracy.

Sallust could be forgiven for thinking that his potential readers had been exposed to quite enough of Cicero's view of the affair and that they were entitled to be given a different perspective. It is true that at one point Sallust describes Cicero as 'the best of consuls' (*Cat.* 43.1), yet this is the very description which, when used by Brutus in a pamphlet on Cato, Cicero himself in a letter to his friend Atticus regarded as faint praise: 'He thinks he is giving me a fine tribute when he calls me "the best of consuls". Which of my enemies has spoken more emptily?' (Cicero, *Letters to Atticus* 12.21.1). Sallust mentions none of Cicero's four Catilinarian speeches except the first, which he describes as 'sparkling' (31.6 *luculentam*): this is the very same adjective that Cicero himself, in the same letter to

Atticus, had used to describe the speech which Cato delivered on 5 December. Moreover, since in Sallust's account it is that speech of Cato (52.2–36) which has displaced Cicero's Fourth Catilinarian, it seems that Sallust is attributing to Cato an importance which Cicero had denied when writing to Atticus.[11] Equally pointed is the fact that Cicero's famous opening address to Catiline in the First Catilinarian ('For how long, then, Catiline, will you exploit our endurance?') is placed by Sallust in the mouth of the villain himself when addressing his fellow conspirators (*Cat.* 20.9 'For how long, then, will you endure these things, most courageous of men?').

Sallust's apparently ambiguous treatment of Cicero contrasts strongly with his treatments of Julius Caesar, his likely bene-factor, and Cato, the future suicide of Utica (see above). After giving us his versions of the speeches which Caesar and Cato delivered in the senatorial debate on 5 December (*Cat.* 51 and 52 respectively), Sallust digresses to provide a contrasting sketch of both individuals (53.2–54.6), whom he describes as the only 'two men of mighty prowess' in his lifetime (53.6 *ingenti uirtute . . . uiri duo*), standing out amidst contemporary degeneracy (53.5). The story of Rome's political and moral decline indeed provides the essential background and impetus for *Catiline's War*. Decline is the subject of a digression in the body of the work (36.5–39.4) and its history is traced in the preface (5.9–16.5), where Catiline is presented as its worst and quintessential symptom (cf. 14.1). The same line seems to have been taken by Catullus roughly ten years before. In Poem 64, his 'miniature epic' on the theme of marriage, Catullus con-cludes with a denunciation of contemporary civil war (lines 397–402):

> But after Earth was stained with crime unspeakable
> And all evicted Justice from their greedy thoughts,
> Brothers poured the blood of brothers on their hands,
> Sons no longer grieved when parents passed away,
> Father prayed for death of son in his first youth
> So as freely to possess the bloom of a new bride.[12]

The last two lines are understood to allude to the allegation, repeated by Sallust (15.2), that Catiline had killed his son in order to be free to marry Aurelia Orestilla, who feared the prospect of acquiring a grown-up stepson. An alternative allegation, that Catiline married his own daughter, features in the description of great criminals in hell which Virgil attributes to the Sibyl in the *Aeneid* (6.623, cf. 8.668–9).[13] In *Catiline's War* Sallust was responding to, and helping to form, a tradition in which Catiline was the epitome of evil.[14]

The Jugurthine War

In his second monograph, an account of the Jugurthine War in Africa (111–105) which he is thought to have been writing in the years 41–40, Sallust both sharpened and extended the picture of Rome's decline (*Jug.* 5.1–2):

> The war I am about to write is that which the Roman people waged with Jugurtha, king of the Numidians, first because it was great and fierce and of only sporadic success, then because that was the first time that the haughtiness of the nobility was confronted – and the latter struggle convulsed everything, divine and human alike, and advanced to such a point of derangement that only war and the devastation of Italy put an end to the citizens' passions.

The first of these reasons centres on Jugurtha himself, who is introduced at the start of the work as a man of *uirtus* or 'prowess' (6.2, 7.2, 8.1, 9.2–3, 10.2, 10.8) and appears almost as an ideal young Roman. But eventual contact with actual Romans and their assurances of Roman corruption (8.1 'at Rome everything was for sale') have the effect of corrupting him. He becomes 'the embodiment of disorder', and his 'manipulation of and affinity with money, deceit, motion, and delay enable him to defer any final settlement, either diplomatic or military, of the war with Rome.'[15] At the same time, however, the Romans gradually learn from Jugurtha how to beat him at his own game (48.1 'Jugurtha . . . recognized that he was being assailed by his own techniques'), and in due course he is double-crossed and betrayed to them (113.3–7). The work thus describes two complementary 'learning curves', each indebted to the other.

Sallust's second reason for choosing to write about the Jugurthine War was that it witnessed the first confrontation with the nobility, whose families had traditionally monopolized the magistracies in general and the consulship in particular. The confrontation was undertaken by Gaius Marius, the 'new man' whose service in the war against Jugurtha acted as a springboard for his first consulship in 107. The monograph ends with Marius as consul for the second time at the very beginning of 104 and with the statement that 'at that time the hopes and resources of the community rested in him'.[16] But we have already been told that in due course Marius would be 'toppled by ambition' (*Jug.* 63.6): after five further consulships, the last of them in 86, he was merely the first in a line of dominant personalities who led up to the civil wars of Sallust's own day. As in *Catiline's War*, the downward course of Roman politics is the subject of a powerful digression embedded in the work (*Jug.* 41–2).[17] The digression, however, seems to offer a rather more complicated analysis than that implied by the preface: Sallust makes it clear that Marius' confrontation with the nobility had been anticipated by that of the Gracchi. While the Gracchi 'had begun to champion the freedom of the plebs and to expose the crimes of the few', the nobility for its part 'confronted the actions of the Gracchi' (42.1). Perhaps Sallust resolved the apparent discrepancy to his own satisfaction by the fact that Marius was successful where the Gracchi failed. Yet, whatever the case, the antagonistic division of Roman society into 'the people' and 'the nobility' maintains in the digression a theme which Sallust had already introduced in his earlier work (*Jug.* 41.5; cf. *Cat.* 38.3–4).

Though modern scholars seem agreed that the Jugurthine War deserves the prominence and significance which Sallust attributes to it, there is perhaps more to his choice of subject than allowed in his preface. The modern phrase 'out of Africa' has as its immediate derivation the elder Pliny, who in his

Natural History referred to 'the common Greek expression that Africa always brings something new' (8.42 *uulgare Graeciae dictum, semper aliquid noui Africam adferre*); but Pliny in his turn was borrowing from Aristotle, who in two works refers to the 'proverb' that Africa is always the source of something new (*Hist. Anim.* 606b20, *Gen. Anim.* 746b7). Though the saying is almost unattested between the times of Aristotle (384–322) and Pliny (AD 23/24–79), its evidently proverbial nature suggests the likelihood that it remained current in popular thought. As has been pointed out,[18] the term 'new' in the proverb connotes 'something strange, even undesirable' or 'revolutionary', and this is exactly how Jugurtha's Numidians are described by Sallust: *Jug.* 46.3 'Metellus had already found out from earlier experience that the Numidian race was untrustworthy, of volatile temperament, and hungry for revolution [*nouarum rerum auidum*]', 66.2 'Their public – as is usually the case, especially with Numidians – was of volatile disposition, rebellious and disaffected, desirous of revolution [*cupidum nouarum rerum*] and hostile to rest and inactivity'. It seems likely that, in choosing to write a monograph about the Jugurthine War, Sallust was at least to some degree taking advantage of popular perceptions of Africa. It was Africa, after all, that had produced Hannibal, whose very name is described as ill-omened by Sallust's younger contemporary, Horace (*Epode* 16.8); and Hannibal's Carthage had been destroyed only thirty-five years before the Jugurthine War started: it was easy to talk of Carthage and Jugurtha in the same breath, as Horace again attests (*Epode* 9.23–6), and indeed Carthage features quite prominently in *The Jugurthine War*. In short, Africa was a country of intrinsic and abiding interest.

And there is of course a further consideration: the historian was no doubt drawn to the subject because of his own personal experiences in Africa in 46–45. But this raises a paradox. Sallust provides an extended description of Africa in chapters 17–19 which he introduces as follows: 'The context seems to demand that I explain briefly the layout of Africa and touch on the peoples with whom our dealings were those of war or friendship.' The modern reader might assume at this point that

Sallust's topographical description would be informed by his governorship of Africa Nova, but not only is there no reference to autopsy in the whole of the account, but, as Sir Ronald Syme remarked, no benefit seems to have derived from the author's presence in the country.[19] Instead, Sallust appeals to a translation of Punic books which were said to have been written by King Hiempsal, a nephew of Jugurtha (17.7). Since modern historians capitalize on autopsy and often go to great lengths to survey personally the land or countryside in which past events have taken place, Sallust's apparent difference strikes today's readers as exceptionally curious and invites questions on the nature of Sallust's historical narratives.

Writing History

When the Catilinarian conspiracy took place in 63, Sallust will have been in his early twenties and, when he came to write his account of it two decades later, he was doubtless able to recall at least the outline of events. At *Cat.* 48.9 he tells us of an allegation which he himself heard Crassus make against Cicero, and at *Cat.* 53.6 he refers to Cato and Julius Caesar as having had their careers within living memory. These are welcome and interesting moments but they are the only traces of autopsy in the work. From where did he derive his information for the bulk of the monograph? When Sallust describes the city of Rome as 'reinforced by watches' against fire (*Cat.* 32.1 *uigiliis munitam*), the expression occurs nowhere else in Latin except in the First Catilinarian, where Cicero had used it to describe the town of Praeneste (1.8 *uigiliis ... munitam*). It therefore seems certain that Sallust had read Cicero on the conspiracy, as one would expect, and that the great frequency of other, far more commonplace, phrases shared by the two authors are to be explained in terms of this reading. Indeed, the phraseological parallels between Sallust and Cicero are such as to demonstrate that the historian was extremely familiar with Cicero's Catilinarian speeches.[20] He was probably also familiar with the other speeches in which Cicero alludes to the conspiracy; with the pamphlet which, as we have seen, Brutus wrote in praise of the younger Cato; and with the *Anticato* which Caesar wrote in response to the latter. But need Sallust have had any more material than these? Is it possible that he approached his first work of history in the manner of a modern writer who, about to compose a monograph on the Second World War, has little else at his disposal except an intimate familiarity with the better known speeches of Winston Churchill?

In 55, the year in which it is assumed that Sallust held the quaestorship, Cicero set out his views on how history should be written (*On the Orator* 2.63–4):

The actual superstructure [of historiography] consists of content and style. It is in the nature of content, on the one hand, that you require a chronological order of events and topographical descriptions; and also that you need – since in the treatment of important and memorable achievements the reader expects (i) intentions, (ii) the events themselves, and (iii) consequences – in the case of (i) to indicate whether you approve of the intentions, of (ii) to reveal not only what was said or done but also in what manner, and of (iii) to explain all the reasons, whether they be of chance or intelligence or impetuousness, and also to give not only the achievements of any famous protagonist but also his life and character. The nature of style and type of discourse, on the other hand, require amplitude and mobility, with a slow and regular fluency and without any of the roughness and prickliness associated with the law-courts. – These points are both numerous and important, but do you see them covered by any of the rules to be found in books entitled *Art of Rhetoric*?

Many readers of this passage have believed that 'Cicero is not expressly advocating a type of historical exposition different from that commonly employed by modern political historians'.[21] Yet Cicero has merely transferred to the writing of history the precise same elements which went into writing the so-called 'narrative' section of a forensic speech: for example, the 'chronological order of events' (*ordinem temporum*), which perhaps sounds particularly appropriate for history, is simply

lifted, and in the same words, from his *On Invention*, an earlier
work on rhetorical theory (1.29 *temporum ordo*). It is significant that Cicero discusses this element under the heading of
'invention' (*inuentio*), a technique in which rhetoricians were
expected to be expert and which Cicero defines as 'the devising
of matter true or lifelike which will make a case appear convincing' (*On Invention* 1.9). In an adversarial system of justice,
such as that practised in ancient Rome, it was inevitable that
the defence and prosecution would say different things. If the
defence alleged that the chronological order of events was ABC,
the prosecution might argue that the order was ACB. One of
these might be true; but, if so, it follows that the other cannot
be true. Cicero's point is simply that, whether or not one of
them is true, both must at least be 'convincing'.[22]

Sallust in his works gives every impression that he has taken
to heart Cicero's advice on the content of historiography. The
prominence which he gives to describing the personalities of
Catiline (*Cat.* 5.1–8) and Jugurtha (*Jug.* 6.1), for example,
seems to correspond to Cicero's insistence on the importance
of giving character sketches of 'any famous protagonist'. However, since the significance of Cicero's discussion lies in his
transfer of rhetorical techniques to historiography, the same
underlying assumptions are transferred also. This immediately
makes sense of Sallust's account of Africa: it was more important that his 'topographical description' (to use Cicero's phrase)
be convincing than that it should claim to be autoptic. 'A man's
own experience', remarked Syme, 'might seem less attractive
and convincing than what stood in literary tradition, guaranteed by time and famous names.'[23] Likewise the autobiographical introduction to *Catiline's War*. Sallust hoped to present to
his readers a convincing case, made stronger by the allusions to
Plato; the fact that his career (as far as one can tell) had been
quite different from his self-presentation is neither here nor
there: collective memory is very often partial and of limited
duration, and the testimony even of eyewitnesses is notoriously
prone to error. Sallust had every reason for confidence that his
self-presentation would be found acceptable; and by the same

token he stood every chance of convincing his readers with his account of a conspiracy which had taken place more than twenty years in the past.

The Jugurthine War was an even more distant event, having begun over seventy years before and now beyond the memory of anyone alive. Scholars have naturally debated what sources Sallust might have used to compile a narrative which in the Latin of the Oxford Classical Text is almost one hundred pages long. The latest commentator on the work, after a largely negative appraisal of the investigations of other scholars, concludes that Sallust himself 'has made a distinctive contribution to the finished work'.[24] This seems to be a euphemistic way of saying that, while the historian no doubt had some kind of framework with which to operate, a significant portion of his narrative was the product of 'invention'. It mattered little whether a given battle took place at X or Y, since each site had a strange local name and no one in Rome would be any the wiser. Nor need Sallust know the details of the battle, since invention 'is simply the "discovery" of what requires to be said in a given situation, the implied theory being that this is somehow already "there" though latent'.[25] There were various stereotypical ways in which battles and other events were expected to be described ('historiographical motifs'[26]); and, if a historian exhausted the possibilities of these, there were always other sources of material to which to resort. At one point during the treacherous events at the town of Vaga, Sallust tells us that 'women and boys on the roofs of buildings vied with one another in casting down rocks and other things with which their location provided them' (*Jug.* 67.1). The vivid detail has the ring of truth precisely because it is a vivid detail; but Sallust has simply adapted a well known moment from the Peloponnesian War as described by the Greek historian Thucydides (2.4.2), when at Plataea in 431 'the women and slaves on the house-tops . . . kept pelting them with stones and tiles'.

Histories

The events of Sallust's last work, the *Histories*, fall between the periods of the Catilinarian conspiracy and the Jugurthine War. His starting point was 78, the year in which Sulla, the former dictator, died; it is also likely to have been the year with which another historian, L. Cornelius Sisenna, brought his (now fragmentary) history of the two preceding decades to a close: if so, Sallust was following the well established convention of starting his work where a previous historian had stopped.[27] The incomplete survival of Sallust's *Histories* – his 'lost masterpiece', in the words of Syme[28] – makes it difficult to know whether he intended to stop at the latest attested date, namely 67, in Book 5. Of the original work, chance has preserved more than 550 items which are conventionally called 'fragments'.[29] These range from single words or phrases (1.151 = 137 'rustic', 131 = 118 'to Corycus', 132 = 119 'at Corycus') through longer phrases or complete sentences (2.17 = 18 'moderate in all other respects except domination', 1.120 = 104 'he took up position in a scrubby and copsy valley') to four whole speeches (1.55 = 48, 77 = 67, 2.47 = 44, 3.48 = 34) and two letters (2.98 = 82, 4.69 = 67).

The problems posed by a fragmentary work are clear and grave.[30] Some 'fragments' are not fragments at all but references or allusions embedded in the text of another author: when Servius, the fourth-century AD commentator on Virgil, says that 'Pelorus is a promontory on Sicily, called, according to Sallust, after the burial of Hannibal's helmsman there' (*Hist.* 4.29 = 25), it is impossible to tell which of these words, if any, is actually Sallustian. Very often a quoting source, even if transmitting an item genuinely Sallustian, does not identify the book of the *Histories* to which the item belongs: if the item is of a reasonable length and/or contains some historical information, an editor may be able to guess roughly where to place it in Sallust's presumed storyline, but often the item is preserved (by a grammarian or scholar of similar interests) for its linguistic curiosity, as with the otherwise unexampled 'scrubby' (*uirgultus*) above, and in such cases an editor will usually have no clue as to the original context of the fragment. Occasionally the ancients' practice of literary allusion will help. A fragment of the *Histories* ('in the manner of a cavalry battle, resorting to and giving up the rear') was placed by Maurenbrecher in the context of fighting in Armenia in Book 4 (75) but by McGushin amongst the 'Fragments of Uncertain Reference' (29). A baffling sentence of Tacitus' *Annals* on fighting in Armenia (6.35.1 'in the manner of a cavalry battle, it was the turn of front and rear') is recognized to allude to this fragment and is followed shortly afterwards by an explanation of the name Mesopotamia (6.37.3 'the plains which, encircled as they are by the renowned streams of the Euphrates and Tigris, have received the name of Mesopotamia'). Since Sallust also has a fragment which explains the same name and which is placed by both editors in Book 4 (77 = 74 'which [the rivers], going in different directions, are widely separated by an area of many miles in the middle; and the land which is surrounded by them is called Mesopotamia'), it seems highly likely that Maurenbrecher was right to place both fragments in close proximity to each other.

In view of the very considerable difficulties presented by the *Histories*, I have translated only the following: (a) some fragments of the preface, (b) a few other more lengthy fragments and (c) the speeches and letters. Sallust's preface was an extremely important text, seemingly more pessimistic than even the monographs, and influencing the preface of Rome's next great historian, Livy. The lengthier fragments are those which require the least in terms of editorial intervention and emendation. The speeches and letters choose themselves, as being both substantial and complete. But it is in the nature of fragments to pose problems. For example, it can be inferred that, either as part of an extended preface or in the form of a digressive flashback, Sallust provided a survey of the previous decades (1.19–53 = 16–46), just as Thucydides had done with his famous 'Pentecontaetia' or summary of the years 480–430 (1.89–119). Then, after the interposition of a single fragment (1.54 = 47), we are given the very first speech (1.55 = 48), which is an attack by the consul of 78, M. Aemilius Lepidus, on Sulla: Lepidus speaks as though Sulla were still in power, yet he had resigned the dictatorship three years before and may even have been dead when the speech which Sallust puts into Lepidus' mouth was delivered.[31] This anomaly is inexplicable without the original narrative context in which the speech was placed.

Style and Attitude

When Sallust died, probably in 35, he left to his great-nephew and adopted son the Horti Sallustiani, the great gardens in Rome which he had evidently acquired and developed with the ill-gotten gains from his year's governorship in Africa.[32] Meanwhile his historiographical legacy attracted widespread comment for the style in which it was written. A younger contemporary – the brilliant but curmudgeonly Asinius Pollio, general, politician, playwright and historian – wrote a book in which he criticized Sallust's writings as being 'smudged with an excessive affectation of archaic words' and alleged that Sallust had employed a research assistant, Ateius Philologus, to make 'a collection of archaisms and figures of speech' for him. These criticisms did not, however, prevent Pollio from employing the same assistant himself when Sallust died, whereupon Ateius advised Pollio (somewhat paradoxically, in the circumstances) that in his own history he should employ 'familiar, unassuming and literal speech and should avoid in particular Sallust's obscurity and boldness in metaphors'.[33] Sallust's attraction to archaisms became notorious and doubtless explains the numerous references to his 'stealing' words from the elder Cato, great-grandfather of the Cato who committed suicide at Utica (see above). Consul in 195 and famously censor in 184, Cato was author of the *Origines*, the first work of history to be written in Latin. One author, now anonymous, directed at Sallust the following couplet: 'You frequent thief of words from ancient Cato, / Crispus, composer of the Jugurthine history.'[34]

Besides metaphors and archaisms, the third feature of Sallust's style to provoke special comment was his brevity: 'that famous Sallustian brevity and abrupt form of speech', as it was described by Quintilian (4.2.45), who elsewhere refers to 'that famously immortal rapidity of Sallust' (10.1.102). During Sallust's lifetime, according to the younger Seneca, 'chopped-off sentences and expressions ending before one expects and an obscure brevity were the fashion' (*Letters* 114.17). Seneca's observation, which indicates that the Sallustian manner was very different from the smooth and ample style recommended for historiography by Cicero (see above), is strikingly reminiscent of what was said about Thucydides by Dionysius of Halicarnassus, the Augustan critic and historian (*On Thucydides* 24):

> The most conspicuous and characteristic features of the author are his efforts to express the largest number of things in the smallest number of words, and to compress a number of thoughts into one, and his tendency to leave his hearer still expecting to hear something more, all of which things produce a brevity that lacks clarity.[35]

Elsewhere in the same chapter Dionysius refers to Thucydides' 'rapidity' and says that 'in his choice of words he preferred a diction that was metaphorical, obscure, archaic and alien instead of that which was in common use and familiar'. In the light of this evidence it is scarcely surprising that ancient readers and critics regarded Sallust as 'a second Thucydides':[36] the distinguishing features of Sallust's style exactly mirror those perceived to characterize his Greek predecessor.

Style was not the only aspect of Thucydides' work on which Dionysius commented. In his *Letter to Pompey* (3) Dionysius wrote as follows:

> Thucydides starts with the incipient decline of the Greek world, something which should not have been done by a Greek and an Athenian . . . In his malice he finds the overt causes of the war in the conduct of his own city . . . The attitude . . . of Thucydides is severe and harsh and proves that he had a grudge against his native country because of his exile. He recites a catalogue of her mistakes, going into them in minute detail.

Sallust for his part had provided, over the course of his three works, an almost continuous account of the years 111 to 63 which entitled him to be called 'the historian of decline and fall'.[37] He was regarded in antiquity as one who 'criticizes his own times and attacks their failings'.[38] We can never know whether Sallust's disaffected history of Rome's decline was motivated by his twice-enforced exile from politics or whether he saw the circumstances of his own life as reflecting those of Thucydides, who had been exiled from his native Athens in 424; but there can be no doubt that the disaffection of his narratives is brilliantly complemented by his adaptation of the harsh and contorted style of Thucydides.

Sallust's historical writing seems to have had an immediate impact, the influence of the *Histories* being detectable in such works of the thirties as Horace's epode on the civil war (16) and the preface to Livy's history.[39] But by the end of that decade the nature of Roman politics had changed completely and for ever: the victory of Octavian (the future Augustus) over Mark Antony at the battle of Actium in 31 ensured that henceforward Rome would be ruled by an autocrat. Obsessively preoccupied with the security of their own position, successive Roman emperors did not welcome historians whose narratives betrayed signs of the disillusion and disaffection with which Sallust was identified. The result was that, though in the late first century AD the epigrammatist Martial (14.191) and the critic Quintilian (2.5.19) could express a high opinion of Sallust, for more than a hundred years no historian of imperial Rome chose to imitate Sallust as his principal model. It was therefore a radical and shocking moment when, early in the second century AD, Tacitus began his *Annals* with the words 'The City of Rome from its inception was held by kings'. The sentence is an allusion to the words with which Sallust had introduced his flashback of early Roman history in *Catiline's War* (6.1): '*The City of Rome . . . was* founded and *held* initially by the Trojans'. In classical literature such opening allusions function as a kind of 'code', alerting readers to the tradition in which a writer is working: readers will have inferred that Tacitus' narrative of the years AD 14 to 68 would in no sense be conformist but would interact with, and capitalize on, the subversive style and voice of Sallust.

The Translation

It should go without saying that it is impossible to reproduce in an English translation the features of Sallust's style which attracted such attention in antiquity. There is simply no way in which a different language can achieve the effect of 'chopped-off sentences and expressions ending before one expects and an obscure brevity'; all I have attempted to do in this new translation is to keep as close to the Latin as is consistent with readability.[40] There is one difficulty in particular which is worth noting. Sallust's analysis of Rome's social, political and moral decline is seen against an idealized system of values and concepts which is especially evident in the prefaces to his works. The key concept in this system is *uirtus*, which may be defined as 'the functioning of *ingenium* to achieve *egregia facinora*, and thus to win *gloria*, through *bonae artes*'.[41] This definition poses problems, however, because most of the terms involved are very difficult to render in English. The word *uirtus* itself is notoriously hard to translate. It is etymologically connected with *uir*, which means 'man': hence the first of the dictionary definitions as 'The qualities typical of a true man, manly spirit, resolution, valour, steadfastness'; since the Romans expected a *uir* to display *uirtus* especially on the battlefield, the word also means 'courage' or 'bravery' and is thus synonymous with *fortitudo*. However, the word also comes to have a wider meaning: 'excellence of character or mind, worth' and 'moral excellence, virtue, goodness' (and hence close in meaning to *probitas*).[42] Wherever possible in the translation I have tried to render *uirtus* by the English noun 'prowess', which means both 'manly courage' and 'exceptional ability or talent';[43] but at *Hist.* 1.55.15 I have felt obliged to be more explicit in using the phrase 'manly prowess' because the speaker, as is clear from the context, is emphasizing the derivation of the word from *uir*.

It may be inferred from the above that in my opinion one

should attempt to render each Latin word by the same English word wherever possible; but, although this is especially desirable when an author is as rigorous in his argumentation as is Sallust in the prefaces to his monographs, a term such as *ingenium* cannot always be translated consistently. *ingenium* means 'disposition, temperament' (as at *Cat.* 5.1) and 'intellect, talent' (as at *Cat.* 2.1): from the latter it comes to be used in a concrete way, 'talent' in the sense of 'a man of talent' (as at *Cat.* 8.4); but the word is also used of the 'inherent quality or character' of things (such as that of a particular countryside, e.g. *Hist.* 3.28 = 15).[44] *facinus* (derived from *facio*, 'I do') means 'a deed': hence one can equally well say *mala facinora* ('wicked deeds', as at *Cat.* 16.1) or *egregia facinora* ('exceptional deeds', as at *Jug.* 2.2). Yet *facinus* by Sallust's time had also come to mean 'a crime' and even, in an extended sense, 'a criminal' (as at *Cat.* 14.1).[45] Sallust, who likes alliteration, several times combines the word with *flagitium*, for which my usual translation is 'outrage'; but clearly it is impossible both to be consistent with these translations and to reproduce the alliteration (hence 'depravity or deed' for *flagitium aut facinus* at *Cat.* 14.2). *bonae artes* constitutes a set phrase meaning 'cultural pursuits, liberal studies'; but *ars* can also mean 'a quality, practice' (as at *Cat.* 2.9) and, in the plural, 'behaviour' (thus equivalent to *mores*, also plural).[46] Though Sallust was not the first author to use *bonae artes* in a moral sense, his repeated deployment of the phrase (e.g. *Jug.* 1.3) is one of his distinguishing characteristics.

Sallust's 'politico-social terminology', as it has been called,[47] is by no means restricted to the cases mentioned so far. *ambitio*, for example, is another key term and, 'though a fault, was nevertheless closer to prowess [*uirtus*]' (*Cat.* 11.1). In this passage *ambitio* seems directly equivalent to the English 'ambition'; but the word is derived from the verb *ambire*, 'to go round', and can also mean 'canvassing (for votes)' and hence, more broadly, 'striving after popularity',[48] which I have rendered by 'ingratiation' (e.g. *Hist.* 2.98.5 = 82.5). In a quite different category is Sallust's predilection for such basic verbs as *facio* (literally, 'I do' or 'I make') and *habeo* (literally, 'I have' or 'I hold'). The younger Seneca (*Letters* 114.17–18) tells an

amusing story about L. Arruntius, the consul of 22, who wrote
a history of the Punic War:

> He was a Sallustian and strained after that style. There is in
> Sallust's work 'he made an army with silver', that is, he procured
> it with money. Arruntius began a love-affair with this, putting it
> on every page: in one place he says 'they made flight for our men',
> and in another 'hearing this made the Panhormitans surrender
> themselves to the Romans'. I only wanted to give you a taste; his
> whole book is shot through with it.

Seneca's letter illustrates vividly the facts that in some cases
(such as the first two) one cannot combine literalness with
intelligibility and that in others (such as the third) an intelligible
literalness fails to do justice to what was evidently an unusual
expression in Latin.[49] Such examples could be multiplied many
times; readers of the translation must constantly try to bear in
mind that Sallust's distinctive vocabulary has a regularity which
is belied by the frequency with which one is obliged to vary
one's rendering in English.[50]

Text and Transmission

The process of translation is inseparable from that of interpretation: if one is to translate a text, one must first have some
confidence that one knows what it means. In the case of Greek
and Latin authors, however, an extra process is involved too:
one needs to be satisfied that the words which are being
interpreted are the words which Sallust wrote. Readers of a
translated Latin text often assume – and generally are not
discouraged from assuming – that their reading matter has
remained in the same state as it was more than two thousand
years ago when its author finished composing it. Yet texts
of such antiquity, whose very survival depended on multiple
hand-written copyings over the centuries, are unstable, often
containing a wide variety of scribal errors which it is necessary
to try to correct. I have based the present translation on the
Oxford Classical Text of Sallust edited by L. D. Reynolds

(1991): on the few occasions where I have diverged from his edition, the divergence has been registered in a note, serving to remind readers that we cannot always be certain of an ancient author's actual words.

Our earliest independent witnesses to Sallust's three works are a few scraps of papyrus which are dated to the fourth or fifth centuries AD and which contain relatively small amounts of text. *Catiline's War* and *The Jugurthine War* have come down to us more or less complete in a variety of manuscripts, of which the two oldest (called P and A) were copied in the ninth century; however, like some of the later manuscripts, P and A depend upon a now lost archetype from which a sizeable section towards the end of *The Jugurthine War* (103.2–112.3) was already missing. (This section has to be supplied from other later manuscripts which have supplemented their texts from another lost archetype.) A further ninth-century manuscript (called V) is responsible for the four speeches and two letters which comprise the longest fragments of the *Histories*; but the almost total loss of the rest of the *Histories* constitutes an apt reminder that the very survival of classical texts to the modern day was never guaranteed.[51]

Despite the eventual loss of the *Histories*, Sallust was one of the most popular and quoted authors in antiquity. The second century AD developed a taste for archaizing which is associated particularly with M. Cornelius Fronto, correspondent of emperors and consul in 143, and Aulus Gellius, author of *Attic Nights*. Both writers were extremely familiar with Sallust's work, which they quote liberally. The spread of Christianity throughout the Roman empire brought Sallust new readers who were attracted by his severe moralizing: well known examples are Jerome and Augustine, whose lives spanned the later fourth and early fifth centuries.[52] 'The fame of Sallust endured to the end,' Syme has remarked. 'The whole range of literature in late antiquity acknowledges his spell, from Ammianus to the *Historia Augusta*, from Church Fathers to the lowly grammarians and scholiasts. Only Cicero and Virgil surpass him in estimation.'[53]

Throughout medieval times interest in Sallust only increased.

Writing in the middle of the ninth century, Lupus of Ferrières in the Loire valley has several references to the historian.[54] The tenth-century Vatican manuscript known as 'N' displays interlinear glosses in Old High German, showing that Sallust was being read intently, and perhaps used in teaching, both in that century and later.[55] If we may judge from the number of copies that were made of Sallust's works (a number which rose even more impressively than that of most other classical authors), there was a dramatic surge of enthusiasm in the eleventh and (especially) the twelfth centuries.[56] William Fitz-Stephen appealed to Sallust's description of Africa (*Jug.* 17–19) in order to defend his own inclusion of a description of London in his Life of Thomas à Becket (L1),[57] for example, while the anonymous author of the *Vita Heinrici IV* 'writes excellent Latin in a Sallustian style . . . Sallust is also the model for parts of the narrative, notably wars and sieges, and has influenced some of the author's key concepts, such as *avaritia* and *fortuna*'.[58] Later, this trend continued throughout the Renaissance and beyond. For the century between 1450 and 1550 Sallust was the most popular ancient historian, attracting the attention of such readers as Machiavelli, and for the next century and a half he was never out of the 'top three'.[59] Justly has it been observed that 'Sallust, whose importance was of the first rank in antiquity for his qualities as historian, thinker and stylist, has continued to radiate in literature.'[60]

NOTES

1. For Caesar's historical work see note 8.
2. The title of the work is disputed. The manuscripts offer a variety of titles including *Bellum Catilinarium* ('The Catilinarian War') and *Bellum Catilinae* ('Catiline's War' or 'War with Catiline'). On the basis of *Cat.* 4.3 'de Catilinae coniuratione' ('on Catiline's conspiracy'), many scholars make that or some similar phrase into a title (thus the OCT has *De Coniuratione Catilinae*, 'On the Conspiracy of Catiline'), despite the lack of manuscript authority. I think that *Bellum Catilinae* is supported both by Sallust's presentation of events as a (civil) war (e.g. *Cat.* 16.4, 17.6, 21.1,

26.5, 29.1, 29.3, 32.1–2, 33.1, 36.1–3, 56–61) and by the late first-century AD critic Quintilian (3.8.9 'Sallustius in bello Iugurthino et Catilinae', 'Sallust in the Jugurthine and Catiline's War').

3. See A. S. Pease, *M. Tulli Ciceronis De Natura Deorum* (1958), vol. 2, pp. 619–20.

4. Details of Sallust's career can be found in any of the standard works, e.g. Syme, *Sallust*, pp. 5–15, 29–59; J. T. Ramsey, *Sallust's* Bellum Catilinae (2nd edn, 2007), pp. 1–5; G. M. Paul, *A Historical Commentary on Sallust's Bellum Iugurthinum* (1984), p. 1; *OCD*, pp. 1348–9.

5. For an excellent account of what life might have been like for non-metropolitan writers see R. Jenkyns, *Virgil's Experience* (1998), pp. 73–127.

6. The expression was also used to describe the first man in a (senatorial or non-senatorial) family to reach the consulship (*OCD*, pp. 1051–2): see in general T. P. Wiseman, *New Men in the Roman Senate 139 B.C.–A.D. 14* (1971).

7. *Cambridge Ancient History* (2nd edn, 1994), vol. 9, p. 772 ('Epilogue' by J. A. Crook, A. Lintott and E. Rawson).

8. Caesar's commentaries are extant and pre-date Sallust's works, but arguably they belong to a different genre from mainstream historiography (see *OCD*, p. 373).

9. *Rhetorica ad Herennium* 1.7 (an anonymous treatise thought to have been composed roughly forty years before Sallust began to write).

10. Translations are my own unless stated otherwise.

11. It is generally believed that Cicero's letters to Atticus had not yet been published by the time that Sallust was writing (see Nepos, *Atticus* 16.3–4); but some letters were in circulation (see e.g. *Atticus* 8.9.1; cf. 16.5.5), and the coincidences seem too great if Sallust was unaware of this particular letter. Cf. how another friend in a letter called Cicero 'patron of everyone' (Cicero, *Letters to Friends* 6.7.4), a description which reappears in a poem of Catullus addressed to Cicero (49.7).

12. Translated by Guy Lee, *The Poems of Catullus* (1990), p. 103.

13. See D. H. Berry, 'The criminals in Virgil's Tartarus: contemporary allusions in *Aeneid* 6.621–4', *Classical Quarterly* 42 (1992), pp. 419–20.

14. Yet, since in the battle scene at the end of the work Catiline is described in seemingly heroic terms, Sallust's account of him is by no means straightforward. See A. T. Wilkins, *Villain or Hero: Sallust's Portrayal of Catiline* (1994).

15. C. S. Kraus, 'Jugurthine Disorder', in *The Limits of Historiography*, ed. C. S. Kraus (1999), p. 220.

16. See D. S. Levene, 'Sallust's *Jugurtha*: an "Historical Fragment"', *Journal of Roman Studies* 82 (1992), pp. 54–5.

17. See T. E. J. Wiedemann, 'Sallust's *Jugurtha*: concord, discord, and the digressions', *Greece & Rome* 40 (1993), pp. 48–57.

18. See H. M. Feinberg and J. B. Solodow, 'Out of Africa', *Journal of African History* 43 (2002), pp. 255–61, to whom all of this information is due.

19. R. Syme, *Tacitus* (1958), p. 126.

20. A selection from the First and Third Catilinarians (references to *Catiline's War* come first): **5.3** patiens inediae, algoris, uigiliae ~ 1.26 illam praeclaram patientiam famis, frigoris, 2.9 frigore et fame et siti et uigiliis; **5.7** conscientia scelerum ~ 1.17 conscientia scelerum; **12.3** templa deorum ~ 1.12 templa deorum; **14.3** manus atque lingua ~ 3.16 neque lingua neque manus; **15.2** uacuam domum ~ 1.14 domum uacuefecisses; **15.5** colos . . . oculi . . . uoltu ~ 3.13 color, oculi, uoltus; **20.9** emori ~ 1.20 emori; **21.1** opis aut spei ~ 3.16 spes atque opes; **26.4** praesidia amicorum ~ 1.11 amicorum praesidio; **28.1** pollicitus . . . ea nocte paulo post . . . salutatum . . . domi suae ~ 1.9–10 illa ipsa nocte paulo . . . pollicerentur . . . salutatum, 32 domi suae; **31.5** in senatum uenit ~ 1.2 in senatum uenit, 1.16 uenisti . . . in senatum; **32.1** in Manliana castra profectus ~ 1.10 proficiscere . . . Manliana castra, 30 in Manliana castra; **32.2** caedem, incendia (also at 43.2, 48.4, 51.9, 52.36) ~ 1.3 caede atque incendiis (also at 1.6, 2.6); **44.5** ~ 3.12; **45.2** occulte pontem . . . legati cum Volturcio ~ 3.5–6 occulte ad pontem . . . legati . . . unaque Volturcius; **46.6** Volturcium . . . introducit ~ 3.8 introduxi Volturcium; **47.1** fide publica ~ 3.8 fidem publicam; **47.3** signa sua cognouissent ~ 3.10 signum cognouit (twice); **47.3** abdicato . . . Lentulus itemque . . . custodiis ~ 3.14 Lentulus . . . abdicasset . . . custodiam . . . itemque; **48.1** mutata mente ~ 1.6 muta . . . istam mentem; **55.1** optumum factu (and elsewhere) ~ 1.29 optimum factu.

21. P. A. Brunt, 'Cicero and historiography', *Studies in Greek History and Thought* (1993), p. 188.

22. For a detailed discussion of the issues raised in this paragraph see my *Rhetoric in Classical Historiography* (1988), pp. 70–116.

23. Syme, *Tacitus*, p. 126.

24. Paul, *A Historical Commentary* (1984), p. 4.

25. D. A. Russell, 'Rhetoric and criticism', *Greece & Rome* 14

(1967), p. 135; reprinted in *Ancient Literary Criticism*, ed. A. Laird (2006), p. 273.

26. This is the term used by Paul in *A Historical Commentary* (1984), p. 5.

27. See J. Marincola, *Authority and Tradition in Ancient Historiography* (1997), pp. 289–92. For Sisenna see also *Jug.* 95.2; and note T. J. Cornell et al., *Fragments of the Roman Historians* (2008).

28. Syme, *Sallust*, p. 179.

29. For an explanation of references to the *Histories* see Abbreviations and References.

30. See P. A. Brunt, 'On historical fragments and epitomes', *Classical Quarterly* 30 (1980), pp. 477–94.

31. Speeches in the Greek and Roman historians are of course composed by the historians themselves and the presence of a speech in a historian's text is no guarantee that a speech was actually delivered on the occasion in question.

32. See K. J. Hartswick, *The Gardens of Sallust* (2004). Sallust's heir was the recipient of an ode from Horace (2.2) and went on to play vital but unpleasant roles under the emperor Tiberius in AD 14 and 17, finally dying in 20 (Tacitus, *Annals* 1.6.3, 2.40.2–3, 3.30.1–3).

33. Suetonius, *On Grammarians and Rhetoricians* 10.2 and 6.

34. Quoted by Quintilian 8.3.29; see also Suetonius, *On Grammarians and Rhetoricians* 15.2, *Augustus* 86.3. For Sallust and Cato see D. S. Levene, *Classical Quarterly* 50 (2000), pp. 170–91.

35. Translations of Dionysius are adapted from W. K. Pritchett, *Dionysius of Halicarnassus: 'On Thucydides'* (1975).

36. Seneca, *Controversiae* 9.1.13, Velleius 36.2, Quintilian 10.1.101. We should remember that Sallust also borrowed episodes and other scenes from Thucydides too (see p. xxiv): see in general T. F. Scanlon, *The Influence of Thucydides upon Sallust* (1980).

37. Syme, *Sallust*, p. 56.

38. Granius Licinianus (2nd century AD), ed. G. Camozzi (1900), p. 59.

39. See e.g. my *Rhetoric in Classical Historiography* (1988), pp. 130–32.

40. My translation of Sallust is intended to be less literal than my translation of Tacitus' *Annals*, although I have not changed my basic principles (for which see *Tacitus: The Annals* (2004), pp. xxii–xxvi). For some further discussion of the issues involved

see my 'Readers and Reception: a Text Case', in J. Marincola (ed.), *A Companion to Greek and Roman Historiography* (2007), pp. 133–44.

41. D. C. Earl, *The Political Thought of Sallust* (1961), p. 11.

42. *OLD* 1a–b, 2a, 3.

43. These definitions are from the *Oxford English Dictionary*.

44. *OLD* 1a, 4a, 5b, 2.

45. *OLD* 1a, 2a–b.

46. *OLD* 6a, 4a.

47. U. Paananen, *Sallust's Politico-Social Terminology* (1972).

48. *OLD* 4a, 1a, 3.

49. It is noteworthy that in *OLD* there are 30 separate meanings for *facio* and 27 for *habeo*.

50. For Sallust's style see Syme, *Sallust*, pp. 240–73, especially pp. 254–67.

51. For the transmission of Sallust's text see L. D. Reynolds in *Texts and Transmission: A Survey of the Latin Classics*, ed. L. D. Reynolds (1983), pp. 341–52.

52. See H. Hagendahl, *Latin Fathers and the Classics* (1958), pp. 292–4 (for Jerome), and *Augustine and the Latin Classics* (1967), pp. 225–44, 631–49.

53. Syme, *Sallust*, p. 301.

54. R. McKitterick, *History and Memory in the Carolingian World* (2005), pp. 194, 274.

55. See K. Zangmeister, 'Althochdeutsche Glossen zu Sallust', *Germania* 20 (1875), pp. 402–3.

56. B. Munk Olsen, 'The production of the classics in the eleventh and twelfth centuries', in C. A. Chavannes-Mazel and M. M. Smith (eds.), *Medieval Manuscripts of the Latin Classics: Production and Use* (1996), pp. 3, 17.

57. J. L. Butrica, 'Classical learning in William FitzStephen's Life of Thomas à Becket', *Studi Medievali* 46.2 (2005), pp. 551–4. 'L1' refers to the start of the description of London.

58. S. Bagge, *Kings, Politics, and the Right Order of the World in German Historiography c. 950–1150* (2002), pp. 314–15 and note 5 there. See further B. Smalley, 'Sallust in the Middle Ages', in *Classical Influences on European Culture A.D. 500–1500*, ed. R. R. Bolgar (1971), pp. 165–75; and note R. M. Stein, 'Sallust for his readers, 410–1550: a study in the formation of the classical tradition' (unpublished dissertation, Columbia, 1977).

59. See P. Burke, 'A survey of the popularity of ancient historians, 1450–1700', *History and Theory* 5 (1966), pp. 135–52, especi-

ally pp. 136–7; P. J. Osmond, 'Sallust and Machiavelli: from civic humanism to political prudence', *Journal of Medieval and Renaissance Studies* 23 (1993), pp. 407–38.

60. R. Poignault (ed.), *Présence de Salluste* (1997), p. 9. This work contains discussions of the reception of Sallust in modern times, including the twentieth century.

Chronological Tables

The Late Republic

(Roman figures in brackets refer to the numbers of consulships)

BC

146	End of Third Punic War; destruction of Carthage
133	Tiberius Gracchus tribune; siege of Numantia ends
123–122	Gaius Gracchus tribune
115	M. Aemilius Scaurus consul
111	L. Calpurnius Bestia consul; Jugurthine War begins
110	Sp. Postumius Albinus consul
109	Q. Caecilius Metellus consul
107	Marius consul (I); Sulla quaestor
106	Cicero born
105	P. Rutilius Rufus consul; Jugurthine War ends; battle against the Cimbri (Arausio)
104–102	Marius consul (II–IV)
101	Marius consul (V); defeats Cimbri (Vercellae)
100	Marius consul (VI)
97	Sulla praetor
91	L. Marcius Philippus consul
91–87	Social (or Marsic) War
88	Sulla consul (I)
88–85	First Mithridatic War
87	Cinna consul (I)
86	Marius (VII) and Cinna (II) consuls; Sallust born
85	Cinna consul (III)
84	Cinna consul (IV); ? Catullus born
83–81	Second Mithridatic War

82–81	Sulla dictator
81–72	Sertorius' war
80	Sulla (II) and Q. Caecilius Metellus Pius consuls
79	P. Servilius Vatia consul
78	M. Aemilius Lepidus and Q. Lutatius Catulus consuls; L. Cornelius Sisenna praetor; death of Sulla; narrative of Sallust's *Histories* starts
77	M. Aemilius Lepidus' revolt
77–71	Pompey in Spain
75	C. Aurelius Cotta consul
74–65	Third Mithridatic War
74	L. Licinius Lucullus and M. Aurelius Cotta consuls
73	C. Licinius Macer tribune
70	Pompey (I) and Crassus (I) consuls; Virgil born
67	Latest attested date in Sallust's *Histories*; Pompey's command against the pirates
66	'First Catilinarian Conspiracy'
66–62	Pompey in the east
65	Horace born
63	Cicero consul; Catilinarian conspiracy
60	'First Triumvirate' (Caesar, Pompey, Crassus)
59	Caesar consul (I)
58–57	Cicero in exile
55	Pompey (II) and Crassus (II) consuls; ? Sallust quaestor
54	? Catullus dies
52	Pompey consul (III); Sallust tribune
50	Sallust expelled from senate
49	Caesar crosses Rubicon, becomes dictator
48	Caesar consul (II); battle of Pharsalus; Pompey murdered; Caesar dictator
46	Caesar consul (III); Sallust praetor, appointed to Africa Nova; Cato commits suicide (at Thapsus); Caesar dictator
45	Caesar consul (IV) and dictator; ? Sallust charged with extortion
44	Caesar consul (V) and dictator *perpetuo*; murdered
43	Triumvirate (Antony, Lepidus, Octavian)

42	Battle of Philippi; ? Sallust, *Catiline's War*
41	? Sallust, *The Jugurthine War*
40	? Sallust starts his *Histories*
35	? Sallust dies
31	Battle of Actium (Octavian defeats Mark Antony and Cleopatra)

The Catilinarian Conspiracy

(references in brackets refer to *Catiline's War*)

63 BC

21 or 22 Oct.	The *senatus consultum ultimum* passed by the senate (29.2)
27 Oct.	C. Manlius takes up arms (30.1)
6/7 Nov. (night)	The conspirators meet at Laeca's house (27.3–4)
7 Nov. (early morning)	Attempt on Cicero's life (28)
8 Nov.	Cicero's First Catilinarian (31.6)
8/9 Nov. (night)	Catiline leaves Rome (32.1)
9 Nov.	Cicero's Second Catilinarian
2 Dec. (night)	The arrest at the Milvian Bridge (45)
3 Dec.	Cicero's Third Catilinarian
4 Dec.	L. Tarquinius' evidence in the senate (48.3–8)
5 Dec.	Senatorial debate (50.3, 50.5–53.1) and Cicero's Fourth Catilinarian; execution of the conspirators (55)

Further Reading

The only book in English which is devoted to Sallust and his work is Sir Ronald Syme's *Sallust*, first published in 1964 and reissued in 2002 with a new Foreword by R. Mellor (University of California Press). There are very helpful commentaries by J. T. Ramsey (*Sallust's* Bellum Catilinae, American Philological Association/Oxford University Press, rev. edn, 2007) and G. M. Paul (*A Historical Commentary on Sallust's Bellum Iugurthinum*, Francis Cairns, 1984): both (especially the former) are aimed at readers who know Latin. On the *Histories* there is P. McGushin, *Sallust: The Histories*, 2 vols. (Oxford University Press, 1992–4). For a historical study of the Catilinarian conspiracy in particular see A. Drummond, *Law, Politics and Power. Sallust and the Execution of the Catilinarian Conspirators* (Steiner, 1995).

The history of the Roman republic's last years has attracted an extraordinary amount of scholarly attention. The classic account remains R. Syme, *The Roman Revolution* (Oxford University Press, 1939), but it is not for the general reader; a more accessible narrative will be found in J. A. Crook, A. Lintott and E. Rawson (eds.), *The Cambridge Ancient History*, Vol. 9 (2nd edn; Cambridge University Press, 1994); there are helpful introductory essays in T. P. Wiseman (ed.), *Roman Political Life 90 B.C.–A.D. 69* (Exeter University Press, 1985); and note most recently J. Osgood, *Caesar's Legacy: Civil War and the Emergence of the Roman Empire* (Cambridge University Press, 2006).

For studies of the major figures of the period see A. Keaveney, *Sulla, the Last Republican* (2nd edn; Routledge, 2005);

T. F. Carney, *A Biography of Caius Marius* (2nd edn; Argonaut, 1970); R. Seager, *Pompey the Great: A Political Biography* (2nd edn; Blackwell, 2002); M. Gelzer, *Caesar: Politician and Statesman* (Blackwell, 1968); Z. Yavetz, *Julius Caesar and his Public Image* (Thames & Hudson, 1983); T. N. Mitchell, *Cicero: The Ascending Years* (Yale University Press, 1979), and *Cicero: the Senior Statesman* (Yale University Press, 1991). Note also P. O. Spann, *Quintus Sertorius and the Legacy of Sulla* (University of Arkansas Press, 1987), and B. C. McGing, *The Foreign Policy of Mithridates VI Eupator, King of Pontus* (Brill, 1986).

There is important material in P. A. Brunt, *The Fall of the Roman Republic and Related Essays* (Oxford University Press, 1988); other studies include M. Beard and M. Crawford, *Rome in the Late Republic* (2nd edn; Duckworth, 1999); P. A. Brunt, *Social Conflicts in the Roman Republic* (Chatto & Windus, 1971); D. C. Earl, *The Moral and Political Tradition of Rome* (Thames & Hudson, 1967); D. F. Epstein, *Personal Enmity in Roman Politics 218–43 BC* (Croom Helm, 1987); F. Millar, *Rome, the Greek World and the East*, Vol. 1: *The Roman Republic and the Augustan Revolution* (University of North Carolina Press, 2002); A. W. Lintott, *The Constitution of the Roman Republic* (Oxford University Press, 1999), and *Violence in Republican Rome* (2nd edn; Oxford University Press, 1999); and R. Seager (ed.), *The Crisis of the Roman Republic* (Heffer, 1969).

Though Sallust is discussed in the numerous books devoted to classical (or Roman) historiography (or historians), many of these books are out of date and – misleadingly, in my view – treat their subject according to the criteria of modern historical writing. For a different perspective see T. P. Wiseman, *Clio's Cosmetics* (Leicester University Press, 1979), and C. S. Kraus and A. J. Woodman, *Latin Historians* (Oxford University Press, 1997). Two recent compendia are J. Marincola (ed.), *A Companion to Greek and Roman Historiography* (Blackwell, 2007), and A. Feldherr (ed.), *The Cambridge Companion to Roman Historiography* (Cambridge University Press, 2008).

CATILINE'S WAR

All persons who are enthusiastic that they should transcend the 1
other animals ought to strive with the utmost effort not to pass
through a life of silence, like cattle, which nature has fashioned
to be prone and obedient to their stomachs. *Our* entire power 2
resides in the mind as well as in the body: we use the mind to
command, the body to serve; the former we share with the
gods, the latter with the beasts. Therefore it seems to me more 3
correct to seek glory with our intellectual rather than with our
physical resources, and, because the very life that we enjoy is
short, to ensure that a recollection of ourselves lasts as long as
possible. The glory of riches and appearance is fleeting and 4
fragile, but to have prowess is something distinguished and
everlasting.

Yet for a long time there was considerable dispute amongst 5
mortals as to whether it was through the power of the body or
the prowess of the mind that military affairs made greater
progress. For, before you begin, deliberation is necessary, and, 6
when you have deliberated, speedy action: hence each element, 7
deficient on its own, requires the help of the other. Initially, 2
therefore, kings (that was the first name which commanders on
earth had) differed from one another, some deploying their
intellect, others their body. That was a time at which people
were still leading a life without any desire: each was satisfied
with what was his. But, after Cyrus in Asia and the Lacedae- 2
monians and Athenians in Greece began to subdue cities and
nations,[1] and to regard the urge for dominion as a reason for
war and to think that the greatest glory resided in commanding
the greatest empire, then at last it was discovered through

dangerous enterprises that in war the intellect has the greatest
3   potential. And, if the mental prowess of kings and commanders
were as effective in peace as in war, human affairs would be
conducted more uniformly and consistently, and you would
not see things swept along in different directions and everything
4   changing and confused. For command is easily held by means
5   of the same qualities as it was acquired initially; but, when toil
is replaced by an attack of indolence, and self-control and
fairness by one of lust and haughtiness, there is a change in
6   fortune[2] as well as in morals and behaviour. Hence command
is always transferred to the best man from the less good.

7   Ploughing, sailing and building are all dependent on prowess.
8   But many mortals, devoted to their stomachs and to sleep,
have passed through life untaught and uncouth, like foreign
travellers; and of course, contrary to nature, their bodies were
a source of pleasure to them, their minds a burden. In the case
of such people, I assess their life and death alike, since silence
9   surrounds each. He alone seems to me to live truly and to enjoy
his existence who, concentrating on some enterprise, finds[3] a
reputation for a distinguished deed or good practice.

Given the great profusion of possibilities, nature shows dif-
3   ferent paths to different people. It is a splendid thing to do well
for the advantage of one's commonwealth;[4] but also to speak
well is not misplaced: it is allowed to one to be distinguished
either in peace or in war; and in many cases both those who
have done deeds and those who have written of the deeds of
2   others are praised. And, even though it is by no means an equal
glory which attends the writer of affairs and their author,[5] it
nevertheless seems, to me at least, especially difficult to write
about the conduct of affairs – first, since deeds have to be
matched by speech, then because, if you criticize failings, most
people think you have spoken from malice and resentment, but,
when you recall the great prowess and glory of good men, each
person accepts with equanimity that which he thinks easy for
himself to do, but considers things beyond that as false, tanta-
mount to fabrication.

3   In my own case, as a young adolescent (like many others) I
was initially swept by enthusiasm towards politics, and there

many things were against me. For instead of propriety, self-denial and prowess, it was daring, bribery and avarice which were thriving; and, even though my mind rejected those things, unaccustomed as it was to wicked practices, nevertheless amidst such great faults my youthful weakness was corrupted and gripped by ambition; and, although I disagreed with the wicked behaviour of others, nonetheless my desire for honours afflicted me with the same reputation and resentment as it did the rest. Therefore, when my mind sought repose from the many miseries and dangers, and I determined that the remainder of my life must be kept far away from politics, it was not my intention to waste the good of my leisure time in lethargy and indolence, nor to spend my life in agriculture or hunting, concentrating on the duties of slaves;[6] but, returning to a project and enthusiasm from which my wicked ambition had detained me, I decided to write of the affairs of the Roman people – selectively, according as each subject seemed worthy of recollection, and with the additional reason that my mind was free from hope, dread and political partisanship. Therefore I shall dispatch, in a few words, the conspiracy of Catiline as truthfully as I am able: for I think his deed especially deserving of recollection owing to the newness of the crime and of its danger. But a few things must be explained about his behaviour and habits before I can begin my narrative.

L. Catilina, born of a noble line, had great strength of both mind and body, but a wicked and crooked disposition. From adolescence, internal wars, slaughter, seizures and civil disharmony were welcome to him, and there he spent his young manhood. His body was tolerant of hunger, cold and wakefulness beyond the point which anyone finds credible; his mind was daring, cunning and versatile, capable of any simulation and dissimulation; acquisitive of another's property, prodigal with his own; burning in desires; his eloquence was adequate, scant his wisdom. The enormity of his mind always desired the unrestrained, the incredible, the heights beyond reach. After the dominion of L. Sulla,[7] he had been assailed by his greatest urge, to capture the commonwealth; and he attached no weight to the methods by which he might achieve it, provided he

7   acquired kingship for himself. His defiant spirit was exercised
    increasingly each day by his lack of private assets and a con-
    sciousness of his crimes, both of which he had augmented by
8   the qualities which I recalled above. He was incited, too, by the
    community's corrupt morals, which were afflicted by those
    worst and mutually different maladies, luxury and avarice.

9   Since there has been occasion to mention the morals of the
    community, the context seems to encourage going further back
    and discussing in a few words the customs of our ancestors at
    home and on campaign, by what means they kept the common-
    wealth and how great it was when they bequeathed it, and how
    it changed gradually from the finest and best and became the
    worst and most outrageous.
6   The City of Rome, on my understanding, was founded and
    held initially by the Trojans, who as fugitives under the leader-
    ship of Aeneas had been wandering with no fixed abode; and
    with them were the Aborigines, a rustic race, without laws,
2   without command, free and unrestricted.[8] After they had come
    together behind a single wall, it is incredible to recall how easily
    – despite the difference in race, their separate languages and
    disparate life-styles – they merged: so short was the time in
    which, owing to harmony, the diverse and wandering multitude
3   had become a community. But, after their state had grown in
    terms of its citizens, customs and territory, and had begun to
    seem quite prosperous and quite powerful, their resources (as
    is the way with most of mortals' affairs) gave rise to resentment.
4   Neighbouring kings and peoples made warlike attempts on
    them, and only a few of their friends were a source of help: the
5   rest were terror-stricken and stayed clear of any danger. But the
    Romans, at home and on campaign, concentrated on quickness,
    preparation, mutual encouragement, confronting the enemy
    and protecting by arms their freedom and their fatherland and
    parents. After, when they had repulsed the dangers by their
    prowess, they brought aid to their allies and friends and
    acquired friendships more by giving kindnesses than by receiv-
6   ing them. They had a statutory command, and the name of the
    command was kingship. A select group, physically infirm in

years but intellectually strong in wisdom, would deliberate in the interests of the commonwealth: they were called 'the fathers',[9] either because of their age or because of the similarity of their caring role. After, the command of the kings, which initially had been to preserve freedom and to increase the commonwealth, transformed itself into haughty domineering:[10] so, with a change of convention, they created for themselves annual commands and paired commanders:[11] they thought that in that way there was the least possibility of the human mind's becoming overbearing through licence.

But that was the period at which each man began to advance himself more and to keep his intellect more at the ready. (For, to kings, the good are more suspect than the wicked, and prowess in another is always a source of fear to them.) It is incredible to recall how much the community grew in a short time after its acquisition of freedom, so great was the desire for glory which had arisen. From the very first, as soon as its young men could tolerate warfare, they learned military practice through hard work in camp, and they took pleasure in attractive armour and military horses rather than in whores and parties. To such men no hard work was unusual, no place rugged or steep, no armed enemy a source of fear: prowess had tamed everything. But the greatest competition for glory was amongst themselves: each hurried to be the one to strike an enemy, to scale a wall and to be observed while doing such deeds; they considered this to be their riches, this to be a good reputation and great nobility. They were hungry for praise, generous with money; they wanted mighty glory, honourable riches. I can recall the places where the Roman people, with only a small unit, routed the greatest of enemy forces; the cities which, though protected by nature, they took by storm – were it not that that subject would take us too far from our project.

But of course Fortune's dominion extends everywhere; she celebrates and obscures everything according to whim rather than reality. The achievements of the Athenians, in my assessment, were perfectly substantial and magnificent, but somewhat less than their reputation maintains; but, because a crop of greatly talented writers[12] was produced there, the deeds of the

4   Athenians are celebrated across the globe as the greatest. Hence
    the prowess of those who did the deeds is considered to be only
    as great as was the ability of distinguished talents to extol it in
5   words. But such a possibility was never open to the Roman
    people, because all their cleverest men were the most enterpris-
    ing in action: no one exercised his intellectual talent without
    his body; all the best men preferred to do rather than to speak,
    and that their own good deeds should be praised by others
    rather than that they themselves should narrate those of others.
9   Hence at home and on campaign good behaviour was culti-
    vated. There was the greatest harmony, very little avarice; jus-
    tice and goodness thrived amongst them not because of laws
2   but by nature. Quarrels, disharmony and conflict were what
    they conducted with the enemy; citizens competed with citizens
    in the area of prowess. They were lavish in supplicating the
3   gods, sparing in the home, faithful to their friends. By two
    qualities – daring in war and, when peace came, fairness – they
4   took care both of themselves and of their commonwealth. The
    greatest proofs I have of these two are as follows: in war,
    punishment was more often inflicted on those who had fought
    against the enemy contrary to command,[13] or who had with-
    drawn too slowly when recalled from battle, than on those who
    had dared to abandon the standards or to retire from their
5   position when beaten; in peace, they exercised command by
    conferring kindness, not causing dread, and, when wronged,
    they preferred forgiveness to pursuit.
10 But, when the commonwealth had grown through hard work
    and justice, and great kings had been tamed in war, and wild
    nations and mighty peoples subdued by force, and Carthage
    – the rival of Rome for command of an empire – had been
    eradicated,[14] and all seas and lands became accessible, then
    Fortune began to turn savage and to confound everything.
2   Those who had easily tolerated hard work, danger and uncer-
    tain and rough conditions, regarded leisure and riches (things
    to be craved under other circumstances) as a burden and
3   a source of misery. Hence it was the desire for money first of
    all, and then for empire,[15] which grew; and those factors were
4   the kindling (so to speak) of every wickedness. For avarice

undermined trust, probity and all other good qualities; instead, it taught men haughtiness, cruelty, to neglect the gods, to regard everything as for sale. Ambition reduced many mortals to 5 becoming false, having one sentiment shut away in the heart and another ready on the tongue, assessing friendships and antagonisms in terms not of reality but of advantage, and having a good demeanour rather than a good disposition. At first 6 these things grew gradually; sometimes they were punished; but after, when the contamination had attacked like a plague, the community changed and the exercise of command, from being the best and most just, became cruel and intolerable.

At first people's minds were taxed less by avarice than by 11 ambition, which, though a fault, was nevertheless closer to prowess: for the good man and the base man have a similar 2 personal craving for glory, honour and command, but the former strives along the true path, whereas the latter, because he lacks good qualities, presses forward by cunning and falsity. Avarice involves an enthusiasm for money (which no wise man 3 has ever desired): as if saturated with a harmful poison, it feminizes the manly body and mind, knows neither limit nor surfeit, and is lessened by neither sufficiency nor insufficiency. But after L. Sulla, having taken the commonwealth by arms, 4 had had a wicked outcome to his good beginning,[16] everyone started to seize and loot; one man desired a house, another land; the victors showed neither restraint nor moderation but did foul and cruel deeds against their fellow citizens. To this 5 was added the fact that, to gain the loyalty of the army which he had led in Asia, L. Sulla had treated it luxuriously and too generously, contrary to ancestral custom.[17] Attractive and pleasurable localities had easily softened the defiant spirits of his soldiers during their periods of leisure: that was the first 6 time an army of the Roman people became accustomed to love-affairs and drink; to admire statues, paintings and engraved goblets; to seize them regardless of whether privately or publicly owned; to despoil shrines and to pollute everything sacred and profane alike. After the soldiers had achieved victory, they left their victims nothing. The reason was that successful situations overwhelm the minds even of the wise; 7

8   still less would those men of corrupt morals moderate their victory.

12   After riches began to be a source of honour and to be attended by glory, command and power, prowess began to dull, poverty to be considered a disgrace and blamelessness to be regarded 2 as malice. In the wake of riches, therefore, young men were attacked by luxury and avarice along with haughtiness; they seized, they squandered; they placed little weight on their own property and desired that of others; they considered propriety and unchastity, divine and human matters, as indistinguishable, 3 and nothing as worth weight or restraint. When you contemplate houses and villas built on the model of cities, it is worthwhile to view the temples of the gods which our ancestors, 4 those most religious of mortals, made. Yet *they* enhanced the shrines of the gods by their devotion, their own houses by their glory, and they took nothing from their defeated victims except 5 a licence to do wrong. But *these* people, on the other hand, the basest of individuals, committed the gravest crime in removing from their allies whatever the victors, most courageous of men, had left them; just as if doing wrong and exercising command 13 were really one and the same thing. Why should I recall that numerous private individuals undermined mountains and paved over the seas[18] – things which are credible to no one 2 except those who have seen them? To such men, it seems to me, their riches were a plaything: when they could have held them with honour, they hurried to misuse them disgracefully. 3 But the lust which had arisen for illicit sex, gluttony and the other refinements was no less: men took the passive role of women, women made their chastity openly available; everywhere, by land and by sea, was ransacked for the sake of feeding; they slept before there could be any desire for slumber: they did not wait for hunger or thirst nor for cold nor tiredness 4 but in their luxuriousness anticipated them all.[19] It was these things which inflamed young men to crime when their private 5 wealth failed: a mentality saturated in wicked practices did not easily forgo its lusts, so its comprehensive dedication to profit and expenditure was all the more prodigal.

In so great and so corrupt a community Catiline kept himself   14
surrounded (it was very easy to do) by hordes of those responsible for every depravity and deed, like bodyguards. Whoever   2
had ravaged his ancestral property by means of his muscle,
stomach or groin; anyone who had run up a huge debt to buy
his way out of some depravity or deed; all those anywhere who   3
were convicted of parricide or sacrilege in the courts (or who
feared the courts in the light of their deeds); those whose muscle
and tongue made provision for them by perjury or civil bloodshed; all, finally, who were agitated by depravity, destitution
and conscience – these were Catiline's nearest and dearest. If   4
there *was* anyone still clear of blame who happened to fall into
friendship with him, he was easily made equal and similar to
the others by daily association and enticements. It was especially   5
the fellowship of adolescents that he sought: their minds – still
impressionable and flexible – were captured without difficulty
by cunning. For, depending on what burning enthusiasm each   6
one had at that age, Catiline presented some with whores,
bought dogs and horses for others, and, finally, spared neither
expense nor his own modesty, provided he could make them
beholden and loyal to himself. I know that there were some   7
who reckoned that the young men who thronged to Catiline's
house treated their chastity as something of little honour; but
the report of this thrived for reasons other than that anyone
had actually found the matter out.

From the very first, Catiline as an adolescent had committed   15
many unspeakable acts of illicit sex – with a noble maiden, with
a priestess of Vesta – and other deeds of this type contrary to
divine and human law. Finally he was captivated by love for   2
Aurelia Orestilla (in whom no good man ever praised anything
but her appearance), but, because she hesitated to marry him
through fear of a stepson of adult years, it is believed for certain
that he killed his son, thereby ensuring an empty house for the
criminal marriage. It is this affair above all which seems to me   3
to have been his reason for speeding up the deed: for his vile   4
spirit – hostile to gods and men – could not be calmed by
wakefulness or repose: to such an extent was his conscience
preying upon his unquiet mind. Hence his bloodless complexion   5

and ugly eyes, and his walk alternating between fast and slow; in short, there was derangement in his demeanour and face.

16   As for the young men whom (as we said above) he had
2   enticed, he taught them wicked deeds in numerous ways. From them he provided false witnesses and signatories; he commanded of them, first, that they should regard loyalty, fortunes and danger as cheap, and then, when he had worn away their
3   reputation and sense of shame, other and still greater deeds. If reasons for wrongdoing were temporarily in short supply, he would nonetheless entrap and butcher the guiltless no differently from the guilty. (It was of course to prevent their muscles or minds from languishing through inactivity that he was gratuitously wicked and cruel instead.)

4   These were the friends and allies on whom Catiline relied; and, both because there was mighty debt across every land, and because many Sullan soldiers – too lavish with their own property, and mindful of the seizures of their old victory – were longing for civil war, he conceived the scheme of an assault
5   upon the commonwealth. There was no army in Italy, and Cn. Pompeius was waging war in the most distant lands;[20] he had high hopes of his own candidacy for the consulship,[21] and the senate was of course not concentrating: conditions on all fronts were settled and calm, but *that* was favourable to Catiline.

17   Therefore, around the Kalends of June[22] in the consulship of L. Caesar and of C. Figulus, it was individuals upon whom he called first: he encouraged some, others he sounded out; he told them of his resources, the unpreparedness of the common-
2   wealth, the great rewards of a conspiracy. When he had ascertained sufficiently what he wanted, he summoned together all
3   those who had the greatest need and the most daring. Of the senatorial order, there assembled P. Lentulus Sura, P. Autronius, L. Cassius Longinus, C. Cethegus, P. and Ser. Sulla (the sons of Servius), L. Vargunteius, Q. Annius, M. Porcius Laeca,
4   L. Bestia, and Q. Curius;[23] apart from them, from the equestrian order, M. Fulvius Nobilior, L. Statilius, P. Gabinius Capito, C. Cornelius;[24] and, in addition, many from the colonies and
5   municipalities – the local nobility. Apart from these, there were

numerous nobles whose participation in this scheme was rather more secret and who were encouraged more by the hope of dominion than by any want or need. As for the young men, 6 the majority (and especially those from the nobility) favoured Catiline's project: those who could have lived a leisurely life in magnificence or ease preferred uncertainty instead of certainty, war to peace. Likewise there were at that period those who 7 believed that M. Licinius Crassus[25] was not unaware of the scheme; and that, because Cn. Pompeius (whom he resented) was leader of a great army, he was willing for anyone's resources to grow in opposition to the latter's power, all the while confident that, if the conspiracy succeeded, he would easily be chief amongst them.

Previously a small number likewise conspired against the 18 commonwealth, and one of them was Catiline; I shall speak 2 about the matter as briefly[26] as I can.

In the consulship of L. Tullus and of M'. Lepidus,[27] P. Autronius and P. Sulla (the designated consuls) had been questioned under the laws of canvassing[28] and punished. A little after, 3 Catiline's prosecution for extortion had prevented him from being a candidate for the consulship,[29] because he had been unable to put forward his name within the prescribed number of days. A contemporary was Cn. Piso,[30] an adolescent from 4 the nobility, of the utmost daring, destitute and factious, who was being spurred by want and wicked habits to disrupt the commonwealth. It was with him that Catiline and Autronius 5 around the Nones of December[31] shared their scheme, and they were preparing to kill the consuls L. Cotta and L. Torquatus on the Capitol on the Kalends of January,[32] and, having themselves seized the fasces,[33] to send Piso with an army to hold the two Spains.[34] But after the discovery of the affair, their response 6 had been to transfer the murderous scheme to the Nones of February,[35] and now they were already devising the destruction 7 not only of the consuls but of numerous senators. And, had not 8 Catiline been too speedy in giving the signal to his allies in front of the curia,[36] the worst deed since the founding of the City of Rome would have been perpetrated on that day. But, because

the armed men had not yet assembled in force, that circumstance caused the scheme to be broken off.

19   Afterwards Piso was sent to Nearer Spain as quaestor with
praetorian power[37] thanks to the efforts of Crassus, because he
2 knew that he was a fierce antagonist of Cn. Pompeius. And yet
the senate had not been unwilling to give him the province,
since it wanted a foul individual to be far away from political
life, as well as because numerous good men saw in him a
bulwark, and at that time Pompeius' power was already a
3 source of fear. But he was the Piso who, during a journey in the
province, was killed by Spanish cavalry whom he was leading
4 as part of his army. There are those who say that the barbarians
were unable to tolerate his unjust, haughty and cruel com-
5 mands; but others that the cavalry, as long-standing and loyal
clients of Cn. Pompeius, attacked Piso with his blessing: the
Spanish had never done such a deed apart from that, they
say, even though they had previously endured many savage
commands. We shall leave the matter undecided between the
6 two; and about the earlier conspiracy enough has been said.

20 When he saw that those whom I recalled a little before had
assembled, Catiline, despite the frequent and detailed discussions which he had had with individuals, nevertheless
believed it would be pertinent to call upon them collectively
and encourage them, so he withdrew to a secluded part of the
house and there, with all witnesses moved well away, he made
a speech of this type:
2   'If your prowess and loyalty had not been demonstrated to
my satisfaction, this favourable circumstance would have fallen
to us in vain, and the high hopes and dominion in our grasp
would have been to no purpose – and I am not a man who
would clutch at uncertainties instead of certainties, aided by
3 cowards of unreliable disposition. But, because I have come to
know, through many great turmoils, that you are courageous
and loyal to me, that is the reason why my spirit has dared to
embark on the greatest and finest of deeds, and also because I
have come to understand that your perception of goodness and

wickedness is the same as mine: wanting and not wanting the 4
same things – that, ultimately, is firm friendship.

'You have already heard before, separately, what I have pon- 5
dered in my mind. Yet my spirit is kindled more and more each 6
day when I reflect what the conditions of life will be if we do not
assert our freedom ourselves. For, ever since the commonwealth 7
passed to the jurisdiction of a powerful few, it has always been
to them that the dues of kings and tetrarchs[38] go, that the taxes
of peoples and nations are paid; the rest of us – all the committed and good, noble and ignoble – have been simply "the
masses", denied favour, denied influence, beholden to those to
whom, if the commonwealth thrived, we would be a source of
fear. Hence all favour, power, honour and riches rest with them 8
or are where they want them; to us they have left the dangers,
rejections,[39] lawsuits and destitution.

'For how long, then, will you endure these things, most 9
courageous of men?[40] Is it not better to die with prowess than
to lose in disgrace a life which is pitiable and dishonourable,
once you have become a plaything of the haughtiness of others?
That is surely true, but, by the faith of gods and men, victory 10
is in our hands! We have the vigour of youth, hearts of valour.
Everything of theirs, by contrast, has been enfeebled by the
years and by riches. Only a start is needed; circumstances will
make light of the rest. What mortal of manly disposition can 11
tolerate the fact that *they* abound in riches which they can pour
into building on the sea and levelling mountains,[41] while *we*
lack the private assets even for necessities? That *they* each link
two or more houses together, while *our* household gods are
nowhere to be found? They buy their pictures, statues and 12
reliefs; they destroy new structures and put up others; in fact,
they plunder and ravage their money by every means at their
disposal, yet, despite the extreme nature of their whims and
lusts, they are unable to achieve victory over their riches.[42] But 13
for us it is want at home and debt abroad, a distressing situation
and the prospect of much worse; what, in the end, have we left,
except the pitiful breath that we breathe?

'Why not, therefore, rouse yourselves? Here, stretching 14

before your eyes, lies that freedom which you have often craved, as well as riches, respect and glory! All these things Fortune has
15 set out as the rewards for the victors. The issue, the moment, the danger, the destitution, the magnificent spoils of war are a
16 greater encouragement to you than any speech of mine. Use me as either commander or soldier: neither my mind nor my body
17 will fail you. These are the very things, I hope, that I shall be discussing with you when I am consul, unless perchance my mind deceives me and you are prepared for servitude rather than for command.'

21 These words were received by men who possessed every wickedness in abundance, but neither substance nor any good prospect; and, although they thought it highly profitable to disrupt the calm, nevertheless many of them demanded that he put forward what the nature of the war would be, what rewards they were seeking by arms and what resource or prospect they
2 had. Then Catiline guaranteed fresh accounts[43] and the pro-scription of the wealthy; magistracies and priesthoods; and seizures and everything else which is yielded by war and by the
3 victors' whim and lust. Apart from that, he said, there was Piso in Nearer Spain, P. Sittius of Nuceria with an army in Mauretania,[44] both of them participants in his scheme; one candidate for the consulship was C. Antonius, who he hoped would be his colleague, a man who was a friend and was hampered by every constraint;[45] alongside him, he himself as
4 consul would make an active start. In addition, he upbraided all good men in insulting terms and praised each of his own followers by name: he reminded one of his destitution, another of his desire, several of their danger or ignominy, and many of the Sullan victory which had provided them with plunder.

5 After he had seen urgency in the spirits of all, and having encouraged them to be concerned for his own candidacy, he dismissed the assembly.

22 (There were contemporaries who said that, when Catiline at the end of his speech was binding his criminal associates by an oath, he had handed round, in bowls, blood from a human
2 body, mixed with wine; then, when everyone after an impreca-tion had tasted it (as customarily happens in sacred rituals), he

had revealed his scheme and said repeatedly that he was doing so[46] with the precise purpose of increasing the likelihood of their mutual loyalty, one being the accessory with another to so great a deed. Yet some reckoned that this and much else had been fabricated by those who believed that the resentment against Cicero, which arose later,[47] would be mitigated by the frightfulness of the crime of those who had been punished. In our view, too little has been found out about the matter in relation to its significance.)

In the conspiracy there was Q. Curius, born in circumstances by no means obscure, deep in depraved deeds, whom the censors had removed from the senate on account of his disreputableness. This individual was no less unreliable than daring: he neither kept silent about what he had heard nor concealed his own crimes; in fact, he attached no weight to anything he either said or did. With Fulvia, a noble woman, he had a long-standing arrangement for illicit sex; but, when he became less welcome to her because through indigence he was less able to be lavish, he suddenly started boastingly to promise her 'the seas and the summits',[48] and sometimes he threatened her with steel if she did not submit to him, and finally he behaved more defiantly than had been his usual custom. But Fulvia, having learned the reason why Curius was unusually overbearing, did not keep secret such a danger to the commonwealth but, though withholding her source, told numerous people what she had heard, in whatever way, about Catiline's conspiracy.

That circumstance in particular inflamed people's enthusiasm for entrusting the consulship to M. Tullius Cicero. For previously many of the nobility had been seething with resentment, believing that the consulship would be (as it were) polluted if a new man,[49] however exceptional, acquired it. But, at the approach of danger, resentment and pride took second place. So, when the elections were held, it was M. Tullius and C. Antonius who were declared consuls. This development had at first shaken the associates in the conspiracy, but Catiline's fury in no way lessened; on the contrary, his agitation increased daily: he prepared arms at strategic locations across Italy; and the money which he had borrowed on his own or his friends'

guarantee he took to a certain Manlius at Faesulae, who afterwards had a chief role in the conduct of the war.[50]

3   This was the period at which he is said to have brought over
to his side very many men of every type, and even some women
too, who at first had borne their mighty expenditure by using
their bodies for illicit sex, but then, when age had placed a limit
only on their profitability and not on their luxury, had run up
4   large debts. Through them Catiline believed he could incite the
City slaves, burn the City, and either bring their husbands over
25 to his side or kill them. (Amongst them was Sempronia,[51] who
2   had often performed many deeds of manly daring. This woman
was quite fortunate in her lineage and appearance, and in her
husband and children besides; learned in Greek and Latin literature, she played the lyre and danced more elegantly than is
necessary for a virtuous woman; and there were many of the
3   other things which abet luxury. Yet, to her, everything was
always dearer than respectability and chastity. Whether she was
less sparing of her money or her reputation, you could not have
easily decided: her lust was so inflamed that she more often
4   sought men than was sought by them; but often before now she
had betrayed her trust, abjured credit, been an accessory to
murder. Through luxury and indigence she had fallen headlong.
5   Still, she was in no way intellectually inept: she could write
verse, produce a joke, and indulge in conversation which was
either restrained or tender or provocative; in fact, she had
considerable wit and considerable charm.)

26   Despite these preparations, Catiline nonetheless became a
candidate for the consulship for the next year,[52] hoping that, if
he were designated, it would be easy for him to use Antonius
at will. Nor was he quiet in the meanwhile, but by every means
2   at his disposal was preparing snares for Cicero. Yet the latter
lacked neither the cunning nor the astuteness for taking pre-
3   cautions. For, from the inception of his consulship, by numerous guarantees made through Fulvia, he had ensured that
Q. Curius (about whom I spoke a little earlier) would betray
4   Catiline's schemes to him; in addition, he had prevailed on his
colleague Antonius, by settling the matter of his province,[53]
not to harbour sympathies against the commonwealth; and he

secretly surrounded himself with bodyguards of friends and
clients. When the day of the elections came and neither   5
Catiline's candidacy nor the snares which he had laid on the
Plain[54] for the consuls had turned out successfully, he decided
to make war and to put everything to the ultimate test, since
what he had attempted in secret had had a harsh and ugly
outcome. Therefore he dispatched C. Manlius to Faesulae and   27
that part of Etruria, a certain Septimius of Camerinum to the
territory of Picenum, C. Iulius[55] to Apulia, and, apart from
them, others to wherever he believed would be strategically
favourable to himself.

Meanwhile at Rome he made simultaneous efforts on many   2
fronts: he set snares for the consul, made preparations for fires,
occupied strategic points with armed men; he himself carried a
weapon, ordered others likewise, and encouraged them always
to concentrate and be prepared. Day and night he hurried and
watched, and was exhausted by neither sleeplessness nor toil.
Finally, when despite his considerable activity no progress had   3
been made, at dead of night he again summoned the chiefs of
the conspiracy through the agency of M. Porcius Laeca, and   4
there,[56] after many complaints about their apathy, he told them
that he had sent Manlius ahead to the crowd which he had
prepared for taking to arms, and likewise other persons to other
strategic points to make a start on the war, and that his own
desire was to set off for the army, if only he could overwhelm
Cicero first: the man was a considerable obstacle to his schemes.
Therefore, while everyone else hesitated in terror, the Roman   28
equestrian C. Cornelius guaranteed his services, and with him
the senator L. Vargunteius, and they decided that a little later
that night with armed men they would call on Cicero as if to
pay their respects and suddenly would stab him, while unpre-
pared, in his own home. But, when Curius realized the great   2
danger threatening the consul, he quickly informed Cicero,
through Fulvia, of the plot being prepared for him. Hence the   3
men were kept from the door; they had undertaken such a deed
in vain.

Meanwhile Manlius in Etruria was galvanizing the plebs,   4
desirous of revolution as they were because of destitution and

the pain of injustice, since during the dominion of Sulla they had lost their land and all their property; and, apart from them, bandits of every type, of whom there were great numbers in that region, and some men from the Sullan colonies,[57] whose lust for luxury meant that they had nothing left from their great seizures.

29   When these things were announced to Cicero, he was affected by a twofold problem – that he could no longer by his personal counsel protect the City from ambush and that he had not found out adequately the size of Manlius' army or its intentions. He therefore referred the matter, already discussed beforehand

2   in rumours amongst the public, to the senate. And so, as often happens in the case of some frightening business, the senate decreed that the consuls should do their utmost 'to prevent

3   the commonwealth from suffering any damage'.[58] That is the greatest power allowed to a magistracy by the senate according to Roman custom: to prepare an army, to wage war, to coerce allies and citizens by every means, and to wield the highest command and jurisdiction at home and on campaign. (Otherwise a consul has the right to none of these things without an order from the people.)

30   After a few days L. Saenius, a senator, read out in the senate a letter which he said had been brought to him from Faesulae, in which it had been written that C. Manlius with a great crowd had taken to arms on the sixth day before the Kalends of

2   November.[59] At the same time (as is usual in such a circumstance) some people announced portents and prodigies, others that assemblies were taking place and arms being carried about, and that at Capua and in Apulia a slave war was stirring.

3   Therefore by a senate's decree Q. Marcius Rex was sent to Faesulae and Q. Metellus Creticus to Apulia and the places

4   round about (they were each commanders in the vicinity of the City, prevented from holding a triumph[60] by the chicanery of a few whose custom it was to sell everything honourable and

5   dishonourable); as for the praetors, Q. Pompeius Rufus was sent to Capua and Q. Metellus Celer[61] to the territory of Picenum, and permission was given them to muster an army in

6   the light of the circumstances and danger. In addition, if anyone

gave information about the conspiracy which had been formed
against the commonwealth, the reward for a slave would be his
freedom and a hundred thousand sesterces, and for a free man
immunity for his involvement and two hundred thousand sesterces; likewise they decreed that the troupes of gladiators   7
should be dispersed to Capua and the other municipalities
according to the resources of each place, and that at Rome
watches should be stationed across the whole City and that the
lesser magistrates should be in charge of them.

The community quaked at these measures, and the face of   31
the City was altered. Instead of the mirth and merriment which
the lasting calm had produced, there was suddenly an assault
from every form of sadness. People hurried and trembled; they   2
did not quite trust any place or any individual; they were neither
waging war nor experiencing peace; and each was gauging the
dangers by his own dread. In addition, women – overcome by   3
a fear of war which, given the magnitude of the commonwealth,
was unfamiliar to them – beat their breasts, held out their hands
to heaven in supplication, expressed pity for their children,
questioned everything, panicked at every rumour, seized upon
everything, and, forgoing their haughtiness and delights, dis-
trusted themselves and their fatherland.

But Catiline's cruel mind maintained its selfsame activities,   4
even though defences were being prepared and he himself had
been questioned by L. Paullus[62] under the Plautian Law.[63]
Finally, for reasons of dissembling or of self-exculpation, as   5
though he had been merely assailed in an altercation, he came
to the senate. Then M. Tullius as consul, whether fearful of the   6
man's presence or affected by anger, delivered a sparkling
speech of benefit to the commonwealth, of which he afterwards issued the written version.[64] But when he had sat down,   7
Catiline, prepared as he was to dissemble everything, with face
downcast and suppliant voice began to demand of the fathers
that they should not believe rashly anything concerning him:
he was sprung from such a family, and he had regulated his life
from adolescence in such a way, that he had good prospects in
every respect; they should not reckon that, as a patrician[65]
whose own and whose ancestors' benefits to the Roman plebs

were very numerous, he needed the destruction of the commonwealth – when it was being safeguarded by M. Tullius, an
8   immigrant citizen of the City of Rome.[66] When he began to
add other insults in addition, everyone heckled him and called
9   him 'enemy' and 'parricide'.[67] Thereupon, in a fury, he said,
'Because I have been trapped and am being driven headlong by
my antagonists, I shall extinguish this fire of mine by demo-
32   lition.'[68] Then he hurtled out of the curia, and home.

There he turned over many considerations within himself,
and, because his snares for the consul had been making no
progress and he realized that the City had been reinforced by
watches against fire, he believed that the best thing to do was
to enlarge his army and, before legions could be enlisted, to
anticipate the many things which would be useful for the war;
so at dead of night[69] he set off with a few men for Manlius'
2   camp. To Cethegus and Lentulus and the others who he knew
were ready and daring, he gave instructions that, by whatever
means they were able, they should strengthen the faction's
resources, hasten the snares for the consul and prepare slaughter
and fire and other deeds of war; he himself would advance on
the City any day with a large army.

3   While these things were happening in Rome, C. Manlius sent
legates from his company to Marcius Rex with instructions of
this kind:

33   'We call upon gods and men to witness, commander, that we
have taken up arms neither against the commonwealth nor to
endanger others but so that we may keep our persons safe from
injury – we who are pitiful and needy, and, through the violence
and cruelty of money-lenders, most of us lacking a fatherland,
all of us in[70] fame and fortune. Not one of us could resort to
the law according to ancestral custom nor, having lost his
patrimony, keep his person free: so great was the savagery of
2   the money-lenders and praetor.[71] Often did your ancestors take
pity on the Roman plebs and, by their decrees, bring help in its
helplessness; and most recently, within our recollection, silver
was paid off in bronze because of the magnitude of debt,[72] with
3   the blessing of all good men. Often did the plebs itself, roused by
an enthusiasm for dominion or by the magistrates' haughtiness,

conduct an armed secession from the fathers.[73] But, as for us, 4
we seek neither command nor riches, which are the cause of all
wars and struggles amongst mortals, but freedom, which no
good man loses except along with his life's breath. We call 5
upon you and the senate to pay heed to the citizens' pitifulness,
to restore the legal protection which the unfairness of the
praetor has snatched away, and not to impose upon us the
necessity of seeking how best we may avenge our blood when
we perish.'

Q. Marcius replied to this that, if there was anything for 34
which they wanted to ask from the senate, they should put
down their arms and set off for Rome as suppliants: the for-
bearance and pity of the senate of the Roman people had always
been such that no one ever sought its aid in vain.

As for Catiline, while on his journey he sent letters to numer- 2
ous consulars and all the best men: he had been entrapped by
false charges; since he could not withstand the faction of his
antagonists, he was yielding to Fortune and setting off for exile
in Massilia,[74] not because he was an accessory to so great a
crime but so that the commonwealth should be calm and no
sedition arise as the result of his struggle.

A quite different letter from this was read out in the senate 3
by Q. Catulus,[75] who said that it had been given to him in
Catiline's name. A copy of it is written below:

'L. Catilina to Q. Catulus. Your exceptional fidelity, known 35
to me by experience and welcome to me in my great dangers,
gives confidence to this commission of mine. For that reason 2
I have decided not to prepare a defence in the case of my
revolutionary scheme;[76] but I *have* determined to put forward,
though from no consciousness of guilt, an explanation, which
(so help me god!) you can recognize as true.

'Goaded by wrongs and aspersions, and because I was 3
deprived of the fruit of my toil and industry and failed to
maintain the position of my rank, I undertook the official cause
of the wretched, as is my habit; it was not that I could not pay
off the debts against my name from my own possessions (or
that the generosity of Orestilla could not pay off those against
others' names from her own and her daughter's funds), but

because I kept seeing unworthy men honoured by the honour of office and I came to realize that I had been disqualified

4 because of a false suspicion. On this account I have followed the hope – quite honourable, given my situation – of preserving what rank I have left.

5 'Though I would like to write more, I am told that force is
6 being prepared against me. As it is, I commit Orestilla to you and entrust her to your fidelity: keep her from harm, asked as you are by your children.[77] Farewell.'

36 Nevertheless he himself delayed for a few days at the house of C. Flaminius in the territory of Arretium,[78] while he furnished arms to a neighbourhood which was already galvanized; then, with the fasces and other insignia of command, he marched

2 to Manlius in his camp. When this was found out at Rome, the senate pronounced Catiline and Manlius enemies and appointed a day before which the rest of their crowd (apart from those condemned on capital charges) could put down

3 their arms with impunity. Apart from that, it decreed that the consuls should hold a levy, that Antonius with an army should speedily pursue Catiline, and that Cicero should act as defender of the City.

4 It was at that period that the empire of the Roman people seemed to me easily at its most pitiful. Although everywhere from east to west had been domesticated by force of arms and was in obedience to it, and domestically both peace and riches (which mortals think of chief importance) were overflowing, nevertheless there were citizens who with hardened hearts set

5 out to destroy both themselves and the commonwealth. For, despite two senate's decrees,[79] no one at all from that great crowd had either revealed the conspiracy through the inducement of a reward or had withdrawn from Catiline's camp.

Such was the violence of the disease and the kind of rottenness
37 which had attacked many of the citizens' spirits. And not only was there the mental derangement of those who were accessories to the conspiracy, but the entire plebs, in its enthusiasm for
2 revolution, approved completely of Catiline's projects. That,
3 indeed, it seemed to do from its own particular habit. For it is

always those in a community who have no resources who resent
the good and extol the wicked, who hate what is old and crave
what is new, who in their hatred of their own circumstances
are enthusiastic for everything to be changed, and who thrive
on disruption and sedition with no concern, since destitution is
a possession easily held without loss. But, in the case of the   4
City plebs, there were many reasons for *its* headlong plight.

First of all, there had flowed into Rome, as if into a bilge,   5
those everywhere whose disreputableness and discontent were
particularly transcendent, and similarly others after losing their
patrimony in disgrace, and finally all who had been driven from
home by depravity or deed. Second, many were mindful of the   6
Sullan victory, and, because they saw some of the troop soldiers
become senators and others so rich that they lived a life of royal
scale and style, each of them hoped that, if he took to arms,
victory would bring him the same.[80] Apart from them, the   7
young men who had endured indigence by the wages of their
hands in the fields had been unsettled by generous public and
private grants and had preferred city leisure to thankless toil.
They and all the others were kept nourished by the public
malady. It is therefore less of a surprise that destitute indi-   8
viduals, with their wicked morals and the highest hopes, paid
the same heed to the commonwealth as to themselves.

Apart from them, those whose parents had been proscribed   9
after the victory of Sulla, whose property had been seized and
whose right to freedom had been curtailed,[81] were naturally
awaiting the outcome of the war with just the same attitude.
In addition, whoever belonged to a different party from the   10
senate's preferred the commonwealth to be disabled rather than
that they themselves should thrive less well. That, indeed, was   11
the malady which after many years had returned to the community. For, after the tribunician power had been restored in   38
the consulship of Cn. Pompeius and of M. Crassus,[82] the utmost
power was acquired by young men whose age and spirit were
those of defiance, and they began to stir up the plebs by accusing
the senate and then to inflame them still more by bribery and
promises: in this way they became personally distinguished and
powerful. It was against them that many of the nobility strove   2

with the utmost effort, apparently on behalf of the senate but
3 in fact for their own greatness. For after those times (to dispatch the truth in a few words), no matter who stirred up
the commonwealth on honourable pretexts (some as though
defending the rights of the people, others to maximize the
authority of the senate), each of them, despite his pretence of
the common good, was competing for his own powerfulness.
4 There was nothing moderate or restrained about their struggle:
39 any victory was enforced cruelly by each of the two sides. But,
after Cn. Pompeius was sent to the maritime and Mithridatic
wars,[83] the resources of the plebs were reduced and the power
2 of the few increased. It was they who held the magistracies,
provinces and everything else: unassailable and flourishing, they
lived a life free from dread themselves but used the courts to
terrify the others, so that the latter during any magistracy of
3 theirs would handle the plebs more peaceably. But, as soon as
circumstances became uncertain and the prospect of revolution
4 presented itself, the old contest stirred their spirits; and, if
Catiline had come away from the first battle the stronger (or at
least on equal terms), assuredly a great catastrophe and
calamity would have overwhelmed the commonwealth, and
those achieving victory would not have been able to enjoy
it for too long before someone still more powerful extorted
command and freedom from them, exhausted and debilitated
as they would have been.

5 There were nevertheless several outside the conspiracy who
initially set off to join Catiline, and amongst them was Fulvius,
a senator's son, who was ordered by his parent to be brought
back from his journey and to be executed.[84]
6   At the same time, at Rome, in accordance with Catiline's
instructions, Lentulus either personally or through the agency
of others was inveigling whomsoever he believed to be suited
to revolution because of behaviour or fortune – and not only
citizens but categories of men of every kind, provided only that
40 they would be useful in the war. Hence he gave to a certain
P. Umbrenus the business of seeking out the legates of the
Allobroges[85] and, if he could, inducing them to join the war:

he thought that, overwhelmed by debt both communally and individually as they were, and also because the Gallic people were naturally warlike, they could easily be drawn to such a scheme. Because Umbrenus had been a businessman in Gaul, 2 he was known to numerous community chiefs and knew them; and so, as soon as he caught sight of the legates in the forum, without delay he enquired briefly about the condition of their community and, as if sympathizing with its plight, began to ask what outcome they expected for their great maladies. When he 3 saw that they complained about the avarice of the magistrates, accused the senate for its complete inability to help them and only awaited death as the remedy for their pitiful state, he said, 'But, if only you are willing to be men, *I* will show you a way of escaping from those great maladies of yours.' When he said 4 this, the Allobroges were drawn to the highest hope and begged Umbrenus to take pity on them: nothing was so harsh or so difficult that they would not do it with the utmost desire, provided that it freed their community from its debt.

He took them to the house of D. Brutus, because it was 5 near the forum and no stranger to the scheme on account of Sempronia (Brutus was away from Rome at the time); in 6 addition he sent for Gabinius, so that his conversation should be invested with greater authority. In the latter's presence he revealed the conspiracy and named the accomplices – and many innocent men of every type besides, so that the legates would take greater heart. Then, when they had promised their services, he sent them home.

But for a long time the Allobroges were uncertain what course 41 of action to adopt. On the one hand, there was the debt, their 2 enthusiasm for war, the great remuneration after the victory in prospect; on the other, greater resources, safe courses of action, certain rewards instead of an uncertain prospect. As they were 3 turning over these considerations, at length the Fortune of the commonwealth prevailed: they revealed the whole affair, 4 exactly as they had learned of it, to Q. Fabius Sanga, on whose patronage the community particularly relied.[86] Cicero, learning 5 of the scheme from Sanga, instructed the legates to make an earnest pretence of enthusiasm for the conspiracy, to approach the other members of it, to give them nice promises and to do their best to render them as red-handed as possible.

42   At roughly the same time there were tremors in Nearer and Further Gaul,[87] likewise in the Picene and Bruttian territory and
2   in Apulia. Those whom Catiline had previously dispatched were stirring up everything simultaneously, without consideration and as if demented: by night-time meetings, by moving arms and weapons about and by hurrying and general agitation, they had
3   caused more fear than danger. The praetor Q. Metellus Celer, after examining their case in the light of the senate's decision, had thrown several of their number in chains; likewise C. Murena in Nearer Gaul, who was in charge of the province as legate.[88]

43   But at Rome Lentulus and the others who were the chief conspirators, having prepared what seemed to them to be a great force, had decided that, when Catiline arrived in the territory of Faesulae[89] with his army, L. Bestia, the tribune of the plebs, should hold a meeting, complain about the actions of Cicero and saddle the best of consuls with the resentment for the gravest of wars: with that as the signal, on the next night the general crowd of conspirators should carry out their own
2   individual tasks. These were said to have been shared out in this way: Statilius and Gabinius with a substantial unit were to fire twelve strategic locations in the City simultaneously, so that in the resulting commotion there would be easier access to the consuls and the others for whom snares were being prepared; Cethegus was to lay siege to Cicero's door and attack him with force; there were to be various killings, particularly of parents by the sons of the families, most of whom belonged to the nobility; and, with everyone stunned by the simultaneous slaughter and fire, they would burst out in Catiline's direction.
3   Amidst these preparations and decisions Cethegus kept up a continual complaint about the apathy of his allies: by their hesitation and daily deferments they were spoiling great opportunities; deeds, not deliberations, were needed at such a dangerous moment; and despite the general listlessness he himself, if only a few would help him, would make an assault on the curia.
4   By nature he was defiant, violent and ready with his muscle; he thought the greatest advantage lay in haste.

As for the Allobroges, in accordance with Cicero's instruction   44
they had a meeting with the others, brought about by Gabinius.
From Lentulus, Cethegus, Statilius and likewise Cassius they
demanded an oath which, once sealed, they could take to their
fellow citizens; otherwise, they said, it would not be easy to
induce them into so great an enterprise. The others, suspecting   2
nothing, gave it; Cassius guaranteed that he would soon come
there, and set off from the City a little before the legates.
Lentulus sent with them a certain T. Volturcius[90] of Croton, so   3
that, before the Allobroges made for home, they could confirm
their association with Catiline by means of mutual pledges of
loyalty. He gave Volturcius a letter for Catiline, a copy of which   4
is written below:[91] 'Who I am, you will realize from him whom   5
I have sent to you. Make sure you reflect on the size of the
calamity in which you are involved, and remember that you are
a man. Consider what your calculations demand: seek help
from everyone, even from the lowest.' In addition he gave oral   6
instructions: since he had been pronounced an enemy by the
senate, what was the point in rejecting the slaves? The preparations which he had ordered in the City were in place; he
himself should not delay in advancing nearer.

When these matters had been conducted in this way, and   45
the night on which they would set off decided, Cicero – who
had been told everything by the legates – commanded the
praetors L. Valerius Flaccus and C. Pomptinus[92] to arrest the
Allobroges' retinue by an ambush at the Milvian Bridge.[93] He
revealed to them the whole affair which was the purpose of
their being sent; and he gave them permission to act in general
as the need required. Being military men, they placed guards   2
without any commotion and, as had been instructed, took over
the bridge secretly. When the legates along with Volturcius   3
reached that point and a shout arose simultaneously from both
sides, the Gauls quickly realized the plan and handed themselves over to the praetors without delay; Volturcius at first   4
encouraged the others and protected himself with a sword
against the crowd; but then, after being deserted by the legates,
he first remonstrated volubly about his safety with Pomptinus
(because he was known to him) and finally, fearful and uncer-

tain of his life, he gave himself up to the praetors as if to an
enemy.

46   After the conclusion of these events, the consul was quickly
2   told everything by messengers; but he was overwhelmed might-
ily by simultaneous concern and delight: he was delighted to
learn that, with the conspiracy revealed, the community had
been snatched from danger; but on the other hand he was made
anxious by the uncertainty of what he should do, now that such
great citizens had been caught in the greatest of crimes: he
believed that punishing them would rest heavily upon himself,
whereas exemption would result in destroying the common-
3   wealth. It was therefore only when he had fortified his spirit
that he ordered Lentulus, Cethegus, Statilius and Gabinius to
be summoned to him; and likewise Caeparius[94] of Tarracina,
4   who was preparing to set off for Apulia to rouse the slaves. The
others came without delay; Caeparius, having left home a little
before, had become acquainted with some information and fled
from the City.

5   The consul himself led Lentulus by the hand into the senate,
because he was a praetor; the rest he ordered to come under
6   guard to the shrine of Concordia. That was where he had
summoned[95] the senate, and, before a large throng of their
order, he introduced Volturcius and the legates; he ordered the
praetor Flaccus to bring along to the same place the document-
box containing the letters which he had received from the
47   legates. Volturcius was asked about his journey, about the letters, and, lastly, what scheme he had had and for what reason.
At first he fabricated variously and dissembled about the conspiracy; after, when he had received an official assurance of
immunity and been ordered to speak, he revealed everything
exactly as it had taken place, and told them that he had been
enrolled as an accomplice by Gabinius and Caeparius only a
few days before and knew nothing more than the legates: he
had merely been accustomed to hear from Gabinius that
P. Autronius, Ser. Sulla, L. Vargunteius and many apart from
2   them were in the conspiracy. The Gauls professed the same and
confuted Lentulus' dissembling on the basis of (apart from his
letter) the conversations which he had been accustomed to hold,

to the effect that the Sibylline books[96] portended kingship at Rome for three Cornelii; that, after Cinna and Sulla previously, he himself was the third for whom possession of the City was fated;[97] in addition, that that was the twentieth year after the burning of the Capitol,[98] and the soothsayers had often responded to prodigies by saying that it would be made gory by civil war. Therefore, after the letters had been read, and only when everyone had acknowledged his own seal, the senate decreed that Lentulus after abdicating his magistracy and the others likewise should be held under house arrest. And so Lentulus was handed over to P. Lentulus Spinther, who was then aedile, Cethegus to Q. Cornificius, Statilius to C. Caesar, Gabinius to M. Crassus, and Caeparius (he had been brought back from his flight a little before) to Cn. Terentius, a senator.[99]

Meanwhile the plebs, which at first had desired revolution and been too much in favour of war, now, with the conspiracy revealed,[100] changed their minds and cursed Catiline's schemes, extolling Cicero to the sky: as though snatched from slavery, they experienced joy and delight. For they thought that, though other deeds of war would lead to plunder rather than to loss, burning was cruel, excessive and especially calamitous for themselves, whose every resource consisted in their daily utensils and accessories for the body.

On the day after that, there had been led into the senate a certain L. Tarquinius,[101] who they said had been setting off for Catiline and brought back from his journey. When he said that he would give information about the conspiracy if he received an official assurance of immunity, he was ordered by the consul to say what he knew, and he told the senate roughly the same as Volturcius about the preparations for burning, the slaughter of the good, the enemy's march; apart from that, he had (he said) been sent by M. Crassus to tell Catiline that he should not be terrified by the arrest of Lentulus and Cethegus and others from the conspiracy but should proceed all the more quickly to advance on the City so that he might restore the spirits of the others and they might be snatched from danger more easily. But, when Tarquinius named Crassus, a noble man of the greatest riches and the utmost power, everyone cried that the informant was false and demanded a motion concerning the matter – some deeming the matter incredible, others because, though they reckoned it true, it seemed that at such a moment so strong a man should be mollified rather than provoked, while very many of them were beholden to Crassus through

6 personal business. And so a crowded senate, when consulted by Cicero, decreed that Tarquinius' information seemed false and he should be kept in chains and given no further opportunity of informing except concerning the person whose scheme

7 it had been that he should lie about so great a matter. (There were at the time those who thought that his information had been devised by P. Autronius so that, once Crassus had been named, the man's power might protect the others through his

8 association in their danger. Others said that Tarquinius had been sent in by Cicero to prevent Crassus from undertaking the patronage of the wicked according to his usual custom and

9 disabling the commonwealth. I later heard Crassus himself declaring that that great aspersion had been imputed to him by Cicero.)

49 At the same time Q. Catulus and C. Piso[102] could not induce Cicero either by pleas or by favour or by reward that C. Caesar should be falsely named by the Allobroges or some other

2 informant. (Each had been conducting serious hostilities with him, Piso because he had been attacked in the extortion court on account of the unjust reprisal of a certain Transpadane,[103] Catulus because he was burning with hatred in the light of his candidacy for the pontificate, since, though of advanced years and having held the most honorific offices, he had been defeated

3 by a young Caesar.[104]) The present circumstance seemed favourable because, with his exceptional private generosity and his very great public donations, the man owed a substantial amount

4 of money. But, when they were unable to induce the consul to such a deed, they made the rounds of individuals and lied about what they said they had heard from Volturcius or the Allobroges; and they had stoked up great resentment against him to such an extent that several Roman equestrians who were on guard with weapons round the shrine of Concordia, induced either by the magnitude of the danger or by the volatility of

their dispositions, threatened Caesar with their swords as he
left the senate, so that their enthusiasm for the commonwealth
should be more conspicuous.

While this was going on in the senate, and while rewards   50
were being decreed to the legates of the Allobroges and to
T. Volturcius on the confirmation of their information, the
freedmen of Lentulus and a few of his clients went by various
routes and started to galvanize the artisans and slaves in the
streets to snatch him away; others sought out those leaders of
the crowds who for a price had been accustomed to ravage the
commonwealth. As for Cethegus, by means of messages he   2
was pleading for daring on the part of his establishment and
freedmen, picked and trained as they were: they should form a
troop and, with weapons, force their way through to him.

When the consul heard of these developments, he deployed   3
guards as the situation and moment suggested and, having
summoned the senate, put before it a motion as to what its
decision was concerning those who had been handed over into
custody.[105] (A little before, a crowded senate had pronounced
that they had acted against the commonwealth. On that   4
occasion D. Iunius Silanus,[106] asked for his opinion first because
at the time he was consul designate, had declared that reprisal[107]
should be exacted from those who were being held in custody,
and from L. Cassius, P. Furius,[108] P. Umbrenus and Q. Annius
besides, should they be caught; and afterwards, influenced by a
speech from C. Caesar, he had said[109] that he would go over to
the opinion of Ti. Nero,[110] who had proposed that, after adding
guards, there should be a motion on the matter.) When Caesar's   5
turn came, he was asked by the consul for his opinion and
spoke words of this type:

'All persons who deliberate on uncertain matters, conscript   51
fathers,[111] should empty themselves of hatred, friendship, anger
and pity. It is not easy for the mind to see the truth when they   2
are in the way, nor has anyone at all ever obeyed whim and
expediency at the same time. When you concentrate your intel-   3
lect, the mind is effective; but, if whim takes over, that domi-
nates and the mind is ineffective. I have a large supply of   4
recollections, conscript fathers, of the occasions when kings

and peoples, induced by anger or pity, deliberated wrongly; but
I prefer to speak of what our ancestors did rightly and properly
5 in spite of the whim in their minds. In the Macedonian War
which we waged with King Perseus,[112] the great and magnificent
community of the Rhodians, which had grown thanks to the
resources of the Roman people,[113] was disloyal and hostile to
us; but, when at the war's end there was deliberation concerning
the Rhodians, our ancestors discharged them unpunished, lest
anyone should say that the war had been begun for the sake of
6 riches rather than an injustice. Likewise in all the Punic Wars,[114]
although the Carthaginians had often done many unprincipled
deeds both in peace and during times of truce, they never
did the same despite their opportunities: they asked what was
worthy of themselves rather than what could be done with
7 justice to an enemy. You must see to it likewise, conscript
fathers, that the crime of P. Lentulus and the others does not
have a greater effect on you than does your own worth, and
that you do not pay more heed to your anger than to your
8 reputation. If a worthy punishment is found in the light of their
deeds, I approve a new counsel; but, if the magnitude of the
crime defeats everyone's intellect, I propose resorting to what
has been provided for by law.

9   'Many of those who gave their opinions before me expressed
their pity for the situation of the commonwealth in a neat and
splendid manner. They itemized what the savagery of war was
like, what befell the conquered: maidens and boys seized, children wrenched from their parents' embrace, the mothers of
families enduring whatever their conquerors pleased, shrines
and homes despoiled, slaughter and burning, and, finally, every-
10 where filled with arms, corpses, gore and grief. But, by the
immortal gods, what was the point of such a speech? To make
you hostile to the conspiracy? *Naturally* a man who has not
been stirred by so great and so frightful an act will be influenced
11 by a speech! No, that is not it; and no mortal at all thinks little
of injuries to himself: in fact, many have regarded them more
12 seriously than is fair. But different allowances are made for
different people, conscript fathers. If the lowly who live life in
obscurity commit wrong through anger, few know of it: their

fame is on the same level as their fortune. But, as for those who
are endowed with some great command and spend their years
at the zenith, all mortals know their deeds. Hence the least   13
allowance is made in the case of the greatest fortune: neither
partiality nor hatred, but least of all anger, is proper; what in   14
the case of others is described as anger is called haughtiness
and cruelty in those who command. *I* think, conscript fathers,   15
that no torture matches the deeds of those men; but many
mortals remember only what comes last, and, in the case of
heinous individuals, they forget their crime and talk only of
their punishment, if it was a little too severe.

   'I know for certain that D. Silanus, a courageous and commit-   16
ted man, said what he said out of partiality for the commonwealth, and that in so great a matter he would not exercise
favour or antagonism: such I know to be the behaviour and the
restraint of the man. But his opinion seems to me, not cruel   17
(for what can be cruel for such men?), but foreign to this
commonwealth of ours. Now naturally it was dread or injustice   18
which drove you as consul designate, Silanus, to declare a new
form of punishment. About fear it is superfluous to talk, since   19
– thanks above all to the diligence of that most distinguished
man, the consul – such substantial guards are under arms. But   20
about punishment I am able to say what is the case, that amidst
grief and pitifulness death constitutes, not torture, but a rest
from affliction: it dissipates all the maladies of mortals, and
beyond it there is no place for either worry or joy. But, by the   21
immortal gods, why to your opinion did you not add the proposal that they should first be chastised by lashes? Because the
Porcian Law[115] forbids it? Yet other laws order that citizens   22
similarly condemned should not have their lives snatched away
but should be permitted exile. Or because lashing is more severe   23
than execution? But what is harsh or too severe for men convicted of such a deed? On the other hand, if it was because it is   24
lighter, how is it consistent to fear the law in a lesser case when
you disregard it in a greater?

   ' "But", it may be said, "who will criticize a decree against   25
parricides of the commonwealth?" – Time, is the answer; or
any day; or Fortune, whose whim governs the world. Whatever   26

happens will befall *those* men deservedly; but *you*, conscript
27   fathers, should reflect on what you decide for others. Every bad
precedent has arisen from some good circumstance; but, when
command passes to those ignorant of it or to the less good, any
new precedent is transferred from the deserving and appropri-
28   ate to the undeserving and inappropriate. The Lacedaemonians
imposed on the defeated Athenians thirty men to handle their
29   commonwealth.[116] At first they began to execute, without trial,
all the worst individuals and those resented by all: the people
30   were delighted and said it was deserved. But after, when their
licence had gradually increased, they killed good and bad indif-
31   ferently at whim and terrified the rest with dread. So a community which had been oppressed by slavery paid a heavy
32   penalty for its foolish delight. In our recollection, who did not
praise Sulla's deed when he ordered the butchering of Damasippus[117] and the others of his kind, whose growth had been to
the detriment of the commonwealth? They said that the factious
criminals who had stirred up the commonwealth by their
33   rebellions had been deservedly executed. But that affair was the
start of a great disaster. For, whenever anyone desired someone's home or villa or, ultimately, his goblet or garment, he did
his best to ensure that the man was listed amongst the pro-
34   scribed. So those for whom Damasippus' death had been a
source of delight were themselves dragged off shortly after, and
there was no end to the butchery until Sulla had satisfied all his
35   supporters with riches. I do not fear these things in M. Tullius'
case nor in these times, but in a great community dispositions
36   are many and varied. It is possible that, at another time and
under another consul in whose hands there is likewise an army,
something false will be believed to be true. When after this
precedent a consul draws his sword in accordance with a
senate's decree, who will decide the ending for him, who will
restrain him?
37   'Our ancestors, conscript fathers, were never destitute of
counsel or daring; nor did haughtiness stand in the way of
their imitating others' institutions, provided only that they were
38   virtuous. They borrowed arms and military weapons from the
Samnites,[118] many of their magistrates' insignia from the Etrus-

cans; in short, they pursued with enthusiasm at home whatever seemed suitable anywhere amongst allies or enemies: they preferred to imitate success rather than resent it. Yet at that very same time, in imitation of Greek custom, they chastised citizens with lashes and exacted the ultimate reprisal from the condemned. But, after the commonwealth had matured and the number of citizens led to thriving factions and the innocent began to be entrapped and other things of this type to take place, then the Porcian Law and other laws were provided, laws by which exile was permitted to the condemned. This I think is an especially good reason, conscript fathers, for our not adopting a new counsel. Naturally those who created so great an empire from small resources had better prowess and wisdom than there is in us, who scarcely retain what has been so well acquired.

'Should they therefore be discharged and Catiline's army be increased? Not at all. But I do propose as follows: that their money should be confiscated and they themselves held in chains in the municipalities which have the most effective resources; that no one afterwards should bring a motion before the senate concerning them nor discuss them in front of the people; and that the senate thinks that whoever acts otherwise shall be acting against the commonwealth and the welfare of all.'

After Caesar had finished speaking, the rest began to express orally their varied agreement with one or other member. But, when M. Porcius Cato[119] was asked his opinion, he delivered a speech of this type:

'Far different is my inclination, conscript fathers, when I contemplate the circumstances of our dangers and when I think over to myself the opinions of several of the members. They seem to me to have spoken about the punishment of men who prepared war against their own fatherland, parents, altars and hearths; but circumstances suggest that we should be wary of those men rather than that we should be deliberating what decision to take against them. Other misdeeds you pursue only when they have already been done; but, unless you see to it that this one does not befall us, you will invoke the courts in vain when it has happened: when a city has been captured, the defeated have nothing left. But, by the immortal gods, I call upon those of you who have always placed more value on your homes, villas, statues and pictures than on the commonwealth: if you want to keep whatever kind of thing it is that you embrace, and if you want to provide yourselves with leisure-time for your pleasures, then rouse yourselves before it is too

6 late and turn your attention to the commonwealth! This is no discussion of taxes or of injustice to our allies; our freedom and life's breath are in doubt.

7   'Often enough, conscript fathers, have I made a long speech before this order; often have I complained about the luxury and avarice of our citizens, and I have many mortals as adversaries

8 for that reason. As I had never granted myself or my instincts any dispensation for committing wrong, it was not easy for me to forgive the misdeeds of someone else on the grounds

9 of his whim. But, even though you attached little weight to such matters, nevertheless the commonwealth stood firm and because of its resourcefulness was able to withstand your neg-

10 lect. As things are now, however, the question is not whether our lives are characterized by good or bad behaviour, nor how great or how magnificent the empire of the Roman people is, but whether these things, however they are perceived, will be

11 ours or – along with ourselves – the enemy's. Is it at this point that someone mentions "mercy" and "pity" to me? We have long since lost the true designations of things: it is because lavishing other people's property is called "generosity", and because daring to do wicked things is called "courage", that

12 the commonwealth lies situated on the very brink. Since that is what the convention is, let them be generous with the fortunes of our allies, let them take pity on treasury thieves; but let them not be lavish with our blood nor, in sparing a few criminals, embark on destroying all good men.

13   'A little earlier, C. Caesar spoke well and neatly before this order about life and death, thinking, I believe, that what is said about the inhabitants of the underworld is false – namely, that along a different route from the good, the wicked dwell in

14 places which are rotten, neglected, foul and fearful. And so he has proposed confiscating the money of those men and holding the men themselves under guard in municipalities, evidently

afraid that, if they were in Rome, they would be snatched away
forcibly either by their associates in the conspiracy or by a hired
crowd. As if there were wicked criminals only in the City and   15
not across the whole of Italy or as if daring were not more
powerful where the resources for defence are less! For those   16
reasons this counsel of his is vain, if it is danger that he dreads
from them; and, if amidst such universal dread he alone is not
afraid, there is all the more need for me to be afraid for myself
and for you. For that reason, when you decide about P. Lentulus   17
and the others, be assured that at the same time you are issuing
a decree about Catiline's army and about all the conspirators.
The more attentively you conduct these matters, the weaker the   18
spirit in those quarters will be; but, if they see you wilt only a
very little, all of them will soon make their defiant presence
felt.

   'Do not think that it was by arms that our ancestors made   19
the commonwealth great from being small. If that were so, *we*   20
would now be seeing it at its finest by far, since we have a
greater supply of allies and citizens, and of arms and horses
besides, than our ancestors did. But it was other things which   21
made them great, and which we no longer have: industriousness
at home, a just empire abroad, and a mind free in deliberation,
beholden neither to wrongdoing nor to whim. Instead of these,   22
we have luxury and avarice, collective destitution and private
wealth; we praise riches and pursue idleness; there is no distinction between the good and the wicked; all the rewards for
prowess are in the possession of ambition. And no wonder: 23
when each of you takes counsel separately for himself, when
you are the slaves of pleasure at home and of money or favour
here – that is how an attack can be made on an abandoned
commonwealth.

   'But these things I pass over. Citizens of the greatest nobility   24
have conspired to burn their fatherland; they summon the
Gauls, a people most hostile to the name of Rome, to war; the
enemy leader and his army are poised over our heads: do you,   25
then, still hesitate and doubt what to do with the enemies
caught inside the walls? I propose that you take pity on them –   26
mere young men who did wrong through ambition – and

27 discharge them still armed![120] Do not let your mercy and pity
28 make you pitiable yourselves, should they take to arms! "Certainly the issue itself is harsh", you say, but *you* "do not fear
it." Yet you do, and very greatly; but through idleness and
soft-heartedness you hesitate, one waiting for another, evidently
trusting in the immortal gods, who have often saved this
29 commonwealth in its greatest dangers. Yet it is not by prayers
and womanly supplications that the help of the gods is acquired;
it is by watchfulness, action and good deliberation that everything ends successfully. When you submit to lethargy and
apathy, you invoke the gods in vain: they are angry and hostile.

30 'In the time of our ancestors, A. Manlius Torquatus during
the Gallic War ordered his own son to be executed because he
31 had fought against the enemy contrary to command;[121] and that
exceptional young man paid the penalty for his unrestrained
courage by death. Do you hesitate over what to decide concerning the cruellest of parricides? Evidently their crime is eclipsed
32 by the other aspects of their lives! Well, spare Lentulus for his
rank – if he ever spared his own chastity and reputation, or any
33 god or man! Pardon the young Cethegus – if he did not make
34 war on his fatherland twice![122] Why should I speak of Statilius,
Gabinius, Caeparius? If anything had ever weighed with them,
they would not have adopted those schemes of theirs for the
35 commonwealth. Finally, conscript fathers, if (as Hercules is my
witness) there were room for error, I would easily allow you to
be put right by the actual events, since you despise words; but
we are trapped on all sides: Catiline with his army is pressing
us at the throat; other enemies are inside the walls and in the
bosom of the City, and no preparation or deliberation is possible in secret. So speed is all the more necessary.

36   'For that reason I propose as follows: that, since the commonwealth has been brought to the greatest danger by the unprincipled scheme of criminal citizens, and since they have been
convicted on the information of T. Volturcius and the legates
of the Allobroges and have confessed to preparing slaughter,
burning and other foul and cruel deeds for citizens and fatherland, reprisal should be exacted on the strength of their

confession, as from those caught red-handed in capital cases, according to the custom of our ancestors.'

After Cato had sat down, all the consulars, and the majority   53
of the senate likewise, praised his proposal and extolled his prowess to the skies. Some upbraided one another with calls of 'coward', but Cato was regarded as 'distinguished' and 'great': a senate's decree was passed in accordance with his proposal.

Whenever I used to read or hear of the very many distinguished   2
deeds which the Roman people did at home and on campaign, on sea and land, it so happened that I liked to consider what factor above all had underpinned such great enterprises. I knew   3
that very often, with only a small unit, they had grappled with great enemy legions; I recognized that, with only small forces, they had waged wars with well resourced kings, and in addition that they had endured violence from Fortune and that in fluency the Greeks had been ahead of the Romans, and in military glory the Gauls. And, whenever I turned over my many thoughts, my   4
conclusion was that the exceptional prowess of a few citizens had accomplished it all and that that was the reason why riches were overcome by poverty, a multitude by a few.

But, after the community had been corrupted by luxurious-   5
ness and indolence, conversely the commonwealth by its own greatness sustained the faults of its commanders and magis-trates, and, as if it had been exhausted by childbirth, at many periods hardly anyone at all in Rome was great in prowess. But   6
within my own recollection there have been two men of mighty prowess yet differing behaviour: M. Cato and C. Caesar. Since the context has now presented them, it is not my intention to pass them over in silence without explaining, to the best of my intellectual ability, the nature and behaviour of each.

Their background, age and eloquence, then, were almost   54
equal; their greatness of spirit was parallel; likewise their glory, different though it was in each case. Caesar was regarded as   2
great for his kindnesses and munificence, Cato for the integrity of his life. The former achieved distinction for his mercy and pity; the latter's strictness had brought him prestige. Caesar   3

acquired glory by giving, by supporting, by forgiving; Cato by granting nothing. In the one, the wretched found their refuge; in the other, the wicked their ruin. The former's complaisance
4 was praised, the latter's steadfastness. Caesar, finally, had made up his mind to be hard-working and vigilant; devoted to the enterprises of his friends, he would neglect his own and refuse nothing that was worth giving; what he desired for himself was a great command, an army, and a new war where his prowess
5 could shine. But Cato's enthusiasm was for restraint, honour,
6 but especially strictness; he did not compete in riches with the rich or in factionalism with the factious, but with the committed in prowess, with the restrained in propriety, with the innocent in self-denial; he preferred to be, rather than to seem, a good man: thus, the less he sought glory, the more it attended him.

55 After the senate (as I have said) had divided in favour of Cato's proposal, the consul, deeming that the best thing to do was to forestall the impending night to prevent any revolutionary move during the course of it, ordered the triumvirs[123] to prepare what
2 the punishment demanded. After the deployment of guards, he personally escorted Lentulus to the gaol; the same was done for
3 the others by the praetors. There is in the gaol a place called the Tullianum, on the left when you have gone up a short way,
4 and sunk into the ground about twelve feet. It is fortified on all sides by walls, and the roof above is spanned by stone vaulting; but neglect, gloom and stench give it a foul and terrifying
5 appearance. That was the place to which Lentulus was taken down, whereupon the executioners of capital cases, whose com-
6 mission it was, broke his neck with a noose. So it was that a patrician from the most distinguished clan of the Cornelii, who had held consular command at Rome, met the end which his be-haviour and deeds deserved. From Cethegus, Statilius, Gabinius and Caeparius punishment was exacted in the same way.

56   While these things were taking place at Rome, Catiline formed two legions from the entire force which he himself had brought and which Manlius had had, the complement of the
2 cohorts being in proportion to the number of soldiers; but then, as volunteers or various of his allies came to the camp, he

distributed them equally and in a short while had filled up the legions with the number of men, although initially he had had no more than two thousand. But from the entire force only 3 about a quarter had been equipped with military arms; the rest had been armed with spears or lances, as chance would have it in each case, while some carried sharpened stakes.

When Antonius was approaching with his army, Catiline 4 made his way through the mountains; sometimes he moved his camp towards the City, sometimes facing Gaul; and he gave the enemy no opportunity to fight: he hoped that any day he would be in possession of great forces, if his allies accomplished their undertakings in Rome. Meanwhile he rebuffed the slaves (great 5 forces of whom had initially been rallying to him), relying on the resources of the conspiracy and at the same time thinking it incompatible with his schemes to be seen to have shared a citizens' cause with runaway slaves.

But, after news reached the camp that the conspiracy had 57 been revealed at Rome and that punishment had been exacted from Lentulus and Cethegus and the others whom I recalled above, many who had been lured to war by the hope of plunder, or by enthusiasm for revolution, slipped away; the rest Catiline led off by forced marches across rugged mountains to the region of Pistoria, his plan being to flee along byways secretly to Transalpine Gaul. But Q. Metellus Celer with three legions was 2 garrisoned in the region of Picenum, and he thought, from the difficulty of his circumstances, that Catiline would be turning over just those plans that we mentioned above. Therefore, when 3 he had discovered his route from deserters, he moved his camp hurriedly and stationed himself at the very base of the mountains where lay the other's descent in his hurry to reach Gaul. Nor was Antonius far away, seeing that with a great army he 4 was following, over more level ground, unencumbered men in flight.[124] But, after Catiline saw that he was shut in by the 5 mountains and enemy forces, that affairs in the City were against him, and that there was no hope of either flight or reinforcements, he deemed the best thing to do in the circumstances would be to test the fortunes of war, and he decided to engage with Antonius as soon as possible.

6   And so, having summoned a meeting, he made a speech of this type:

58   'I have found, soldiers, that words do not supply prowess and that neither is an apathetic army made committed, nor a cowardly one courageous, by a speech from its commander.

2   Whatever daring resides in the heart of each man by nature or habit, it is usually visible to the same degree in war. It would be pointless to exhort the man who is roused by neither glory

3   nor danger: the fear in his heart blocks his ears. Yet I summoned you for a few words of advice, and at the same time to explain the reasoning behind my plan.

4   'You know, soldiers, the size of the disaster which Lentulus' ineptitude and apathy have brought on himself and on us, and how I could not set off for Gaul while I was awaiting

5   reinforcements from the City. You all understand now, as well

6   as I do, the position our affairs are in. Two enemy armies – one towards the City, the other towards Gaul – stand in our way; a lack of grain and of other things prevents our being any longer

7   in this place, even if we really had the heart for it. Wherever we

8   decide to go, the route must be opened up with steel. Therefore I advise you to be courageous and prepared in spirit, and, when you enter the battle, to remember that in your hands you carry riches, honour and glory, to say nothing of freedom and the

9   fatherland. If we win, the world will be safe for us: we shall have access to supplies in abundance, municipalities and colonies; but, if we yield through dread, those same things will

10   be against us: neither place nor friend will protect the man who has not been protected by his arms.

11   'Besides, soldiers, the constraint looming over us and them is different. Our struggle is for fatherland, for freedom, for life;

12   theirs is a superfluous fight, for the power of a few. Therefore attack all the more daringly, mindful of your old-time prowess.

13   It was open to you to lead a life of the utmost disgrace in exile; some of you, having lost your property, could have anticipated

14   wealth from other quarters in Rome; but, because those alternatives seemed foul and intolerable to true men, you decided to

15   follow this path. If you wish to abandon it, daring is required:

16   no one but the victor exchanges war for peace. For to expect

safety in flight, when you turn away from the enemy the arms
which protect your body, that indeed is madness. In battle there   17
is always the greatest danger for those whose fear is greatest;
but to have daring is like a barrier.

'When I contemplate you, soldiers, and when I assess your   18
deeds, I am gripped by a great hope of victory. I am encouraged   19
by your spirit, your age and your prowess, to say nothing of
that constraint which makes even cowards courageous. The   20
enemy is present in numbers, yet the narrowness of the place
prevents them from surrounding us. But, if Fortune begrudges   21
you your prowess, make sure you neither gasp your last without
taking vengeance nor be captured and butchered like cattle,
but, fighting in the manner of true men, leave the enemy with
a bloody and grievous victory.'

When he had said this, after only a brief delay he ordered the   59
trumpets to sound and he led his organized ranks down to a
level area. Then, after dismissing everyone's horses so that the
soldiers should enjoy greater heart with the risks levelled out,
he personally on foot organized his army to suit both the area
and his forces. As the plain lay between the left-hand moun-   2
tains and the rugged rocks on the right, he set eight cohorts in
front and placed the remainder and their standards in reserve
in closer order. From these he withdrew to the front line all the   3
centurions and re-enlisted men, as well as all the best armed of
the troop-soldiers. He ordered C. Manlius to take charge on
the right, a certain Faesulan on the left; he himself, together
with his freedmen and attendants, took his stand by an eagle
which C. Marius was said to have had in the Cimbrian War.[125]

On the other side C. Antonius had an ailment of the feet,   4
and, because he could not take part in the battle, he entrusted
his army to M. Petreius,[126] his legate. The latter placed the   5
veteran cohorts, which he had conscripted because of the emergency, in front, and behind them the rest of the army in reserve.
He personally went about on horseback, calling each man by
name, encouraging, and asking them to remember that their
struggle was against unarmed bandits in defence of their fatherland and children, their altars and hearths. As a military indi-   6
vidual who had been in the army with great glory for more

than thirty years as tribune or prefect or legate or praetor, he
knew the majority personally and their courageous deeds: these
he recalled, inflaming the soldiers' hearts.

60   When Petreius, with every reconnoitre completed, gave the
signal on the bugle, he ordered his cohorts to advance slowly;
2   the enemy army did the same. But, after a point had been
reached where the battle could be joined by the skirmishers,
they converged quickly with the loudest of shouts, standards at
the offensive; they laid aside their lances: the action was con-
3   ducted with the sword. The veterans, mindful of their old-time
prowess, pressed fiercely at close quarters; the enemy, in no
way cowardly, resisted: the struggle was one of the greatest
4   violence. Meanwhile Catiline was active in the front line with
his unencumbered troops: he helped the flagging, summoned
the fit to take over from the injured, made every provision,
fought hard himself, and often struck the enemy: he performed
simultaneously the duties of committed soldier and good commander.

5   When Petreius, contrary to what he had expected, saw the
great strength of Catiline's exertions, he led his praetorian
cohort into the enemy's centre and, having caused great confusion there, killed them as well as others who resisted in
various other places; then, from the flanks on both sides, he
6   attacked the rest. Manlius and the Faesulan fell fighting
7   amongst the foremost; as for Catiline, after he saw his forces
routed and himself with only a few left, mindful of his lineage
and his own old-time status, he rushed into the thickest of the
enemy and there, fighting, was stabbed.

61   But it was only when the battle was over that you could have
perceived properly what daring and what strength of purpose
2   there had been in Catiline's army. Almost everyone, after gasp-
ing his last, protected with his body the place which he had
3   taken by fighting when alive. Nevertheless a few, whom the
praetorian cohort had scattered from the centre, had fallen over
a somewhat wider area, yet all of them with frontal wounds.
4   Catiline, however, was discovered far from his own men
amongst the corpses of the enemy, still breathing a little and
retaining on his face the defiance of spirit which he had had

when alive. In fact, from that entire force, no freeborn citizen 5
was captured either in battle or in flight: they had no more 6
spared their own lives than those of the enemy.

Yet neither had the army of the Roman people achieved a 7
delightful or bloodless victory: all the most committed had
either fallen in the battle or retired seriously wounded. As for 8
the many who had emerged from the camp for the purposes of
viewing or plundering and were turning over the enemy corpses,
some discovered a friend, others a guest or relative; likewise
there were those who recognized their own personal antagonists. Thus, throughout the entire army, delight, sorrow, grief 9
and joy were variously experienced.

THE JUGURTHINE WAR

False is the complaint which the human race makes about its 1
nature, namely, that it is weak and of short duration and ruled
by chance rather than by prowess. On the contrary, you would 2
find, after reflection, that nothing else is greater or more out-
standing, and that what human nature lacks is industriousness
on man's part rather than strength or time. But it is the mind 3
which is the leader and commander of the life of mortals. When
it proceeds to glory along the path of prowess, it has potency,
power and distinction in abundance and does not need fortune,
which is unable to bestow probity, industriousness and other
good qualities on anyone or to snatch them away. But, if the 4
mind has been taken captive by perverse desires and has sunk
to idleness and bodily pleasures, it enjoys its destructive urge
for a short while but then, when strength and time and intellect
have ebbed away through lethargy, the 'frailty of nature' is the
accusation which is made: those responsible transfer the blame
from themselves to 'events'. Yet, if men's concern for good 5
things matched the enthusiasm with which they seek what is
foreign to them and disadvantageous and is often even dangerous and destructive, they would not so much be ruled by circumstance as rule it themselves, and would advance to a level of
greatness where they became, instead of mortal, everlasting in
glory.

For, just as the race of man is composed of body and soul, 2
so everything, including each of our own enthusiasms, takes
after the nature of the body in some cases and in others that of
the mind. Thus a radiant appearance and great riches, as well 2
as bodily strength and all other things of that kind, dissipate in

a short time; but exceptional deeds of the intellect are, like the
3 soul, immortal. Ultimately, the advantages of the body and of
fortune end as surely as they began, and all of them rise and
fall, grow and decline; but the mind – incorruptible, everlasting,
the ruler of the human race – moves and controls everything and
4 yet is not itself controlled. All the more surprising, therefore, is
the perversity of those who devote themselves to the joys of the
body and live their lives in luxuriousness and apathy but allow
their intellect – and nothing else in the nature of mortals is better
or more important – to languish from neglect and lethargy,
especially since there are so many varied mental qualities by
which the utmost distinction is achieved.

3   Yet at the present time the least desirable products of those
qualities seem to me to be magistracies and commands and, in
short, any concern for public affairs, because the honour of
office is not bestowed on prowess, and those who have come
into possession of it wrongfully are neither secure nor are they
2 more honourable because of it. For, on the one hand, to rule
your fatherland or its subjects[1] by force, even though you could
do so and might correct their faults, is nevertheless perilous,
especially since all changes of circumstance presage slaughter,
3 exile and things generally expected of an enemy. On the other
hand, to strive in vain and, while tiring oneself out, to acquire
4 nothing but hatred is the ultimate madness – unless by chance
one is gripped by the dishonourable and destructive urge of
relinquishing one's dignity and freedom as a favour to the
power of a few.[2]

4   As for other activities which are performed by the intellect,
that which is of especially great benefit is the recording of the
2 conduct of affairs. Because many have spoken of its excellence,
I think that that aspect can be passed over, and also lest anyone
should reckon that, through overbearingness, I am elevating
3 my own form of enthusiasm by praising it. And I believe that,
because I have decided to live my life away from politics, in
some quarters the name of idleness will be placed upon this
great and beneficial work of mine – at least amongst those who
think that the height of industriousness resides in greeting the
4 plebs and seeking their favour by giving dinner-parties.[3] But if

these people reflect on the kind of men who were unable to reach magistracies at the time when I acquired them, and on the types of men who arrived in the senate later on, they will inevitably reckon that I changed my mind with good reason rather than through apathy, and that greater advantage will accrue to the commonwealth from my inactivity than from the activities of others. For I have often heard that Q. Maxumus 5 and P. Scipio and also other distinguished men of our community used to say that, when they gazed at the images of their ancestors, their spirit burned intensely for prowess.[4] Yet one 6 may be sure that it is not *that* wax nor its configuration which has such power in it,[5] but that it is through the recording of historical affairs that that flame grows in the breasts of exceptional men, not dying down until their own prowess matches such fame and glory. By contrast, who in the world 7 today, given the present state of morality, does not compete with his ancestors in riches and expenditure instead of probity and industriousness? Even new men,[6] who previously used to outstrip the nobility in prowess, now strive for command and office stealthily and through banditry rather than by means of good qualities – as if the praetorship and consulship and 8 everything else of that kind were intrinsically distinguished and magnificent, and the perception of them were not dependent upon the prowess of those who shoulder them. – But, in my dis- 9 taste and weariness at the community's morals, I have proceeded too freely and in too much depth; I now turn[7] to my project.

The war I am about to write is that which the Roman people 5 waged with Jugurtha, king of the Numidians, first because it was great and fierce and of only sporadic success, then because that was the first time that the haughtiness of the nobility was confronted – and the latter struggle convulsed everything, 2 divine and human alike, and advanced to such a point of derangement that only war and the devastation of Italy put an end to the citizens' passions. But, before making a start on a 3 topic of this kind, I shall trace back a little beyond it, so that everything may be clearer and plainer to understand.

In the Second Punic War,[8] in which the attrition of Italy's 4

resources by Hannibal, leader of the Carthaginians, was the
greatest since the name of Rome achieved greatness, Masinissa,
the king of the Numidians, was received in friendship by
P. Scipio (who was afterwards given the surname 'Africanus'
for his prowess[9]) and did many distinguished deeds of a military
nature. The result was defeat for the Carthaginians and capture
for Syphax,[10] whose great empire in Africa was strong and
extensive; and the Roman people bestowed on the king, as a
5 gift, all the cities and territories he had taken by force. Hence
Masinissa's friendship remained honourably loyal to us; but his
6 command ended with his life. Then the kingdom was held by
his son Micipsa alone, since the latter's brothers, Mastanabal
7 and Gulussa, had been taken off by disease. He begat Adherbal
and Hiempsal; and he kept Jugurtha (a son of his brother
Mastanabal but left without entitlement by Masinissa because
he had been born to a concubine) in his house in the same style
as his own children.

6   When Jugurtha first reached adolescence, he was powerfully
strong, of becoming appearance but, above all, forceful in intellect. He did not surrender himself to corruption by luxuriousness and idleness but, as is the custom of his race, rode horses,
threw the javelin, competed with his contemporaries at running,
and, though he outstripped them all in glory, was nevertheless
dear to them all. In addition, he spent much of his time in
hunting and was the first, or amongst the first, to strike down
a lion and other wild beasts. A man of action above all, he
spoke but rarely of himself.

2   Although Micipsa had initially been delighted at all of this,
reckoning that Jugurtha's prowess would bring glory to his
kingdom, nevertheless, when he realized that, with himself at
an advanced age and his children still small, the young man
was continuing his development, he was severely shaken by
all the activity and he started to turn things over in his mind.
3   What terrified him was the thought that mortal nature is hungry
for command and impetuous to satisfy the mind's desires;
there was also the opportunity provided by his own age and
that of his children, something which drives even average men
off course in their hope of plunder; and, in addition, the

Numidians' burning enthusiasm for Jugurtha, which made him worry that rebellion or war might arise if he were to kill such a man by cunning.

Trapped by these problems, he saw that a man so well liked 7 by his compatriots could not be overwhelmed by force or snares; but, because Jugurtha was ready with his muscle and had an appetite for military glory, he decided to cast him in harm's way and by this means to put fortune to the test. So, 2 when during the Numantine War Micipsa was sending auxiliary cavalry and infantry for the Roman people,[11] he hoped that Jugurtha would easily come to grief either through flaunting his prowess or through the enemy's savagery; and he placed him in charge of the Numidians whom he was sending to Spain. But the affair turned out very differently from what he had 3 calculated. For Jugurtha, with his energetic and keen intelli- 4 gence, came to understand the nature of P. Scipio,[12] who was the Roman commander at the time, and the behaviour of the enemy. By working very hard and taking great pains, as well as by the most deferential obedience and frequent encounters with danger, he had soon reached such a degree of distinction that he was overwhelmingly dear to our men[13] and the greatest source of terror to the Numantines. And indeed he was both 5 committed in battle and good at strategy, a very difficult combination: the latter is generally accustomed to engender fear through foresight, the former rashness through daring. Hence 6 the commander used Jugurtha to conduct almost every harsh task, counted him amongst his friends, and made him increasingly welcome each day, since no advice or project of his was ever in vain. To this was added his generosity of spirit and 7 shrewdness of intellect, by means of which he had joined many of the Romans to himself in a close friendship.

At that time in our army there were numerous new men and 8 nobles for whom riches were more an influential consideration than goodness and honourableness; factious at home, influential with the allies, distinguished rather than honourable, they fired Jugurtha's by no means average mind with the repeated promise that, if King Micipsa died, he alone would acquire command of Numidia: in him there was the greatest prowess,

2 they said, and at Rome everything was for sale. But after P. Scipio, on the destruction of Numantia, had decided to dismiss his auxiliaries and to return home himself, he made a magnificent presentation and speech of praise to Jugurtha before the assembled army, and then led him away to his head-quarters and there warned him in secret that he should cultivate the friendship of the Roman people through official rather than through private channels and should not acquire the habit of bribing people: it was dangerous to buy from a few what belonged to the many. If he was prepared to persevere with his own qualities, then glory and kingship would come to him of their own accord; but, if he moved forwards too fast, his very

9 own money would cause him a precipitate fall. Having spoken

2 thus, he dismissed him with a letter to take to Micipsa. Its purport was this: 'The prowess of your Jugurtha in the Numan-tine War was the greatest by far, something which I know for certain will be a joy to you. His services make him dear to us; we shall strive with the utmost effort to ensure that he is the same to the senate and the Roman people. On the basis of our friendship I congratulate you: you have a man worthy of your-self and of his grandfather Masinissa.'

3   When the king learned from the commander's letter that what he had heard by rumour was the case, he changed his mind, shaken not only by the man's prowess but also by his popularity: he proceeded to overwhelm him with acts of kind-ness and immediately adopted him and established him as heir

4 along with his sons in his will. But when a few years later he realized that the end of his life was near, enfeebled as he was by illness and age, he is said to have spoken words of this kind to Jugurtha in the presence of friends and relatives and of his sons Adherbal and Hiempsal too:

10   'When you were little, Jugurtha, and had lost your father and were without hope and without resources, I took you into my kingdom, reckoning that because of my kindnesses I would be no less dear to you than if I had begotten you; and that

2 circumstance has not played me false. For – to pass over your other great and exceptional achievements – when you returned very recently from Numantia, you honoured both me and my

kingdom with your glory, and by your prowess you turned the Romans from being merely our friends to being our greatest friends. In Spain the name of our family has been restored. Lastly – what is a very difficult thing amongst mortals – you have overcome resentment with your glory.[14]

'Now, because nature is bringing my life to its close, by this 3 right hand and by your loyalty to the kingdom I advise and beseech you to hold dear these men who are your relatives by birth and your brothers through my kindness, and not to prefer to have an alliance with strangers rather than to hold on to those allied by blood. Neither armies nor treasures are the 4 bulwarks of a kingdom, but friends, whom you can neither coerce by arms nor procure with gold: it is by duty and loyalty that they are acquired. Who is more friendly than brother with 5 brother? What stranger will you find loyal, if you are an enemy to your own? For my part, I hand to you all a kingdom which 6 will be strong, if you are good, but, if evil, weak. In harmony, small things grow; in disharmony, the greatest are dissipated.

'But as you, Jugurtha, are the first in age and wisdom, it is 7 your responsibility, before it is theirs, to ensure that nothing turns out differently: in every contest it is the more resourceful who, even if he is the recipient of an injustice, nevertheless seems, because of his greater power, to be its perpetrator. As 8 for you, Adherbal and Hiempsal, pay attention and respect to such a man as this; imitate his prowess and strive to ensure that I am not thought to have adopted better children than I have begotten.'

Although Jugurtha understood that the king had uttered 11 fabrications, and he himself had quite different things on his mind, nevertheless he replied generously in accordance with the occasion.

A few days after, Micipsa died. After a magnificent perform- 2 ance of the rites for him in the royal manner, the princes met together to debate all items of business amongst themselves. But Hiempsal, who was the youngest of them, being naturally 3 defiant and even before then despising Jugurtha's ignobility because he was inferior to them on his maternal side, sat on Adherbal's right to prevent Jugurtha's being the middle of the

three (which amongst the Numidians is regarded as an honour).
4 But then, worn down by his brother's pleas that he should bow
5 to age, he transferred reluctantly to the other side. Thereupon,
as they were discussing many things about the administration
of command, Jugurtha amongst other items interjected that all
the decisions and decrees of the last five years should be
rescinded, for during that time Micipsa had been enfeebled by
6 age, he said, and mentally infirm. Hiempsal then replied that
he agreed, for it was only within the last three years, he said,
that the other had himself arrived on the royal scene through
7 adoption. This statement went deeper into Jugurtha's heart
8 than anyone deemed at the time. So from that moment onwards,
under the strain of anger and dread, he toiled and planned, and
in his mind he considered only how Hiempsal might be seized
9 by cunning. When progress was too slow and there was no
calming his defiant mind, he decided to accomplish his project
by whatever means.

12   At the first meeting of the princes which I recalled above, it
had been agreed, because of their differences, that the treasures
should be divided and the boundaries of their individual com-
2 mands be established. For each of these two matters a time was
decided, the earlier for the distribution of the money. Meanwhile the princes settled themselves in various places near to
3 the treasures. But Hiempsal by chance had use of a house in
the town of Thirmida which belonged to the closest lictor[15] of
Jugurtha, for whom he had always been a dear and well liked
figure. Now that the man was offered fortuitously as an agent,
he loaded him with promises and induced him to go to his
house as though visiting his property and to procure counterfeit
keys to the gates (the real ones were customarily delivered to
Hiempsal[16]); but, when the moment demanded it, he himself
4 would arrive with a large unit. The Numidian soon carried out
his instructions and, as he had been told, admitted Jugurtha's
5 soldiers by night. After they had burst into the living-quarters,
they spread out to look for the king, killing some as they slept
and others as they ran up, investigating recesses, breaking open
closed areas, and causing confusion everywhere with their noise
and commotion – while in the meantime Hiempsal was dis-

covered hiding in the hut of a serving woman, where, in his
initial panic and unfamiliarity with the place, he had fled. The   6
Numidians, as they had been ordered, delivered his head to
Jugurtha.

Report of such a deed soon received publicity across the   13
whole of Africa. Adherbal and all who had been under
Micipsa's command were overcome with dread. The Numidians divided into two parties: Adherbal's followers were the
more numerous, but the other side's were better in battle. So   2
Jugurtha armed as many troops as he could; some cities he
brought under his command by force, others voluntarily; and
he made preparations to command the whole of Numidia.
Although Adherbal had sent legates to Rome to tell the senate   3
about the slaughter of his brother and his own circumstances,
nevertheless, relying on the number of his soldiers, he prepared
for an armed struggle. But, when it came to a contest, he was   4
defeated: he fled to the province[17] and then hurried to Rome.

Thereupon Jugurtha, now that he had completed his plans   5
with the acquisition of the whole of Numidia, reflected on his
deed at leisure and began to be afraid of the Roman people and
to have no hope at all against their anger except in the avarice
of the nobility and his own money. And so, within a few days,   6
he sent legates to Rome with a quantity of gold and silver,
directing them first to satisfy his old friends with gifts, then to
find new ones, and finally not to delay in procuring whatever
they could by bribery. But, when the legates arrived in Rome   7
and in accordance with the king's direction sent great gifts to
their hosts and to others whose authority in the senate carried
weight at that time, such a change occurred that, from being
an object of the greatest resentment, Jugurtha acquired access
to the favour and goodwill of the nobility. With the induce-   8
ments of hope in some cases and of reward in others, they
canvassed individual members of the senate, striving to ensure
that the measures against him would not be too severe.

When the legates were sufficiently confident, therefore, on an   9
appointed day both parties were given access to the senate. We
have been led to understand that on this occasion Adherbal
spoke in this way:

14   'Conscript fathers, when my father Micipsa was dying he
directed me to regard only the governance of the kingdom of
Numidia as my own, while its jurisdiction and command rested
with you; at the same time I should strive to be of the greatest
use to the Roman people at home and on campaign; I should
consider you to take the place of my relatives and of my in-laws:
if I did that, I would have the kingdom's army, riches and
2   defences resting on your friendship. It was while I was carrying
out the directions of my parent that Jugurtha, the most criminal
of all men whom the earth supports, treated your command
with contempt and banished me – the grandson of Masinissa
and already at birth the ally and friend of the Roman people –
from my kingdom and my every fortune.

3   'For my own part, conscript fathers, I was destined to reach
this degree of wretchedness: therefore, I could only wish that
my seeking your help were in return for my own acts of kindness
rather than those of my ancestors, and, above all, that I were
due kindnesses from the Roman people that I did not need, or,
failing this, that, if they had to be required, I were taking
4   advantage of them as my due. But, because probity is scarcely
a protection by itself and what kind of man Jugurtha would be
was not in my hands, I have fled to you, conscript fathers, to
whom (something which is most distressing to me) I am com-
5   pelled to be a burden rather than of use. Other kings, if beaten
in war, have been received by you in friendship or, when in a
position of uncertainty, have sought an alliance with you; but
our family established its relationship with the Roman people
during the Carthaginian War, at which time their good faith
6   rather than their good fortune was our aim. Do not allow its
progeny, conscript fathers, to seek help from you in vain.

7   'If I had no reason for a successful request besides my
wretched fortune (a short while ago I was a king, powerful in
lineage, reputation and forces, but now I am disfigured by my
afflictions and wait resourceless upon the resources of others),
nevertheless it was always a characteristic of the sovereignty of
the Roman people to prevent injustice and not to allow anyone's
8   kingdom to grow through crime. Yet I have been ejected from
the territory which the Roman people gave to my ancestors,

from where my father and grandfather, with you at their side, evicted Syphax and the Carthaginians. It is your kindnesses which have been snatched from me, conscript fathers, it is you who have been flouted in the injustice done to me. Oh, how 9 wretched I am! Is it to this, my father Micipsa, that your kindnesses have come, that the annihilator of your stock is precisely the one whom you made equal with your children and a partner in the kingdom? Will our family therefore never be at rest? Will it always be involved in blood, steel and flight? As 10 long as the Carthaginians were unscathed, it was with good reason that we bore every savagery: with an enemy on our flank and you, our friends, far away, all our hope resided in arms. But, after that plague had been ejected from Africa, we were delighted to pursue peace, since we had no enemy save any whom you might have ordered. Yet here, quite unexpectedly, 11 is Jugurtha! Carried away by his unendurable daring, criminality and haughtiness, and having killed the brother of mine who was likewise his relative, he first made that man's kingdom the reward for his crime; afterwards, when he could not use the same cunning to capture me (who, given the existence of your empire, was expecting anything other than violence or war), he made me, as you see, an outcast from my fatherland and home, resourceless and deep in wretchedness, with the result that I was safer anywhere than in my own kingdom.

'My thinking, conscript fathers, was always the same as the 12 statement I had heard from my father – namely, that those who diligently cultivated your friendship undertook a considerable task but were by far the safest of all. Our family did what it 13 could to assist you in every war; our security in peacetime is in your hands, conscript fathers. My father left two of us 14 brothers; he deemed that through his acts of kindness the third, Jugurtha, would be joined to us. One of those is killed; I have scarcely escaped the heinous hands of the other. What am I to 15 do? Where precisely am I to resort to in my unhappiness? All protection from my family has been extinguished. My father, as was inevitable, succumbed to nature; from my brother, who least deserved it, a relative has snatched away his life through crime; my other in-laws, friends and relatives have been

variously overwhelmed by one slaughter or another: captured
by Jugurtha, some have been crucified, some thrown to beasts,
and the few who are still left breathing have been shut away in
darkness, leading a life of sorrow and grief which is worse than
any death.

16   'If everything which I have lost, or which has changed from
friendship to hostility, remained unscathed, nevertheless, if
some evil had befallen me unexpectedly, I would still be implor-
ing you, conscript fathers, whom it behoves, by virtue of the
greatness of your empire, to be concerned with all cases of
17   justice and injustice. But as it is, an exile from fatherland and
home, alone and lacking all honourable means, where am I to
resort to or on whom should I call? Nations or kings? They are
all hostile to our family on account of your friendship. Is there
anywhere I can go where there are not very many enemy monu-
ments of my ancestors? Can anyone who was once an enemy
18   of yours take pity on us? Finally Masinissa instilled in us,
conscript fathers, not to cultivate anyone except the Roman
people, not to entertain new alliances or treaties: we would
enjoy any amount of strong protection in your friendship, he
said; and, if there was a change in the fortunes of this empire
19   of yours, our inevitable fall would be at your side. Through
prowess and by the gods' will you are great and resourceful;
everything is favourable and obedient to you: all the more easily
can you make injustices to your allies your concern.

20   'My one fear is that Jugurtha's personal friendship may drive
some men off course who are unfamiliar with it. I hear that
they have been striving with the greatest effort and canvassing
and overwhelming you with their pleas to individuals not to
decide about him in his absence without his case being heard;
that they are saying my words are fabrications and I am only
pretending flight when I could have remained in the kingdom.
21   Well, I wish that I could see an identical pretence from him,
whose heinous deed has cast me into such wretchedness, and
that eventually, either amongst you or amongst the immortal
gods, there may arise a concern for human affairs! Assuredly,
the man whose crimes have brought him his present defiance
and distinction would then be tortured by every evil and would

pay a severe penalty for his heinousness to our parent, for the killing of my brother and for my own wretchedness.

'Although you, brother dearest to my heart, are the least 22 deserving of persons to have your life snatched away from you prematurely, nevertheless I *now* think your fate should be a reason for delight rather than for pain: for, along with your 23 breath, you have lost, not a kingdom, but flight, exile, want and all the present afflictions which overwhelm me. In my unhappiness, cast headlong from my father's kingdom into such evils, I present a spectacle of the human condition, uncertain what to do, whether to pursue the injustices done to you while needing help myself, or to pay heed to the kingdom when my power over life and death depends upon the resources of others. Would that dying were an honourable outcome to my circum- 24 stances and that I would not rightly seem contemptible if, worn out by evil, I gave in to injustice. As things are, it is neither pleasant to live nor possible to die without shame.

'Conscript fathers, for your own sake, for that of your chil- 25 dren and parents, for that of the sovereignty of the Roman people, help me in my wretchedness, confront injustice, do not allow the kingdom of Numidia – which is yours – to waste away through the criminal shedding of our family's blood.'

After the king had finished speaking, Jugurtha's legates 15 replied briefly, relying on bribery rather than on their case: Hiempsal had been killed by the Numidians on account of his savagery, they said; Adherbal, after he had been overcome in a war of aggression in which the initiative had been his, was complaining that he had not had the ability to perpetrate injus- tice; Jugurtha was asking the senate not to think him a different person from the one familiar at Numantia, and not to give precedence to the words of an antagonist over his own deeds. Then each party left the curia.

The views of the senate were immediately sought. The sup- 2 porters of the legates, to say nothing of the majority of the senate who had been perverted by their influence, treated Adherbal's words with contempt and extolled in praise the prowess of Jugurtha: using their influence, their powers of speech and in fact every means, they strove on behalf of a

3 stranger's outrageous criminality as if for their own glory. But
   the few for whom goodness and fairness were dearer than riches
   voted for helping Adherbal and for avenging Hiempsal's death
4 severely – most of all Aemilius Scaurus,[18] a noble, energetic
   and factious, hungry for power, honour and riches, yet craftily
5 concealing his flaws. After he had seen the king's notorious and
   shameless bribery, he was afraid that (as happens in such a
   situation) such tainted freehandedness[19] might inflame resentment, and so he held back from his habitual craving.

16 Yet victory in the senate went to the party which preferred
2   rewards or favour to the truth. A decree was passed that the
    kingdom which Micipsa had held should be divided by ten
    legates between Jugurtha and Adherbal. The chief of the del-
    egation was L. Opimius, a distinguished man who was powerful
    in the senate at that time because in his consulship, after the
    killing of C. Gracchus and M. Fulvius Flaccus, he had enforced
    the nobility's victory over the plebs with extreme harshness.[20]
3   Although Jugurtha had regarded him as amongst his antagon-
    ists at Rome, he nevertheless welcomed him very punctiliously
    and, with many gifts and promises, ensured that the man put
    the king's advantage before his own reputation, his own credit
4   – in short, all his own interests. Assailing the other legates in
    the same way, he made several his captives; only a few con-
5   sidered their credit dearer than money. In the division, the part
    of Numidia which touches Mauretania and which had more
    resources in terms of land and men was handed to Jugurtha;
    the other part, which was more valuable in appearance than in
    practice and had more harbours and was better furnished with
    buildings, became the possession of Adherbal.

17 The context seems to demand that I explain briefly the layout
    of Africa and touch on the peoples with whom our dealings
2   were those of war or friendship; but I could not easily narrate
    anything certain concerning the places and nations which are
    less visited for reasons of heat, harshness or desert; the rest
    I shall dispatch in as few words as possible.
3   In the division of the globe, the majority have considered
    Africa in a third part, though a few that there are only Asia and

Europe, with Africa in Europe.[21] As its boundaries it has the   4
strait between Our Sea and the Ocean to the west,[22] and a
sloping expanse to the east, an area which the inhabitants call
Catabathmos.[23] The sea is savage and harbourless; the ground   5
productive of crops, good for cattle, infertile for trees; from the
sky and on land there is a dearth of water. The typical person   6
is physically healthy, quick, tolerant of hard work; the majority
perish from old age (save for those who are killed by the sword
or beasts), for it is not often that anyone is overcome by disease.
In addition there are very many animals of a noxious kind.

As for which mortal beings held Africa initially and which   7
arrived later or how they intermingled with one another, I shall
say all this in as few words as possible, and, although it differs
from the tradition which obtains amongst the majority, it nevertheless accords both with what was translated for me from the
Punic books which were said to be King Hiempsal's[24] and with
the opinion of the denizens of the land as to what is the case.
But the proof of the matter will rest with its authors.

Initially Africa was held by the Gaetulians and Libyans, rough   18
and uncouth peoples whose food was the flesh of wild animals
and fodder from the ground, as for cattle. They were ruled   2
neither by customs nor by law or anyone's command; wanderers and rovers, they took whatever abode night compelled
them to have. But, after Hercules (as the Africans think) died   3
in Spain, his army – composed as it was of various peoples –
quickly dispersed once it had lost its leader and many on all
sides began to seek the command for themselves. From their   4
number, Medes, Persians and Armenians crossed by ship to
Africa and occupied the areas closest to Our Sea – except that   5
the Persians were more on the near side of the Ocean, and they
used the upturned hulls of ships for huts, because there was
neither timber in the fields nor the chance of buying from the
Spaniards or bartering with them: the distance by sea and   6
their ignorance of the language kept them from trading. They   7
gradually associated the Gaetulians with themselves through
marriage, and, because in their constant testing of territory
they had sought one area after another, they called themselves
Nomads.[25] (Even now the buildings of the rural Numidians,   8

which they term 'mapalia', are elongated and roofed over with
9   curved sides, like the keels of ships.) As for the Medes and
Armenians, they were joined by the Libyans (for they were
situated nearer the African sea, whereas the Gaetulians were
more under the sun, not far from the torrid zone), and they
quickly had towns: for, divided from Spain by only the strait,
10   they had become accustomed to mutual bartering. The Libyans
gradually corrupted their name, in the barbarian tongue calling
them Mauri instead of Medes.

11   The Persians' state soon developed, and later, now with the
name Numidians, they left their parents on account of their
large numbers and took possession of the area closest to Carth-
12   age, which is called Numidia. Then, with each party relying on
the other,[26] they forced their neighbours under their command
by means of arms or dread and conferred on themselves a
glorious name – more particularly those who had reached Our
Sea, the Libyans being less warlike than the Gaetulians. Finally,
the lower part of Africa was mostly taken possession of by the
Numidians, and all the conquered passed into the race and
name of those in command over them.

19   Afterwards the Phoenicians – some to diminish the numbers
at home, others in a desire for empire – inveigled the plebs and
others who were hungry for revolution, and founded Hippo,
Hadrumetum, Leptis and other cities on the sea coast; these
soon grew considerably, becoming variously a protection or
2   adornment for their mother-cities. (About Carthage I think it
better to remain silent than to say too little, since time warns
me to hurry elsewhere.)

3   At Catabathmos, the area which divides Egypt from Africa,
the first place – going with the sea's current[27] – is Cyrene, a
colony of Thera,[28] and then the two Syrtes and Leptis between
them, and thereafter the Altars of the Philaeni, an area facing
Egypt which the Carthaginians regarded as the boundary of
4   their empire.[29] Then come other Punic cities. The other areas
up to Mauretania are held by the Numidians; nearest to the
5   Spains[30] are the Mauri. Past Numidia, we have been led to
understand, the Gaetulians dwell, some of them in huts, others
6   in a more uncouth fashion as wanderers; and that beyond them

are the Ethiopians, and then the regions scorched by the torrid heat of the sun.

In the Jugurthine War most of the Punic towns, and the 7 territory which the Carthaginians had held most recently,[31] were administered by the Roman people through magistrates; a large number of the Gaetulians, and the Numidians as far as the River Muluccha, were under Jugurtha; all the Mauri[32] were commanded by King Bocchus, who was generally ignorant of the Roman people apart from their name and likewise previously unknown to us either in war or peace.

About Africa and its inhabitants enough has been said for 8 the requirements of the context.

After the division of the kingdom the legates withdrew from 20 Africa and Jugurtha, contrary to his inmost fear, saw that he had acquired the reward of his crime: deeming that what he had been told by his friends at Numantia was certain, namely that everything at Rome was for sale, and at the same time fired by the promises of those whom he had satisfied with gifts shortly before, he turned his attention to the kingdom of Adherbal. Though he was fierce and warlike himself, his target was 2 peaceable, unwarlike, of placid disposition, vulnerable to wrongdoing, fearful rather than fearsome. So he invaded the 3 other's territory unexpectedly with a large unit, seized many mortals along with cattle and other plunder, burned buildings, and made hostile advances in numerous areas with his cavalry; then with his whole host he took himself back to his kingdom, 4 reckoning that Adherbal, shaking with indignation, would use his muscle to requite the wrongs done to himself – and that that would be the pretext for war.

But, because the latter reckoned he was no match in arms, 5 and he relied on the friendship of the Roman people rather than on the Numidians, he sent legates to Jugurtha to complain about his wrongdoing. And, although they brought back only insults, he nevertheless decided to tolerate anything rather than have recourse to war, because his previous attempt had turned out badly. But Jugurtha's desire was in no way diminished 6 thereby, since in his mind he had already invaded the whole of

7 the other's kingdom. So it was not with a plundering unit (as before) but after the assembling of a great army that he began to wage war and quite openly to seek command of the whole
8 of Numidia. Wherever he went, he devastated cities and fields; drove away plunder; and magnified both the courage of his own men and the terror of the enemy.

21 When Adherbal realized that things had advanced to the point where he either had to abandon his kingdom or retain it by arms, of necessity he assembled troops and advanced to
2 confront Jugurtha. For a while their two armies bivouacked not far from the sea near the town of Cirta, and, because it was the end of the day, battle did not begin. But, when the night was much advanced (though there was still only a dim light), the Jugurthine soldiers at a given signal invaded the enemy camp and put to flight and routed men who were either half-asleep or in the act of taking up arms. Adherbal with a few cavalrymen fled to Cirta and, had there not been a crowd of civilians[33] who kept the pursuing Numidians from the walls, the war between the two kings would have been begun and concluded in a single
3 day. As it was, Jugurtha surrounded the town and proceeded to storm it with penthouses and towers and machines of every type, hurrying above all to anticipate the timing of the legates who he had heard had been sent by Adherbal to Rome before the battle started.

4 But, after the senate had learned of the war, three junior legates for Africa were chosen to approach both kings and to announce, in the words of the senate and the Roman people, that their wish and vote was that they should abandon arms and debate about their differences at law rather than by war: that would be a dignified solution both for themselves and for
22 them.[34] The legates arrived in Africa all the more quickly because, while they were preparing to set out, news of the battle's having taken place and of the siege of Cirta was heard
2 in Rome (although the rumour was kind[35]). When Jugurtha had listened to their speech, he replied that nothing was greater or dearer to him than the authority of the senate: from adolescence he had striven for the approval of all the best people; it was by

prowess, not by wickedness, that he had pleased P. Scipio, the most eminent of men; it was for the same qualities, not because of any dearth of children, that he had been adopted by Micipsa into the kingdom. But, the more numerous his good and com- 3 mitted deeds, the less did his temperament tolerate wrongdoing. Adherbal, he said, had ambushed his life with his cunning; and, 4 when he had realized, he had gone to confront the crime; the Roman people would be acting neither properly nor in the interests of morality if they barred him from the law of nations.[36] Finally, he said, he would soon be sending legates concerning all these matters to Rome. So each party withdrew; 5 there was no opportunity of summoning Adherbal.

When Jugurtha deemed that they had left Africa, and he 23 could not storm Cirta by force because of the nature of the place, he encircled its walls with a rampart and ditch, con- structed towers and reinforced them with garrisons; besides this, he made attempts either by force or with cunning day and night; to the defenders of the walls he held out the prospect of rewards or terror alternately; his own men he roused to prowess by exhortation: in short, he concentrated on making every preparation. When Adherbal realized that his entire fortune 2 was situated on the very brink, with an enemy on the offensive and no hope of help, and that because of a dearth of necessities the war could not be drawn out, he chose two particularly energetic members of those who had fled with him to Cirta: by making numerous promises and expressing pity for his own plight, he encouraged them to go through the enemy's siege- works to the sea at its nearest point and thence to Rome.

The Numidians carried out his orders within a few days. In 24 the senate they read out Adherbal's letter, the purport of which was this:

'It is not my fault that I often send advocates to speak to you, 2 conscript fathers, but the violence of Jugurtha compels it: so great an urge for my annihilation has attacked him that he has no thought either for you or for the immortal gods but wants my blood before all else. This is now the fifth month that I – an 3 ally and friend of the Roman people – have been held fast by

armed siege, and neither the kindnesses[37] of my father Micipsa
nor your decrees are any help to me: whether I am under keener
pressure from steel or starvation I do not know.

4　　'My fortune discourages me from writing further about Jugurtha (and long before now it has been my experience that little
5　credibility is shown to the wretched) – except that I realize
that he is aiming at more than me alone and that he has no
expectations of your friendship and my kingdom at the same
time. Which of these he reckons the more important is hidden
6　from no one. Initially he slaughtered my brother Hiempsal;
then he evicted me from my ancestral kingdom. Of course the
wrongs which may have been done to us are nothing to you;
7　but now it is *your* kingdom which is in his armed grasp; and it
is *I*, whom you placed in command of the Numidians, whom
he has shut in and is besieging. The value he placed on your
8　legates' words is clear from the danger I am in. What – except
9　force from you – is left to move him? I could wish that both what
I am now writing and the complaints which I made previously in
the senate were groundless, rather than that my wretchedness
should lend credibility to my words.

10　　'But because I was born specifically to be an advertisement
for Jugurtha's crimes, I no longer pray to be spared death or
affliction but only the command of an enemy and physical
torture. Pay what heed you please to the kingdom of Numidia,
which is yours; but rescue me from heinous hands – for the
sakes of the sovereignty of your empire and of the loyalty of
friendship, if there lingers amongst you any memory of my
grandfather Masinissa.'

25　　When this letter had been read out, there were those who
proposed that an army be sent to Africa and Adherbal be helped
as soon as possible; there should in the meantime be discussion
2　about Jugurtha because he had not obeyed the legates. But
those same supporters of the king[38] strove with the utmost
3　effort to prevent such a decree from being passed. Thus the
public good (as is usual in the majority of affairs) was overcome
4　by personal favour. Nevertheless, legates were chosen for Africa
who were nobles more senior in age, former leaders of high

office: amongst them was M. Scaurus, about whom we recalled above, a consular and, at the time, the senate's leader.

Since the matter was a cause of indignation, as well as because they were being implored by the Numidians, they boarded ship within three days; then, landing soon at Utica, they sent a letter to Jugurtha: he should come to the province[39] as speedily as possible; they had been sent to him by the senate. When he learned that distinguished men, whose authority he had heard was powerful in Rome, had arrived to oppose his project, he was at first shaken, driven in different directions by his dread and by his urge: he feared the anger of the senate if he did not obey the legates; conversely his instincts, dazzled by desire, were sweeping him towards his criminal project. Nevertheless, given his greedy disposition, it was the crooked plan which was victorious. Therefore, throwing his army round Cirta, he strove with the utmost force to burst in, hoping especially that, if the enemy's unit were extended, he would find the opportunity for victory either by force or by cunning. But, when things progressed otherwise and he could not achieve his aim of gaining control of Adherbal before meeting the legates, he came to the province with a few cavalry lest, by delaying further, he should inflame Scaurus, whom he dreaded most of all. And, although grave threats were contained in the announcement of the senate's words because he was not desisting from the siege, nevertheless after many a wasted speech the legates departed in failure.

After news of this was heard in Cirta, the Italians (by whose prowess the walls were being defenced[40]), confident that in the event of a surrender they would be inviolable owing to the greatness of the Roman people, urged Adherbal to hand over himself and the town to Jugurtha and to bargain only for his life; everything else would be the concern of the senate. But, although he deemed that anything was worth more than the word of Jugurtha, nevertheless, because the power of compulsion rested with the Italians if he objected, he surrendered as they had proposed. Jugurtha's first act was the torture and execution of Adherbal; then he killed indiscriminately all the adult Numidians and such businessmen as encountered his armed men.[41]

27   After this became known at Rome and the matter began to be discussed in the senate, the same agents of the king tried to minimize the hideousness of his deed by interrupting and procrastinating, often through their personal influence, some-
2   times through altercation. And, had not C. Memmius – the tribune designate of the plebs, a fierce man and hostile to the power of the nobility – informed the Roman people that a few factious persons were doing their best to get Jugurtha pardoned for his crime, then assuredly all indignation would have dissipated owing to the postponement of the debates: such was the
3   power of the king's influence and money. But, since the senate, conscious of its failing, feared the people, Numidia and Italy were decreed by the Sempronian Law to be the provinces for
4   the next consuls;[42] the consuls were declared as P. Scipio Nasica and L. Bestia Calpurnius: Calpurnius was allotted Numidia,
5   Scipio Italy. Then an army was enrolled for transportation to Africa, and military pay and other things which would be useful for war were decreed.

28   On hearing this news contrary to his expectations (since it had stuck in his mind that at Rome everything was for sale), Jugurtha sent his son and two friends with him as legates to the senate, and he directed them – as he had those whom he had sent after killing Hiempsal[43] – to conduct a financial offensive
2   against every mortal being. After they drew near to Rome, the senate was consulted by Bestia as to whether it was acceptable for Jugurtha's legates to be received within the walls; and they decreed that, unless they had come to surrender the kingdom and its master, they should withdraw from Italy within ten
3   days. The consul ordered an announcement to be made to the Numidians in accordance with the senate's decree; and so, their mission unaccomplished, they departed for home.

4   Meanwhile Calpurnius, having procured his army, chose as his legates some factious nobles by whose authority any delinquencies of his would, he hoped, be upheld (amongst them was Scaurus, about whose nature and bearing we recalled above).
5   For in our consul there were many good qualities of both mind

and body, all of which were hamstrung by avarice: tolerant of hard work, with a keen intelligence, adequately far-sighted, not unfamiliar with war, staunchest of all in the face of dangers and resentment.[44]

The legions travelled through Italy to Regium and were   6
ferried from there to Sicily and onward from Sicily to Africa. Calpurnius, having procured his supplies, initially made a keen   7
entry into Numidia and took many mortal beings and several cities in the fighting. But, when Jugurtha by means of legates   29
began to tempt him with money and to demonstrate the bleakness of the war that he was managing, his mind, diseased as it was by avarice, was easily turned. Moreover, as his ally and   2
manager in all his plans he took on Scaurus: although at the beginning – and despite many of his faction having been bribed – he had attacked the king very fiercely, nevertheless he was diverted by a large amount of money from the good and honourable to crookedness. At first Jugurtha tried to purchase   3
only a delay in the war, reckoning that in the meanwhile he would achieve something at Rome by payment or favour. But, after he heard that Scaurus had become an accomplice in the business, he was led to hope very much that peace would be restored, and he decided to deal in person with them concerning all the terms. (But meanwhile, to establish trust, the consul sent   4
Sextius, a quaestor, to Vaga, a town of Jugurtha's, the pretext being to receive the grain which Calpurnius had openly commanded of the legates, because, given the delay in the surrender, a truce was being observed.[45]) In accordance with his decision   5
the king therefore came to the camp and, having said a few words in the presence of the council about the indignation at his deed and that he should be received in surrender, he conducted the rest of his negotiations secretly with Bestia and Scaurus; then on the next day, with opinions having been sought 'on a collective basis'[46] (so to speak), he was received in surrender. But, as had been commanded before the council, thirty ele-   6
phants, cattle and many horses, together with a small weight of silver, were handed over to the quaestor. Calpurnius set off   7
for Rome to preside over the elections. In Numidia and in our army peace was observed.

30   After rumour had given publicity to events in Africa and
how they had come about, in every assembly area in Rome
observations were made about the consul's deed. Amongst the
plebs there was grievous indignation, the fathers were troubled:
there was little agreement whether they should give their
approval to such an outrage or overturn the consul's decree.
2   What particularly inhibited them from the good and true course
was the powerfulness of Scaurus, because he was said to be the
3   initiator and Bestia's ally. But during the senate's hesitations
and delays C. Memmius, about whose frankness of disposition
and hatred of the nobility's powerfulness we spoke above, used
public addresses to urge the people to vengeance, warned them
not to abandon the commonwealth or their own freedom, and
pointed out to them the many haughty and cruel deeds of the
nobility: in short he concentrated on inflaming the spirit of the
4   plebs in every way. Because at that period in Rome Memmius'
fluency was brilliant and powerful, I reckon it fitting to write
down one of his very many speeches, and specifically I shall say
what he delivered in his public address after Bestia's return, in
words of this type:

31   'The many considerations which discourage me from
addressing you, Citizens, if it were not that enthusiasm for the
commonwealth overcomes everything, are the resources of a
faction,[47] your own submissiveness, the absence of legality, and
above all the fact that innocence is more a matter of danger
2   than of honour. For it is certainly displeasing to say how you
have been the plaything of the haughty few for the past fifteen
years, how foully and how unavenged your defenders have
perished, how your spirit has been undone by apathy and leth-
3   argy – you who do not rise up even now, when your antagonists
are vulnerable, and who still fear those to whom you ought
4   to be a source of terror. Yet, although these things are so,
nevertheless my spirit compels me to confront the powerfulness
5   of the faction. At least I shall be deploying the freedom which
has been handed down to me by my parent; but whether I do
so in vain or to some purpose is in your hands, Citizens.
6   'What I do not encourage is that you should go on the armed
offensive against injustices, which your ancestors often did;

there is no need at all for violence, for secession.[48] What is
necessary is that they themselves should go headlong to destruction in their own way. After Ti. Gracchus, who they said was   7
preparing for kingship, was slain,[49] commissions of enquiry
were held against the Roman plebs; after the slaughter of
C. Gracchus and M. Fulvius,[50] likewise many mortal beings
from your order were executed in gaol: to each disaster an end
was put, not by law, but by their whim. But let us grant that   8
restoring to the plebs their own rights was a preparation for
kingship, and that whatever cannot be avenged without the
bloodshed of citizens was justly done. In earlier years you were 9
silently indignant that the treasury was pillaged, that kings and
free peoples paid tax to a few nobles,[51] and that it was the same
people who had their hands on both the highest glory and the
greatest riches. Nevertheless, they did not consider it sufficient
to have undertaken with impunity such deeds as these; and so
in the end the laws, your sovereignty, all things divine and
human were handed over to your enemies. Nor are those who   10
have done these things ashamed or repentant, but the braggarts
stride past your faces, flaunting their priesthoods and consulships, and some of them their triumphs, as if these possessions
were an honour, not plunder. Slaves who have been procured   11
for cash do not endure unjust commands from their masters;
do you, Citizens, who have been born into command, tolerate
slavery with equanimity? Who *are* those who have taken over   12
the commonwealth? The most criminal of beings, with gory
hands and monstrous avarice, guilty and haughty in full and
equal measure, for whom loyalty, dignity, devotion, and everything honourable and dishonourable is a source of profit. Some   13
of them, as their bulwark, have the fact that they have slain
tribunes of the plebs; others have unjust commissions of
enquiry; the majority have the fact that they have perpetrated
slaughter against you. Hence the worst of evil-doers are the   14
safest: they have transferred the dread from their crime to your
apathy,[52] and the sameness of their desires, hatreds and dreads
has forced togetherness upon them all, something which is   15
friendship amongst good men but factiousness amongst bad.
If you had as much concern for freedom as they burn for   16

domination, the commonwealth would certainly not be in the process of being ravaged, as it is now, and your kindnesses[53] would be in the hands of the best men, not the most daring.

17 For the sake of procuring justice and establishing sovereignty, your ancestors twice took over the Aventine in armed secession;[54] will you not strive with the utmost effort on behalf of the freedom which you have received from them, and all the more rigorously in that it is a greater disgrace to lose an acquisition than not to have acquired it at all?

18   'Someone will say, "What, therefore, do you propose?" That we must requite those who have betrayed the commonwealth to the enemy! – not by muscle or force, which it is more unworthy for you to perpetrate than for them to encounter, but by commissions of enquiry and the evidence of Jugurtha him-

19 self. If he has really surrendered, he will of course be obedient to your orders; but, if he treats them with contempt, you will surely consider what sort of peace or surrender it is which results in impunity for Jugurtha for his crimes, the greatest riches for the powerful few and damage and disgrace for the

20 commonwealth – unless by chance you have not had your fill of their domination even yet and you derive less pleasure from these present times than from those when kingdoms, provinces, laws, rights, judgements, war and peace, and finally all things divine and human were in the hands of a few, whilst you, the Roman people, unconquered by your enemies, commanders of all other nations, considered it enough merely to cling on to life (for which of you dared to reject slavery?).

21   'Although I for my part reckon it is quite outrageous for a man to have suffered injustice with impunity, nevertheless I would with equanimity allow you to pardon those most criminal of beings because they are citizens, were it not that com-

22 passion will end in your destruction. For it is insufficient for *them*, given the measure of their unreasonableness, to have acted badly with impunity if you do not wrest from them the licence so to act in future;[55] and for *you* there will remain everlasting anxiety when you realize that you must either be

23 slaves or use your muscle to cling on to freedom. For, as regards trust or harmony, what hope is there of them? They want to

dominate, you to be free; they to perpetrate injustices, you to prevent them; finally, they treat our allies like enemies, and enemies as allies. Is it possible that, given such divergent mentalities, there can be peace or friendship?   24

'Therefore I advise and encourage you not to leave so great   25 a crime unpunished. This is no embezzlement of the treasury that has been perpetrated, nor has money been seized from the allies by force, matters which, though serious, are nevertheless considered as nothing because of their regularity. Rather, the authority of the senate has been betrayed to the fiercest of enemies, as has your command been betrayed; at home and on campaign the commonwealth has been put on sale. Unless these   26 matters are the subject of enquiry, unless there is vengeance against the malefactors, what will be left except that we live in obedience to those who have done these things? For doing with impunity what one likes – *that* is being a king.

'What I do not encourage, Citizens, is that you should prefer   27 your fellow citizens to have acted wrongly rather than correctly; but you should not proceed to destroy good men through pardoning bad. In addition to this, it is much better in a common-   28 wealth to be unmindful of a good deed than a bad: the good man becomes only more sluggish when you neglect him, but the bad more immoral. In addition to this, if there be no injus-   29 tices, you will not often need help.'

By often saying these and other words of this type, Memmius   32 persuaded the people that L. Cassius,[56] who was praetor at the time, should be sent to Jugurtha and, after the issue of an official pledge, should bring him to Rome so that the offences of Scaurus and the others whom he was indicting for taking money might be revealed more easily by means of evidence from the king.

While these things were being done in Rome, those whom   2 Bestia had left in charge of the army in Numidia followed the practice of their commander and perpetrated a great many utterly outrageous deeds. There were some who, bribed by   3 gold, handed back to Jugurtha his elephants; others sold him deserters; some drove plunder from pacified areas: so great was   4 the violence of the avarice which, like some rottenness, had

5   attacked their spirits. But, after the bill was carried by C. Mem-
    mius and the entire nobility was stunned, the praetor Cassius
    set off for Jugurtha and persuaded him, fearful though he was
    and distrusting his situation because of a guilty conscience,
    that, because he had surrendered to the Roman people, he
    should not prefer to experience their strength rather than their
    compassion. Privately he also issued his own pledge, which the
    other considered of no less value than the official one: such at
    that period was the reputation of Cassius.

33   Therefore, Jugurtha came with Cassius to Rome in as piti-
2   able an attire as possible, contrary to his royal dignity. And,
    although he himself possessed great strength of purpose,
    reassured by all those whose powerfulness or criminality had
    enabled him to do everything that we mentioned above,[57] he
    procured C. Baebius, a tribune of the plebs, with a large sum
    so that the latter's shamelessness might protect him against
3   justice and every wrongdoing. But, after calling a meeting at
    which the plebs was hostile to the king (some demanded that
    he be led in chains, others that, unless he revealed his accom-
    plices in crime, reprisal[58] should be exacted from him as an
    enemy according to ancestral custom), C. Memmius, giving
    more thought to impressiveness than to anger, calmed their
    emotions and softened their spirits and finally reassured them
    that, as far as he was concerned, the official pledge would not
4   be violated. After, when silence fell and Jugurtha was produced,
    Memmius began to speak, recalling the man's deeds at Rome
    and in Numidia and establishing his crimes against his father
    and brother: although the Roman people realized who his
    helpers and agents in those activities were, he said, he neverthe-
    less preferred them to have it at first hand from 'him over
    there':[59] if he revealed the truth, he could rest considerable hope
    in the faith and clemency of the Roman people; but, if he
    remained silent, he would not save his associates but would
    destroy himself and his hopes.

34   When Memmius had finished speaking and Jugurtha was
    ordered to reply, C. Baebius, the tribune of the plebs of whose
    bribing by money we spoke above, then ordered the king to
    keep silent; and, although the crowd at the meeting, blazing

strongly, terrified him with its shouting, appearance, frequent
aggression, and all the other reactions which tend to be produced by anger, nevertheless his shamelessness won. So the   2
people were proved a laughing-stock and withdrew from
the meeting; for Jugurtha, Bestia and the others at whom the
enquiry was aimed, confidence increased.

There was at that period in Rome a certain Numidian by the   35
name of Massiva, the son of Gulussa and grandson of Masinissa, who, because he had opposed Jugurtha in the dispute
between the kings, had left his fatherland as a fugitive when
Cirta had surrendered and Adherbal been killed. This was the   2
man whom Sp. Albinus, who held the consulship with Q. Minucius Rufus in the year after Bestia,[60] persuaded to seek the
kingdom of Numidia from the senate, on the grounds that he
was of Masinissa's stock and that Jugurtha was the object of
resentment and fear on account of his crimes. Hungry to wage   3
war, the consul preferred to take every initiative rather than let
things languish; and to him fell Numidia as his province, to
Minucius Macedonia. After Massiva began to implement his   4
plans and Jugurtha found insufficient support amongst his
friends (some were inhibited by guilt, others by notoriety and
fear), the latter commanded Bomilcar, who was the closest
and most loyal to him, to procure by payment (the way he had
concluded many deals) ambushers for Massiva and to kill the
Numidian – preferably by stealth but, failing that, by any
method at all. Bomilcar quickly carried out the king's instruc-   5
tions and by means of men who were skilled at such tasks he
reconnoitred the other's comings and goings and, in short, all
his places and times; then, when the circumstances required it,
he laid his ambush.

One of the number who had been prepared for the slaying   6
of Massiva approached him rather inadvisedly. Although he
succeeded in butchering him, he was himself arrested and – to
general encouragement, especially from the consul Albinus – he
provided evidence. Bomilcar, as companion of one who had   7
come to Rome under an official pledge, became a defendant
more in accordance with equity and right than the law of nations.
But Jugurtha, the clear culprit in a crime of such magnitude,   8

did not cease to contend against the truth, until he became
aware that resentment at the deed was beyond his influence and
9 money. Therefore, although in the earlier proceedings[61] he had
given fifty of his friends as sureties, he took thought for his
kingdom rather than his sureties and sent Bomilcar secretly to
Numidia, fearing that his other compatriots would have an
attack of dread and would not obey him if reprisal were exacted
from Bomilcar. And within a few days he himself set off for the
same destination, having been ordered by the senate to withdraw
10 from Italy. After he left Rome, however, it is said that he often
looked back silently in that direction, finally saying that 'it was a
city for sale and soon to be doomed – if only it found a buyer'.

36   Meanwhile Albinus, resuming the war, hurried to transport
to Africa supplies, pay and other things which would be useful
for the soldiers; and he himself set out immediately, so that by
arms, surrender or whatever means he might conclude the war
2 before the time of the elections, which was not far off. Jugurtha,
on the other hand, protracted everything, made one reason for
delay after another, promised surrender and then pretended
dread, yielded to pressure and a little later, lest his men should
lose heart, applied it himself: in this way, by the alternate delays
3 of war and peace, he toyed with the consul. (In fact there were
those who reckoned that Albinus at the time was not unaware
of the king's plan and who did not believe that, after so much
haste, ineptitude rather than cunning was the reason why the
4 war had been protracted so easily.) When with the passing of
time the day of the elections approached, Albinus left his
brother Aulus as propraetor[62] in camp and departed for Rome.
37   At that period in Rome the commonwealth was being dis-
2 rupted hideously by tribunician rebellions. P. Lucullus and
L. Annius, tribunes of the plebs, were striving to continue their
magistracy despite resistance from their colleagues – a dispute
3 which was hindering the entire year's elections. The delay led
Aulus, who we said above had been left as propraetor in camp,
to hope either that he would conclude the war or that, because
of the terror inspired by his army, he would take money from
the king: he therefore summoned the soldiers from winter quarters for an expedition in the month of January,[63] and by forced

marches through the harshness of winter he arrived at the town
of Suthul, where the king's treasures were. Although it could   4
be neither taken nor besieged, owing to the savagery of the season
and the advantageousness of its position (around its wall, which
was situated on the brink of a mountain precipice, a muddy plain
had formed into a swamp in the winter floods), nevertheless,
either for the sake of pretence – to add to the king's alarm – or
dazzled by the desire of gaining the town for its treasures, he
brought up penthouses, threw up a mound and hastened along
other measures which would be useful for his project.

But Jugurtha, knowing the foolishness and inexperience of   38
the legate,[64] cunningly encouraged his madness, repeatedly dispatched legates in supplication, and, with apparent evasiveness,
personally led his army through an area of denes[65] and along
tracks. Finally he drove Aulus, with the hope of terms, to   2
forsake Suthul and to follow his seeming retreat into remote
regions. Meanwhile, by means of crafty individuals, he tried to   3
influence the army day and night, bribing some centurions and
leaders of squadrons[66] to desert and others to abandon their
positions at a given signal. After he had arranged all this to his 4
liking, at dead of night he unexpectedly surrounded Aulus'
camp with a host of Numidians. The Roman soldiers were   5
stunned by the unaccustomed confusion, some taking up arms,
others hiding, others reassuring the terrified. There was trepidation in every quarter: a substantial force of the enemy, a sky
darkened by night and clouds, double-edged danger; in short,
whether it was safer to flee or to remain was uncertain. Of the   6
number who we said had been bribed a little earlier, a cohort
of Ligurians with two squadrons of Thracians and a few troop
soldiers crossed to the king, and a front-rank centurion of the
third legion allowed the enemy to enter at the fortification
which he had undertaken to defend; and that was where all the
Numidians burst in. In a foul flight, many of them throwing   7
away their arms, our men occupied a nearby hill; night-time   8
and the plunder in the camp prevented the enemy from capitalizing on their victory. Then on the next day Jugurtha spoke   9
in a dialogue with Aulus: although he held him and his army
in the grip of starvation and steel, he said, nevertheless he was

mindful of human affairs and, if the other made a treaty with
him, he would send them all unscathed under the yoke; besides
that, he was to withdraw from Numidia within ten days.
10 Although these words weighed heavily and were full of outrage,
nevertheless, because the alternative was the dread of death,
peace was agreed in accordance with the king's pleasure.

39   But, when this was discovered at Rome, dread and distress
overwhelmed the community: some grieved for the glory of the
empire, others – unaccustomed to the circumstances of war –
feared for freedom. Aulus was the object of everyone's hostility,
especially those who had achieved frequent distinction in war,
because, though armed, he had sought salvation by disgrace
2 rather than by muscle. For these reasons the consul Albinus,
fearing the indignation and subsequent danger resulting from
his brother's failure, consulted the senate about the treaty. (And
yet, in the meantime, he enlisted reinforcements for the army,
sought auxiliaries from the allies and those of the Latin name[67]
3 – in short, he did everything to save time.) The senate, exactly
as was right, decreed that no treaty could have been made
4 without an order from itself and the people. The consul, prevented by the tribunes of the plebs from transporting with him
the forces which he had procured, set off within a few days for
Africa: for the whole army, as had been agreed, had been
withdrawn from Numidia and was wintering in the province.
5 After he arrived there, although his burning intention was to
pursue Jugurtha and remedy the indignation against his
brother, nevertheless, finding that command was lax and that
the soldiers had been corrupted by reckless licentiousness (quite
apart from their flight), he decided that, given the possibilities,
there was nothing he could do.

40   Meanwhile at Rome C. Mamilius Limetanus, a tribune of
the plebs,[68] published a bill before the people to the effect that
there should be an enquiry into those on whose advice Jugurtha
had ignored the senate's decrees; those who, while on legation
or in command, had taken money from him; those who had
handed back elephants and deserters; and likewise those who
2 had made terms with the enemy concerning peace or war. Partly
from guilt, and partly dreading the dangers of party resentment,

they[69] could not openly oppose the bill without admitting that those and similar actions had their approval: therefore, they secretly prepared obstacles through their friends and especially through individuals of the Latin name and Italian allies. But it is incredible to recall the measure of the plebs' determination and the vehemence with which they ordered the bill through, more from hatred of the nobility, for whom its penalties were being prepared, than from any concern for the commonwealth: so great was the passion of partisanship. Everyone else was therefore stunned by dread; but, in the midst of the plebs' delight and the rout of his own side, and with the community still trembling even then, M. Scaurus, who we have said above was Bestia's legate,[70] ensured that, since three commissioners were required by the Mamilian bill, he himself was created as one of their number. But the enquiry was conducted harshly and violently in accordance with rumour and the whim of the plebs: just as the nobility had often been seized by the overbearingness which arises from favourable circumstances, so at that period was the plebs.

The custom of parties and factions and, then, of all evil practices arose at Rome a few years before from inactivity and an abundance of those things which mortals consider to be priorities. For before the destruction of Carthage[71] the Roman people and senate managed the commonwealth placidly and restrainedly between them. There was no struggle amongst citizens either for glory or for domination: dread of an enemy maintained the community in its good practices. But, when that source of alarm left their minds, recklessness and haughtiness – things, to be sure, which favourable circumstances attract – made their entrance. So the inactivity which in adverse circumstances they had craved was, once acquired, more harsh and bitter.[72] For the nobility began to turn their rank, and the people their freedom, into matters of whim: every man for himself appropriated, looted and seized. So the whole was split into two parties, and the commonwealth, which had been neutral, was rent apart.

But it was the nobility which derived more power from

factiousness; the plebs' strength, amorphous as it was and dis-
7 persed amongst a great number, had less potency. The conduct
of war and of domestic matters rested on the decision of a few;
in the same hands were the treasury, provinces, magistracies,
glories and triumphs; the people were oppressed by soldiering
and want, while commanders and a few others snatched the
8 plunder of war; and meanwhile the parents or small children
of every soldier whose neighbour was more powerful were
9 driven from their abode. So avarice, accompanied by powerfulness, attacked without limit or restraint, it tainted and devastated everything, it attached neither weight nor sanctity to
10 anything, until it caused itself to fall headlong. For, as soon as
some of the nobility were discovered who would put true glory
before unjust power, the community began to quake and civil
dissension to arise, like a convulsion of the earth.

42   For, after Ti. and C. Gracchus (whose ancestors had contributed much to the commonwealth in the Punic and other wars[73])
had begun to champion the freedom of the plebs and to expose
the crimes of the few, the nobility – guilty and therefore stunned
– confronted the actions of the Gracchi, sometimes through the
allies and those of the Latin name, at other times through the
Roman equestrians, whose hope of sharing[74] had divided them
from the plebs; and first they executed Tiberius by the sword,
then, after a few years, Gaius, embarked as he was on the same
course – the one a tribune, the other a triumvir for the founding
2 of colonies; and, with the latter, M. Fulvius Flaccus.[75] Admittedly, in their desire for conquest, the Gracchi did not show a
3 sufficiently moderate spirit; but it is preferable to be conquered
in a moral manner than to conquer injustice in an immoral
4 one.[76] Therefore the nobility, capitalizing on their conquest
according to their whim, annihilated many mortal beings by
the sword or by exile and made themselves more fearful than
powerful for the future – a circumstance which has often been
the downfall of great communities, in that one side wants to
conquer the other by whatever means and to exact from the
conquered too bitter a vengeance.

5   However, if I were prepared to discuss the parties' aims and
the behaviour of the whole community point by point or in

accordance with their significance, time would fail me sooner than material. For that reason I return to my project.

After Aulus' treaty and our army's foul[77] flight, Metellus and   43
Silanus as consuls designate[78] had divided the provinces
between themselves and Numidia had fallen to Metellus, a fierce
man and, though opposed to the people's party, nevertheless of
a consistent and unblemished reputation. When he first entered   2
upon his magistracy, deeming that everything else would be
shared with his colleague, he gave his attention to the war
he was about to wage. Therefore, distrusting the old army, he   3
enlisted soldiers, summoned support from all round, procured
arms, weapons, horses and the other equipment of soldiering,
and in addition supplies in abundance – in short, everything
which is generally of use in a variable and extremely demanding
war. Every effort to accomplish all this was made by the senate   4
through its authority, by the allies and those of the Latin name
and the kings[79] through their spontaneous dispatch of auxiliaries, and finally by the whole community through its utmost
enthusiasm. And so, when everything had been procured and   5
arranged to his liking, he set off for Numidia – to the high
hopes of the citizens, both on account of his good qualities and
especially because he was temperamentally invincible in the face
of riches and it was the avarice of magistrates which previously
in Numidia had worn down our resources and increased those
of the enemy.

But, when he arrived in Africa, the army which was handed   44
to him by the proconsul Sp. Albinus was idle, unwarlike, tolerant of neither danger nor hard work, readier with its tongue
than its muscle, a plunderer of the allies and itself plunder for
the enemy, maintained without command and discipline. So the   2
new commander derived more anxiety from the soldiers' bad
behaviour than help or good hope from their numbers. Never-   3
theless, although the delay to the elections[80] had reduced the
time for campaigning and he thought that the citizens' minds
would be concentrated on the expected outcome, Metellus
decided not to have any contact with the war until he had
compelled the soldiers to work hard under the discipline of

4   their ancestors. For Albinus had been stunned by the disaster
    to his brother Aulus and his army, and, having decided not to
    leave the province, he mostly maintained the soldiers in station-
    ary camp for the length of the campaigning time that he was in
    command, except when the stench or need for fodder forced a
5   change of location. Yet there were no fortifications, nor were
    watches deployed in the military manner; everyone left the
    standards as they pleased; camp-followers, mingling with the
    soldiers, wandered around day and night; and, roving about,
    they devastated the land, laid siege to villas, competed to drive
    off livestock and menials as plunder and to exchange them with
    traders for imported wine and other such; in addition, they sold
    the official rations of grain and each day traded for bread: in
    short, whatever iniquities of apathy and luxury can be men-
    tioned or imagined, they were all in that army – and more
    besides.

45 Yet I discover that in so awkward a situation Metellus was
    no less great and wise a man than in the face of the enemy (such
    was the control with which he moderated his course between
2   ingratiation and savagery); and that in an edict he removed first
    the props of their apathy: no one should sell bread or any other
    cooked food in camp; no camp-followers should accompany
    the army; no spearman or troop soldier should keep a slave or
    baggage-animal in camp or in the column; and that he set a
    narrow limit on other things. Besides this, he moved camp daily
    on sideways routes,[81] he fortified it with rampart and ditch just
    as if the enemy were in the vicinity, he set frequent watches and
    went round them personally with his legates; likewise in the
    column he was sometimes at the front, sometimes at the rear,
    and often in the centre, to ensure that no one broke rank, that
    when advancing they were massed around the standards, and
3   that the soldiery carried food and arms. In this way, by the
    prevention of offences rather than by punishment, he soon
    toughened his army.

46 Meanwhile, Jugurtha heard from messengers what Metellus
    was doing, and, at the same time having been informed from
    Rome about the man's blamelessness, he started to distrust his
    own situation and now at last tried to make a real surrender.

He sent legates with supplicatory offerings to the consul to beg   2
only for the lives of himself and his children; all else should be
surrendered to the Roman people. But Metellus had already   3
found out from earlier experience that the Numidian race was
untrustworthy, of volatile temperament and hungry for revolution. And so he approached the legates separately, one after   4
another; by trying to influence them gradually and (when he
knew that they were receptive to him) by substantial promises,
he persuaded them to hand Jugurtha over to him – preferably
alive, but, failing that, dead. Yet openly he ordered them to
announce to the king what would accord with the latter's
wishes.

Then, after a few days, his army concentrating and comba-   5
tive, he himself proceeded into Numidia, where, so far from
there being a scene of war, the huts were full of people and
there were livestock and farmers in the fields; from their towns
and mapalia[82] officers of the king proceeded to meet them,
ready to give them grain[83] and to carry supplies – in short, to
do everything they were commanded. Yet Metellus did not for   6
that reason advance with his column any the less protected,
but exactly as if the enemy were in the vicinity, reconnoitring
everything over a wide area in the belief that the signs of
surrender were mere show and that a place was being tested for
ambush. Hence he himself, with the unencumbered cohorts as   7
well as a select unit of slingers and archers, was at the front; in
the rear his legate C. Marius[84] with the cavalry was in charge;
on each flank he had distributed the auxiliary cavalry to the
tribunes of the legions and the prefects of the cohorts, so that
the light-armed troops mixed in with them could repel the
enemy's cavalry wherever it approached. For in Jugurtha there   8
was such cunning and such experience of terrain and soldiering
that it was regarded as uncertain whether he was more deadly
when absent or present, when bringing peace or war.

Not far from the route along which Metellus was marching,   47
there was the Numidian town by the name of Vaga, the most
frequented market for merchandise in the whole kingdom,
where many mortal beings of Italian stock had become accustomed to dwell and trade. Here the consul installed a garrison,   2

both to test if they would allow it and for the advantages of its position. In addition, he commanded them to stockpile grain and other things which would be useful for the war, deeming (what the circumstances suggested) that the throng of businessmen would both help the army with supplies and act as a protection for the things already procured.

3   During these activities Jugurtha was simply more unstinting, sending legates in supplication, begging for peace, surrendering everything to Metellus apart from the lives of himself and his

4   children. The consul sent them home just like the earlier ones, having first lured them into betrayal; he neither rejected nor guaranteed the peace which the king was demanding, and, during the resulting interval, awaited what the legates had

48 promised. But, when Jugurtha compared Metellus' words with his deeds, he recognized that he was being assailed by his own techniques: words of peace were repeatedly announced, but the reality was the harshest of wars, his largest city under occupation, his land known to the enemy, the hearts and minds of his compatriots assailed. Compelled by the necessity of circum-

2   stance, he decided on armed struggle. Having therefore reconnoitred the enemy's route, and being led to hope for victory by the advantageousness of the place, he prepared the greatest possible number of forces of all types and by means of secret tracks forestalled the army of Metellus.

3   In the part of Numidia which Adherbal had received in the division,[85] there was a river rising in the south by the name of Muthul, from which there was a mountain twenty miles distant on a parallel course,[86] forsaken by nature and human cultivation. But from the middle of it,[87] reaching an immense distance, there sprang a kind of hill which was covered in wild olive and myrtle and other types of tree that grow in arid and

4   sandy ground. In the middle there was a plain which, owing to the dearth of water, was desert apart from the areas near the river: these were planted with copses and frequented by live-

49 stock and farmers. It was on this hill, then, which we have said stretched on a sideways route,[88] that Jugurtha extended his line of men and took up position. He put Bomilcar in charge of the elephants and some of the infantry forces and told him what to

do; he himself with all the cavalry and select infantrymen was nearer the mountain, where he placed his men.[89]

Then he went round the individual squadrons and man- 2 iples,[90] advising and entreating that they should be mindful of their old-time prowess and victory and should defend themselves and their kingdom from the avarice of the Romans: the struggle would be with men whom they had previously conquered and sent beneath the yoke; their leader had changed, but not their spirit; he had provided for his own men everything which a commander ought – a superior position, and that in the hand-to-hand fighting it would be the knowledgeable against the incompetent, not lesser numbers against greater or the callow against better warriors. Accordingly, they should 3 prepare themselves and concentrate on attacking the Romans at the given signal: that day would either validate all their toils and victories or would be the start of the greatest miseries. Additionally, in the case of those whom he had singled out for 4 money or honour on account of some military deed, he reminded each of them individually of his kindness and pointed them out to the others; in short, by using guarantees, threats and entreaties as was appropriate to the temperament of each man, he motivated them all in different ways – while in the meantime Metellus could be seen descending the mountain with his army, oblivious of the enemy.

At first Metellus was uncertain what the unusual scene 5 showed (horses and Numidians had taken up their positions in the bush: they were not completely hidden, given the stuntedness of the trees, and yet were not clearly identifiable, since men and military standards were obscured both by the nature of the place and by camouflage); then, quickly realizing the ambush, he halted his column for a brief while. There and then 6 he rearranged the ranks, drawing up the line as a threefold support on the right flank (which was nearest the enemy), distributing slingers and archers between the maniples, and placing all the cavalry on the edges; and, after a necessarily brief exhortation to the soldiers, he led the line down into the plain with its vanguard now sideways on, exactly as he had drawn it up.[91] But, noticing that the Numidians were motionless 50 and not descending the hill, and since the time of year and lack of water led him to fear that his army might be overcome by thirst, he sent the legate P. Rutilius[92] with the unencumbered cohorts and part of the cavalry ahead to the river to pre-empt the place by means of a camp, reckoning that the enemy would delay his own march with frequent attacks and sideways battles and, because they lacked confidence in their arms, would test

2 the soldiers' tiredness and thirst. Then he himself advanced gradually, making allowances for the situation and terrain as he had when descending the mountain; he kept Marius behind the vanguard, while he himself was with the cavalry on the left wing, who had become the vanguard in the column.

3   But, when Jugurtha saw that the end of Metellus' column had gone past the first of his own men, he used a garrison of about two thousand infantry to occupy the area of the mountain where Metellus had descended, to prevent its becoming a refuge and subsequently a protection for any retreating opponents.

4 Then suddenly he gave the signal and attacked the enemy. Some Numidians slaughtered those in the rear, others made assaults from left and right: their presence and pressure were ferocious, and in every quarter they disrupted the ranks of the Romans – amongst whom even the stauncher ones, when encountering the enemy, were bewildered by the irregularity of the battle, being wounded themselves only from long range and having no

5 opportunity of striking back or fighting hand to hand. When a Roman squadron began a pursuit, Jugurtha's cavalry, following his earlier instructions, did not retreat in a body or in the same direction but dispersed in as many different ways as possible.

6 So, whenever they were unable to deter the enemy from pursuit, with their superior numbers they simply surrounded their scattered pursuers from the rear or flanks; and, whenever the hill was more advantageous for flight than the plain, the Numidians' horses were of course on familiar ground and easily made their way through the bush, while the harshness and unusualness of the terrain held our men back.

51   Yet in fact the whole scene of activity was fluctuating, unpredictable, foul and wretched: separated from their own men, some gave way, others pursued; there was no regard for stan-

dards or ranks: wherever anyone was overtaken by danger, there he made a stand and resisted; arms and weapons, horses and men, enemies and citizens were all mixed up; nothing was done according to plan or command: chance ruled everything.

And so it was that much of the day had passed and even then 2 the outcome was uncertain. Finally, with everyone wilting from 3 the toil and heat, Metellus saw that the Numidians' pressure was less and he gradually gathered his soldiers together, restored the ranks and placed four legionary cohorts against the enemy infantry (a large part of whom had wearily taken up position on higher ground). At the same time he begged and 4 urged his soldiers not to falter or allow a fleeing enemy to win: they[93] had neither camp nor fortification for which to make in retreat; everything rested on arms. As for Jugurtha, he too did 5 not remain quiet in the meanwhile: he circulated, encouraged, resumed the battle, and with picked men tried every possibility himself, helped his fellows, pressed enemy waverers, and by fighting at long range contained those whom he found to be staunch. In that way the two commanders, the most eminent 52 of men, were conducting a personal struggle, well matched themselves but with ill-matched resources: on Metellus' side 2 there was the prowess of his soldiers but adverse terrain; for Jugurtha everything else was favourable apart from his soldiers. Finally the Romans, knowing that they had no place of refuge 3 and would not be allowed by the enemy to fight (and it was now evening), made their way uphill as they had been instructed. With the loss of their position the Numidians were 4 routed and put to flight. A few died; many were saved by their speed and the enemy's ignorance of the area.

Meanwhile, when Bomilcar (who we said above had been 5 put in charge of the elephants and some of the infantry by Jugurtha) was passed by Rutilius, he gradually led his men down to level ground and, while the legate quickly proceeded to where he had been sent ahead,[94] he prepared his line quietly (as the situation demanded) and did not leave off reconnoitring what the enemy was doing anywhere. After he learned that 6 Rutilius had now taken up position and had nothing to distract him, and at the same time that the shouting from Jugurtha's battle was increasing, he was afraid that the legate might find out the situation and go to assist his troubled colleagues: he therefore extended his line (which in his distrust of his soldiers' prowess he had positioned in close order) along a broader front to block the enemy's route, and in that manner he advanced towards Rutilius' camp.

53   The Romans noticed unexpectedly a great mass of dust (the fact that the land was planted with copses cut off their view). At first they deemed that the arid ground was being whipped up by the wind; but after, when they saw that it remained consistent and was approaching ever closer (as the battle-line moved), they realized the situation, hurriedly seized their arms and stood before the camp as was being commanded of them.

2   Then, when the enemy had come nearer, both sides clashed
3   with a loud shout. The Numidians delayed only so long as they thought the elephants would help them; but, when they saw that they had been impeded by the branches of the trees and, scattered as a result, were being surrounded, they took flight and many of them, throwing away their arms, left unharmed, helped by the hill or night-time (which was already approach-
4   ing). Four elephants were captured; all the rest – forty in number
5   – were killed. As for the Romans, although they were tired by their march and the work on the camp and the battle, neverthe-less, because Metellus was delaying longer than expected, they advanced to meet him, drawn up in formation and concentrat-
6   ing (the cunning of the Numidians allowed no laxity or slack-
7   ness). When there was not much distance between them, each party, like an enemy, at first caused alarm and confusion in the other by its noise in the dark night; and a lamentable deed was almost perpetrated through carelessness, except that cavalry were sent ahead on both sides and reconnoitred the situation.
8   And so dread was suddenly replaced by joy: the soldiers called delightedly to one another, they described and listened to their experiences, each man praised his own courageous deeds to the sky. Such is the way of human affairs: in victory even cowards can boast, but in adversity even the good are disparaged.

54   Remaining in the same camp for four days, Metellus restored the wounded with care, made presentations in the military

manner to those who had earned them in battle, praised and gave thanks to them all in a meeting, and urged them to approach in a similar spirit the trivialities which were left: there had already been enough fighting for victory; their remaining toils would be for plunder. Nevertheless, in the meanwhile, he 2 dispatched deserters and other suitable individuals to discover where in the world Jugurtha was and what he was planning, whether he was accompanied by only a few men or had an army, and how he was bearing himself in defeat. But the man 3 had retired to an area of denes that was naturally well protected, and there he was collecting an army which was larger in numbers but dull and weak, more expert in the land and live-stock than in war. This came about thanks to the fact that, 4 apart from the royal cavalry, no Numidian at all follows the king in his flight: each man departs to wherever his spirit takes him, and that is not considered an outrage to soldiering. Such is the way of their customs.

Therefore, when Metellus saw that the king's spirit was still 5 defiant even then, that a war was resuming which could not be waged except at the latter's whim, and as well that his own struggle with the enemy was unequal (since the loss to them in being conquered was less than that to his own men in conquer-ing), he decided that the war must be waged not by battles or in the line but by another method. And so he went to the 6 wealthiest areas of Numidia, devastated the land, captured and burned many strongholds and towns which were carelessly fortified or without a garrison, and ordered the adults to be killed and everything else to be plunder for the soldiers. Such was the alarm that many mortals were surrendered as hostages to the Romans, and grain and other things which would be useful were provided in abundance; wherever the situation demanded it, a garrison was installed.

These activities terrified the king much more than did the 7 battle fought unsuccessfully by his own men: he whose whole 8 hope rested on flight was being compelled to pursue, he who had been unable to defend favourable territory was now being compelled to wage war in unfavourable. Nevertheless, he 9 adopted the plan which seemed the best of the possibilities: he ordered the majority of his army to wait where it was, while he himself with picked cavalry pursued Metellus and, having escaped notice by moving at night along untrodden routes, 10 suddenly attacked the Romans as they roved about. Numbers of them fell unarmed, many were captured, no one at all escaped uninjured; as for the Numidians, they withdrew, as ordered, to the nearest hills, before help could come from the camp.

55   Meanwhile at Rome great joy arose on the news of Metellus' exploits and how he was conducting himself and his army according to ancestral custom, how in adverse terrain he had still been victorious through prowess, was in possession of enemy land and had compelled Jugurtha – bragging as he had been in consequence of Albinus' ineptitude – to place his hope 2 of salvation in the desert or in flight. And so the senate decreed supplications to the immortal gods in return for his successful deeds; the community, previously trembling and anxious about the outcome of the war, reacted delightedly; Metellus acquired a distinguished reputation.

3   He therefore concentrated all the more on striving for victory, lost no time in any way, but still took care not to become vulnerable to the enemy anywhere, mindful that resentment 4 follows after glory. So, the more distinguished he became, the more cautious he was, and after his ambush by Jugurtha did not spread out his army to plunder: when he needed grain or fodder, the cohorts along with all the cavalry acted as escort; 5 but the land was devastated more by fire than by plundering.He 6 led part of the army himself, Marius the rest:[95] they made camp in two places with not much distance between them; 7 when force was needed, they all appeared; but, to increase the enemy's flight and alarm along a broader front, they acted 8 separately. And all the time Jugurtha was in pursuit across the hills, seeking a time or place for fighting along whichever route he had heard the enemy would come, contaminating the fodder and water-sources (of which there was a dearth), revealing himself sometimes to Metellus and at others to Marius, assailing the rear of the column and immediately returning to the hills, in turn threatening one group after another, neither offering

battle nor permitting inaction but only keeping the enemy from their project.[96]

When the Roman commander saw that he was being exhausted by such cunning and that the enemy was not allowing the chance of a fight, he decided to assault the great city, by the name of Zama, which was the citadel in the part of the kingdom where it was situated, deeming (something which his action would demand) that Jugurtha would come to the aid of his troubled colleagues and that there would be a battle there. But the other, learning from deserters what was being planned, forestalled Metellus by forced marches. He urged the townsfolk to defend their walls, giving them deserters as assistance (the staunchest category of the king's forces, because they could not prove false); in addition, he guaranteed that at the right moment he would arrive in person with an army. So, after making these arrangements, he withdrew to an area as hidden as possible and after a short while found out that Marius with only a few cohorts had been sent for fodder on a detour to Sicca, a town which had been the very first to defect from the king after his unsuccessful battle. He went there by night with picked cavalry and in the gateway started a battle with the Romans just as they were coming out; at the same time, in a loud voice, he urged the Siccenses to surround the cohorts from the rear: Fortune was giving them the chance of a distinguished deed, he said; if they did it, his own life thereafter would be lived in his kingdom, and theirs in freedom without dread. And, had not Marius hurriedly marched forward and left the town, all or a large part of the Siccenses would have changed loyalties: such is the volatility with which Numidians behave. But as for the Jugurthine soldiers, though they were supported for a while by the king, nevertheless, when the enemy started to press with greater force, they turned fugitive and withdrew with a few losses.

Marius arrived at Zama. Situated in a plain, the town was protected by workmanship rather than by nature, lacking no resource, rich in arms and men. Therefore Metellus, having made arrangements to suit the occasion and locality, surrounded the entire walls with his army and commanded his

3 legates where each should be in charge. Then, at a given signal, a great shout arose simultaneously on all sides; and yet that circumstance did not terrify the Numidians: in ferocious con-
4 centration they remained unperturbed. The battle began. On the Roman side, depending on the temperament of each man, some fought at long range with bullet or stones, others drew close and either undermined the wall or attacked it with ladders,
5 desiring to get to grips with the battle; in reply, the townsfolk rolled rocks onto those nearest and threw burning stakes and
6 lances as well as pitch mixed with sulphur and pinewood. But not even those who had remained at a distance were sufficiently protected by their timidity: many were wounded by javelins discharged by launcher or hand, and both the brave and the cowardly shared an equal danger but unequal repute.

58 While this struggle was continuing at Zama, Jugurtha unexpectedly attacked the enemy camp with a substantial unit. Since those who were on guard were relaxing and expecting
2 anything other than battle, he burst through the gate. Stunned by a sudden dread, each of our men took thought for himself according to his character: some fled, others seized their arms,
3 a large proportion were wounded or killed. But out of the whole number not more than forty, mindful of the Roman name, formed a troop and, seizing a place slightly more elevated than the rest, could not be dislodged from it by the greatest force but threw back weapons thrown from long range and, being few against many, experienced little disappointment. And, if the Numidians approached nearer, then they really showed their prowess and with the greatest force slaughtered and routed them and put them to flight.
4 In the meantime, while Metellus was conducting affairs with the utmost ferocity, he heard an enemy shout in the rear and then, turning his horse, he noticed that a flight was taking place
5 in his direction, which indicated that it was his compatriots. He therefore quickly sent all the cavalry to the camp and C. Marius too with the allied cohorts at once, and he begged him tearfully, by their friendship and by the commonwealth, not to allow any disgrace to remain in a victorious army or the enemy to depart
6 unpunished. The other soon carried out his instructions. But

Jugurtha, hindered by the camp's fortifications (some men were toppling headlong over the rampart, some in their haste were obstructing one another in the narrows), retired after many losses to a well protected area.

As for Metellus, his business unfinished, he returned to the   7
camp after nightfall with his army. On the next day, therefore,   59
before he emerged for the assault, he ordered all the cavalry to ride in front of the camp in the area where the king's arrival would be; he allocated the gates and their vicinities to the tribunes; then he himself went to the town and, as on the previous day, attacked the wall. Meanwhile, Jugurtha suddenly   2
fell on our men from a concealed position: those who were placed nearest to him were terrified and disrupted for a short while, but the rest speedily came to their aid; and yet they   3
would not have been able to resist the Numidian for too long,[97] had it not been for the fact that a combination of infantry and cavalry was wreaking a great disaster upon him in the encounter. Relying as they were on the former, the latter[98] did not (as is customary in a cavalry battle) pursue then withdraw but clashed with their horses head-on, entangling and disrupting the line. In this way they presented their waiting infantry with an almost defeated enemy.[99]

At the same time at Zama the struggle was continuing with   60
great violence. Wherever a legate or tribune was in charge, there the effort was at its most ferocious, and no one placed more hope in another than in himself; and the behaviour of the townsfolk was comparable. There was assault or preparation in every quarter; both sides more hungrily wounded the other than protected themselves; shouts were mixed with encourage-   2
ment, delight with groans, and the noise of arms likewise rose to the sky; on both sides weapons flew. But, whenever the   3
enemy relaxed the fight just a little, those who were defencing the walls concentrated on viewing the cavalry battle. You would   4
have noticed them sometimes delighted, sometimes panicking, depending on Jugurtha's situation at the time, and, as if they could be heard or seen by their own men, some offered advice, others encouragement, or gave hand signals or strained with their bodies, moving them this way and that as if avoiding or

5 throwing weapons. When Marius realized this (he was in charge in that area), he deliberately moderated his actions and pretended misgivings about the enterprise, allowing the Numidians
6 to observe the king's battle unperturbed. When they were gripped in this way by concern for their fellows, he suddenly attacked the wall with great violence. Having mounted on ladders, the soldiers had already almost seized the top when the townsfolk ran up and released stones, fire and other weapons
7 as well. At first our men resisted; then, when the ladders were shattered one after another and those standing on them were dashed to the ground, the rest left in whatever way they could, a few of them unharmed, a large number enfeebled by wounds.
8 Finally night broke up the battle on both sides.

61   After Metellus saw that his project was in vain, that the town would not be taken, that Jugurtha would not fight except from ambush or on his own ground, and that the summer season had now passed, he withdrew from Zama and installed garrisons in those cities which had defected to him and were adequately
2 protected by their locality or walls; the rest of his army he settled for the winter in the part of the province[100] nearest to
3 Numidia. Unlike others, he made no concessions to rest or luxury during that time but, because armed warfare was making little headway, he prepared to set ambushes for the king through his friends and to take advantage of their treachery in place of arms.
4   It was therefore Bomilcar – who had been at Rome with Jugurtha and, despite the giving of sureties, had subsequently escaped justice over the execution of Massiva – whom he approached with many promises, because his very great friend-
5 ship gave him the greatest opportunity of betrayal.[101] Metellus first contrived that the man should come to him secretly for talks, and then gave him a pledge that, if he handed Jugurtha over to him alive or dead, he would be given immunity by the senate and all his own possessions – easily persuading the Numidian, who was not only of untrustworthy temperament but also dreading that, if there were peace with the Romans, he might himself be handed over for reprisal as part of the conditions.
62   As soon as there was an opportunity, the man approached Jugurtha, who was in a state of anxiety and lamenting his

fortune; he advised him and tearfully entreated him to make provision at long last for himself, his children and the Numidian people who deserved so well of him: they had been defeated in every battle, their land had been devastated, many mortals had been captured and slaughtered, the kingdom's resources had been shattered; already there had been enough trial of the soldiers' prowess and of fortune; he should beware lest, while he hesitated, the Numidians took thought for themselves. With these and other such words he induced the king's mind towards surrender. Legates were sent to the commander to say that Jugurtha would do what he was commanded and without any terms would hand over himself and his kingdom into Metellus' trust. The latter quickly ordered all those of the senatorial order to be fetched from winter quarters; he held a council with them and others whom he considered suitable. So, in accordance with a decree of the council in line with ancestral custom, by means of legates he commanded from Jugurtha two hundred thousand pounds' weight of silver, all his elephants and a considerable quantity of his horses and arms. After this was done without delay, he ordered all the deserters to be bound and brought to him; a large number was brought, as had been ordered; a few had departed to King Bocchus in Mauretania as soon as the surrender had begun.

Now that Jugurtha had been despoiled of arms, men and money, and since he was being called in person to Tisidium to receive his commands, he began to change his mind again and, because of his guilty conscience, to fear his just deserts. Finally, after many days spent in uncertainty (sometimes in his disgust at adversity he regarded anything as better than war, at others he reflected to himself how heavy a fall it would be from king to slave), and despite the fruitless loss of many great sources of security, he took up war afresh. And at Rome the senate, when consulted about the provinces, had decreed Numidia to Metellus.

At Utica during the same time, while Marius happened to be supplicating the gods with victims, a soothsayer had said that great and marvellous things were portended for him: accordingly, he should rely on the gods and turn his dreams into

reality; he should make as many trials of fortune as possible;
2 everything would turn out successfully. For his part, Marius
had already been agitated by a great desire for the consulship,
to obtain which he had, except for an ancient family, everything
else in abundance: industry, probity, a great knowledge of
soldiering, and a temperament which was remarkable in war
but restrained at home, unconquered by cravings or riches,
hungry only for glory.

3   Born and raised for the whole of his boyhood at Arpinum,
as soon as he was of an age to endure soldiering he occupied
himself with active service, not with Greek fluency or city
refinements: thus, surrounded by good practices, his sound
4 disposition quickly matured. As soon as he sought the military
tribunate from the people, though many did not know his face,
he was easily known for his deeds and so was declared by
5 all the tribes. From that magistracy onwards, he subsequently
acquired for himself a series of others, and in every power he
always behaved in such a way that he seemed worthy of a
6 greater one than that which he was holding. Nevertheless,
despite the man he was up to that point (afterwards he was
toppled by ambition), he did not dare to seek the consulship:
at that time other magistracies were conferred by the plebs, but
the consulship was still passed from hand to hand by the nobles
7 between themselves. No new man was so distinguished or had
such exceptional deeds to his credit that he was not considered
unworthy of that honorific office and as if tainted.

64   When Marius saw that the diviner's words were pointing in
the same direction as he was being urged by his heart's desire,
he asked Metellus for a discharge so as to seek office. Although
the latter had plenty of prowess, glory and other qualities to
be coveted by good men, nevertheless he was possessed of a
contemptuous mentality and – the affliction common to the
2 nobility – haughtiness. And so, at first shaken by the unusual
circumstance, he marvelled at his plan and, as if in friendship,
warned him not to embark on anything so misguided or to hold
ideas above his station: not everything was to be desired by
everyone, he said; he ought to be sufficiently pleased with his
own circumstances; in short, he should beware of seeking from

the Roman people something which would rightly be denied
him. After he had said these and other such things and Marius'   3
mind was unchanged, Metellus replied that, as soon as his
official activities allowed it, he would do what he was asking.
And it is maintained that afterwards, in response to repeated   4
and more frequent requests, he said that Marius should be in
no hurry to depart: he would seek the consulship soon enough
alongside his own son. (At the time the latter was about twenty
years old and was soldiering in the same place as a cadet of his
father's.[102]) The effect of this remark was to inflame Marius
strongly – both towards the honorific office to which he aspired
and against Metellus.

So it was with desire and anger – those worst of counsellors   5
– that he went on his way. He refrained from no word or deed,
provided it served his ambition: he kept under a more lax
discipline than previously the soldiers of whom he had charge
in winter quarters; amongst the businessmen, of whom there
was a large number at Utica, he spoke about the war accusingly
as well as braggingly: if only half the army were entrusted to
him, he said, he would have Jugurtha in chains within a few
days; things were being deliberately protracted by the commander, because, as a foolish man of regal haughtiness, he
enjoyed command too much. All these words seemed the more   6
convincing to them because their private assets had been
undone by the prolongation of the war, and no speed is
adequate for one's heart's desire.

Besides, there was in our army a certain Numidian by   65
the name of Gauda, a son of Mastanabal and grandson of
Masinissa, whom Micipsa had entered in his will as a secondary
heir and who was enfeebled by diseases and for that reason
of somewhat diminished responsibility.[103] When he asked   2
Metellus if he might place his chair next to him according to
royal custom, and afterwards for a squadron of Roman cavalry
as a bodyguard likewise, each had been denied – the honour on
the ground that it belonged only to those whom the Roman
people called kings, the guard on the ground that it would be
disgraceful for Roman cavalry if they were handed over as
retainers to a Numidian. This was the distressed figure whom   3

Marius approached and urged that, with help from himself, he should seek to punish the commander for these insults. In a supportive speech he extolled one who, on account of his diseases, was of insufficiently firm mind: he was a king, he said, a great man, grandson of Masinissa; if Jugurtha were captured or slaughtered, he would have command of Numidia without delay: that could happen quite soon, if he himself were sent to

4 the war as consul. And so he induced both him and the Roman equestrians (both soldiers and businessmen), in some cases by his personal intervention, in many by the hope of peace, to write to their connections in Rome about the war, attacking Metellus in harsh terms, and to demand Marius as commander.

5 So the consulship was sought for him with the most honourable of endorsements from many mortal beings. At the same time, that was the period at which, with the nobility routed by the Mamilian law, the plebs was elevating new men. Thus for Marius all was going well.

66 In the meantime Jugurtha, having abandoned his surrender and started war, made every preparation with great care, lost no time, gathered an army, tried to win over – either by alarming them or by the prospect of rewards – the communities which had defected from him, fortified his positions, re-made or bought arms, weapons and other things which he had lost in the hope of peace, enticed the Romans' slaves and used money to influence the men actually in the garrisons – in short, he left nothing untouched or restful but was active on all fronts.

2 Therefore the people of Vaga, where Metellus had initially installed a garrison during Jugurtha's peace-making, were worn down by the king's supplications and, not willingly estranged from him previously, the leaders of the community entered into a conspiracy. (Their public – as is usually the case, especially with Numidians – was of volatile disposition, rebellious and disaffected, desirous of revolution and hostile to rest and inactivity.) Then, after arranging things amongst themselves, they decided upon the third day because it was a festival celebrated across the whole of Africa, with the prospect of reckless

3 recreation rather than alarm. When the time came, they invited the centurions and military tribunes and the prefect of the town

himself, T. Turpilius Silanus, to their various houses. All of them, except Turpilius, they butchered at their banquets; afterwards they attacked the soldiers, who, given the day and the absence of any command, were roving around unarmed. The 4 plebs did the same, some of them instructed by the nobility, others roused by an enthusiasm for such matters and, ignorant of the policy decisions, happy enough with the turmoil itself and revolution. The Roman soldiers, their unexpected dread 67 making them uncertain and uncomprehending what to do first, were in a state of trepidation: they were kept from the citadel of the town, where their standards and shields were, by the enemy's garrison, and from flight by the earlier closing of the gates; in addition, women and boys on the roofs of buildings vied with one another in casting down rocks and other things with which their location provided them. So it was impossible 2 to take precautions against the twofold danger or for resistance to be offered by the most courageous against this weakest of groups. Good men and bad, the committed and the unwarlike, were butchered indifferently and unavenged. In that harshest 3 of situations, with the Numidians at their most savage and the town closed on all sides, the prefect Turpilius was the only one of all the Italians to escape uninjured. Whether that was due to a sympathetic host or to terms[104] or to chance, we have not adequately discovered; but, because in that great calamity a life of turpitude[105] was more important to him than the soundness of his reputation, he has left an impression of iniquity and infamy.

After Metellus had discovered about the events which had 68 taken place at Vaga, he sorrowfully withdrew from sight for a while. Then, when anger merged with his depression, he lost no time in going to avenge the wrongdoing with the greatest care. To coincide with the setting of the sun, he prepared and 2 led out the legion with which he was wintering and as many Numidian cavalry as possible, and around the third hour on the next day he arrived at a plain which was surrounded by a rather more elevated area. There he told his soldiers, who were 3 tired from their forced march and now generally refractory, that the town of Vaga was no more than a mile away: they

should endure with equanimity their remaining task, in as much as they were exacting punishment on behalf of their fellow citizens, the most courageous and most wretched of men. In
4 addition, he gave them a generous prospect of plunder. With their spirits stirred in this way, he ordered the cavalry to go first along a broad front, the infantry in the closest order possible, and their standards to be hidden.

69 When the Vagenses noticed an army coming against them, deeming (as was the case) that it was Metellus, they first closed the gates; then, when they saw that no fields were being devastated and that those who came first were Numidian cavalry, they thought that it was Jugurtha instead and went out to meet
2 him with great joy. At a suddenly given signal, some of the cavalry and infantry slaughtered the crowd which had poured out of the town; others hurried to the gates; some seized the towers: anger and the hope of plunder proved more powerful
3 than weariness. So the Vagenses had only two days of delight after their treachery: their great and wealthy community was
4 all given over to punishment or plunder. Turpilius, the prefect of the town whom we pointed out above as being the only one at all to have escaped, was ordered by Metellus to plead his case; after he had failed adequately to clear himself, he was condemned, beaten and paid the penalty with his life (for he was a citizen from Latium[106]).

70 During the same time Bomilcar, at whose instigation Jugurtha had begun the surrender which he abandoned in dread,[107] became suspected by, and was himself suspicious of, the king: he therefore desired revolution, sought a cunning way to destroy
2 the man and racked his brains day and night. Finally, in his various attempts, he formed an alliance with Nabdalsa, a noble man, of great wealth, distinguished and well liked by his compatriots, who was accustomed generally to lead an army separately from the king and to carry out all the things which Jugurtha, tired as he was or in the grip of greater concerns, found excessive. As a result the man had come by glory and
3 wealth. According to their joint plan, therefore, a day was arranged for an ambush; it was agreed that all other prep-
4 arations would be made as the situation demanded.[108] Nabdalsa

set off for his army, which he had been ordered to keep between the Romans' winter quarters to prevent the land from being devastated by the enemy with impunity. But afterwards, stunned by the magnitude of the deed, he did not arrive on time and his dread started to hamper the affair. Therefore Bomilcar, both desirous of finishing their project and led by his ally's fear into a state of anxiety lest the latter should abandon their old plan and find a new one, sent a letter to him through trustworthy individuals in which he accused the man of softness and ineptitude, invoked the gods by whom he had sworn, and warned him not to allow Metellus' rewards to turn ruinous: Jugurtha's extermination was at hand, he said; the only issue was whether he perished through Metellus' prowess or their own: accordingly, he should reflect to himself whether he preferred rewards or torture.

But, when the letter was delivered, Nabdalsa was tired after physical exercise and happened to be resting in bed, where, learning of Bomilcar's words, he was overcome first by concern and then (as is customary with depression) by sleep. There was a certain Numidian who took charge of his business, loyal and well liked and a participant in all his plans except the most recent. Having heard that a letter had been delivered, and deeming from habit that his services or talent would be needed, he entered the tent, picked up the letter which the other (now fast asleep) had carelessly placed above his head on the cushion, and read through it; then, quickly realizing the ambush, went to the king. A little after, Nabdalsa woke up and, when he did not find the letter and realized everything that had taken place, he first tried to pursue the informant and then, after that proved fruitless, went to Jugurtha to placate him. He said that his treacherous dependant had anticipated what he had been planning to do himself; tearfully he besought him, by their friendship and by his own previous acts of loyalty, not to consider him suspect of such a crime. In response the king replied placidly, differently from what he was thinking. After Bomilcar and many others whom he found out to be allies in the ambush were killed, he suppressed his anger in case any mutiny should arise from the business. And after that juncture Jugurtha never experienced a restful day or night: he never fully trusted any place, mortal being, or time; he dreaded citizens and enemies alike; he looked all round him and panicked at every noise; he rested at a different place each night, often contrary to his royal dignity, while sometimes, roused from sleep, he would seize his arms and cause a commotion: thus the alarm which agitated him resembled derangement.

73   Therefore, when Metellus learned from deserters about the fate of Bomilcar and the revelation of the information, he once again lost no time in making every preparation as though for a
2   fresh war. Overwhelmed by Marius' requests concerning his journey, and at the same time deeming that a reluctant and aggrieved individual would scarcely be useful to him, he sent
3   him home. And at Rome the plebs, learning of the letters which had been sent about Metellus and Marius, had willingly
4   accepted their contents about both of them. The commander's nobility, which was previously a source of dignity, became one of resentment; but the other's humble lineage had brought him goodwill. Yet in each case it was rather party enthusiasms than
5   their personal good or bad features which guided people. In addition, rebellious magistrates[109] stirred up the public, indicted Metellus on a capital charge at every meeting and treated
6   Marius' prowess to exaggerated celebration. Finally, the plebs were so inflamed that all the craftsmen and rustics, whose means and credit depended on their hands, left their work and crowded round Marius, considering his honour as being before
7   their own needs. So after a long period – to a stunned nobility – a new man was handed the consulship.[110] And afterwards, when the people were asked by T. Manlius Mancinus, a tribune of the plebs, whom they wanted to wage war with Jugurtha, their order at a crowded meeting was Marius. But, a little before, the senate had decreed Numidia to Metellus; that fact was rendered void.

74   At the same time, Jugurtha had lost his friends (most of whom he had executed himself, while the rest had fled in alarm, some to the Romans, others to King Bocchus), and, since the war could not be waged without managers and he considered it dangerous to test the loyalty of new ones (given such treachery

from the old ones), his behaviour was unpredictable and shift-
ing. No circumstance or plan or any man at all satisfied him:
he changed his routes and officers daily; sometimes he went
against the enemy, sometimes into the desert; often he placed
his hope in flight and, a little after, in arms; he was uncertain
whether to trust the prowess or the loyalty of his compatriots
less: hence, wherever he aimed, circumstances were against him.
Amidst these delays of his, Metellus suddenly showed himself   2
with his army. The Numidians were prepared and drawn up by
Jugurtha to suit the moment; then the battle began. In the area   3
of the fighting where the king was present, there a struggle took
place for a time; but all his other soldiers were routed and put
to flight in the first encounter. The Romans took possession of
a certain number of standards and weapons, and only a few of
the enemy: for usually it is their feet rather than their weapons
which save the Numidians in every battle.

After that flight Jugurtha was simply more immoderate in his   75
distrust of his own resources, and with some defectors and part
of his cavalry he reached the desert and then Thala, a great and
wealthy town, where most of his treasures were and his sons
were having much of their boyhood training. Metellus dis-   2
covered this and, although he had learned that between Thala
and the nearest river there was an arid and desolate region fifty
miles across, nevertheless – hoping to finish the war if he gained
possession of the town – he prepared to overcome all its harshness and even to conquer nature. He ordered all the baggage-   3
animals to be relieved of their packs except for ten days' grain;
otherwise, only leather bags and other items suitable for water
were to be carried. Besides this, he rounded up from the fields   4
as much of the tame livestock as he could, and on them he put
vessels of every type, but especially wooden ones collected
from the Numidians' huts. In addition, he commanded the   5
neighbouring peoples (who had surrendered to Metellus after
the king's flight) that each of them should carry as much water
as possible, and he prescribed where and when they should be
ready; and he himself loaded baggage-animals from the river,   6
which we have said above was the nearest water to the town.
Thus equipped he set off for Thala.

7   Then, when he reached the point of which he had given advance notice to the Numidians, and the camp had been pitched and fortified, it is said that so large a volume of water suddenly came down from the sky that it alone was more than
8 enough for the army. Besides this, the supplies exceeded his expectations, because the Numidians (like many after a recent
9 surrender) had concentrated on their duties. But the soldiers, from religious scruple, preferred to use the rain, and it added greatly to their courage: they deemed that the immortal gods were caring for them. Then, on the next day, contrary to what
10 Jugurtha had thought, they arrived at Thala. The townsfolk, who had believed themselves protected by the harshness of their region, were stunned by this great and unusual achievement, yet were in no way more sluggish in their preparations for war. Our men acted similarly.

76   But the king, believing that nothing was now impossible for Metellus (who by his industry had conquered everything – arms and weapons, place and time, in short, Nature herself, the commander of all else), fled by night from the town with his children and a large part of his money. And afterwards he did not delay more than a single day or a single night in any one place; he pretended that his haste was a function of his activity, but in fact he feared betrayal, which he thought he could avoid by speed: any plans of that type, he believed, depended upon
2 inaction and opportunity. As for Metellus, when he saw that the townsfolk were concentrating for battle and that the town was protected by earthworks and position, he surrounded the
3 walls with a rampart and ditch. Then, at the two most suitable points of those possible, he brought up penthouses, threw up a mound and, installing towers on top of the mound, he safe-
4 guarded the work and those managing it; in response to these measures, the townsfolk lost no time in their preparations: in
5 short, nothing was omitted by either side. Finally, forty days after their arrival, the Romans – worn out by their considerable toil earlier and their battles – took possession only of the town:
6 all the plunder had been destroyed by deserters. The latter, when they saw that the wall was being struck by battering-rams and that their fortunes were dashed, carried to the royal resi-

dence the gold and silver and other items which are considered priorities. There, laden with wine and banqueting, they destroyed in flames both them and the residence and themselves; and the punishment which they had dreaded if conquered by the enemy they willingly paid themselves.

At the same time as the capture of Thala, legates from the town of Leptis had come to Metellus begging him to send a garrison and prefect there: one Hamilcar, a noble and factious individual, was enthusiastic for revolution, they said, and against him neither the commands of magistrates nor the laws had any effect; unless Metellus hurried, both their own personal safety and the Romans' allies would be in the utmost danger. (For, from the very beginning of the Jugurthine War, the Leptitani had already sent to the consul Bestia and later to Rome messengers to ask for an alliance of friendship; then, when their request had been granted, they had always remained good and loyal and had performed diligently everything commanded by Bestia, Albinus and Metellus.) And so they easily obtained what they were seeking from the commander: four cohorts of Ligurians were sent there, and C. Annius as prefect.

The town was founded by the Sidonians, who we understand had arrived in that region by ship as fugitives, on account of civil disharmony. It is situated between the two Syrtes, whose name derives from their essential feature. They are the two bays almost at the edge of Africa,[111] dissimilar in size but of a similar nature, where the areas nearest to the land are very deep, while the rest are as chance decides, sometimes simply deep, sometimes shallow in a storm. For, when the sea starts to swell and to turn savage in the wind, mud and sand and huge rocks are swept along by the waves: thus the face of the locality changes with the wind, and the Syrtes are named after this 'sweeping'.[112] Intermarriage with the Numidians transformed only the language of that community; most elements of its laws and culture were Sidonian, which they retained all the more easily because they lived their lives far from the command of the king. Between them and the crowded parts of Numidia there lay many desolate regions.

Because we have arrived in this area by way of the Leptitani's activities, it does not appear unseemly to recall an exceptional and marvellous deed of two Carthaginians: the locality has put us in mind of it.

2   In the period when the Carthaginians exercised command in most of Africa, the Cyrenaeans too were great and wealthy.
3   The territory between them was of sand, uniform in appearance: there was neither river nor mountain to distinguish their boundaries, a circumstance which involved each of them in a great
4   and prolonged war. After legions as well as fleets had been routed and put to flight on both sides many times, and each had worn down the other to some extent, they became afraid that a third party might soon attack the weary conquered and conquerors: during a truce, therefore, they reached an agreement that on a certain day legates would set out from home: the place in which they met each other would be regarded as
5   the common boundary of each people. So from Carthage were dispatched two brothers whose name was Philaenus, and they quickly embarked on their journey. The Cyrenaeans went more slowly. Whether that happened from lethargy or chance I hardly
6   know. In fact in that locality storms are accustomed to hold one up no differently from at sea: when the wind rises and dislodges the sand from the ground in places which are level and devoid of vegetation, the sand is whipped up with great force and is accustomed to fill the mouth and eyes: with one's
7   view cut off in this way, one's journey is delayed. After the Cyrenaeans saw that they were somewhat behind, and they dreaded punishment at home for having mismanaged the affair, they accused the Carthaginians of having left home ahead of time, they confused the issue – in short, they preferred anything
8   to departing in defeat. But, when the Poeni sought an alternative condition, provided it was fair, the Greeks gave them a choice: either the Carthaginians should be buried alive at the place which they were seeking as a boundary for their people or they themselves, under the same condition, would advance to the
9   place they wanted. The Philaeni approved the condition and sacrificed themselves and their lives for their commonwealth:
10   hence their burial alive. The Carthaginians consecrated altars

in that place to the Philaeni brothers, and other honours were established at home for them. Now I return to my theme.

After Jugurtha on the loss of Thala had come to think that nothing was sufficiently secure against Metellus, he set off with a few men across the great deserts and reached the Gaetulians, a wild and uncultivated race and at that time ignorant of the Roman name. He gathered their large numbers into one place and gradually accustomed them to being in ranks, following standards, recognizing command, and likewise doing generally military things. Besides this, he used great gifts and still greater promises to induce those nearest to King Bocchus to be enthusiastic on his own account, and with their help he approached the king and drove him to start a war against the Romans. (That was all the more easy and straightforward thanks to the fact that at the beginning of this present war Bocchus had sent legates to Rome to ask for a treaty of friendship – a development which, though highly advantageous at the start of a war, had been prevented by the few who, dazzled by avarice, had a habit of selling everything honourable and dishonourable. And, even before this, Bocchus' daughter had married Jugurtha.[113] But that connection is considered trivial amongst the Numidians and Moors, because each individual has as many wives as possible depending on his wealth – some ten, others more, but kings yet more. So their number results in divided loyalties: none is ranked as a partner, all are uniformly cheap.) Their armies met in a place agreed by both sides. Then, after an exchange of pledges, Jugurtha fired Bocchus' spirit by a speech: the Romans were unjust, profoundly avaricious, the common enemy of all; they had the same motive for war with Bocchus as with himself and with other peoples – the lust for empire – and they were opposed to all monarchies; now it was himself, but shortly before it had been the Carthaginians and likewise King Perseus;[114] and afterwards whoever seemed to be wealthiest would be the Romans' enemy. After these and other such words, they set their course for the town of Cirta, because Metellus had placed there his plunder, captives and baggage. Jugurtha deemed that either capturing the city would be

worthwhile or, if the Roman leader came to help his men, his
4 own side would compete with him in battle. For the single
object of his crafty haste was to spoil the peace enjoyed by
Bocchus, lest the continued delay should lead him to prefer an
alternative to war.

82   After the commander learned about the kings' alliance, he
offered no opportunity of fighting either rashly or (as he had
been accustomed to do when Jugurtha had been defeated frequently in the past) irrespective of locality; but, after fortifying
his camp, he waited for the kings not far from Cirta, deeming
that it was better to fight from an advantage once he had got
to know the Moors (since they were the recent addition to the
2 enemy). Meanwhile, he was informed in a letter from Rome
that the province of Numidia had been given to Marius; he had
heard earlier that he had been made consul. More stunned by
these developments than was proper or honourable, he neither
kept back his tears nor moderated his language; exceptional as
he was in his other qualities, his toleration of depression was
3 too weak. Some interpreted this as haughtiness, others that a
good disposition had been inflamed by insult, many that, with
victory now achieved, it was being snatched from his grasp; as
for ourselves, we are satisfied in the knowledge that he was
tortured more by the honour to Marius than by the injustice to
himself, nor would he have borne it with such distress if the
province of which he was deprived were being handed to someone other than Marius.

83   Hampered by his pain, and because it seemed foolish to
concern himself with another's affair at his own risk, he sent
legates to Bocchus to demand that he should not become an
enemy of the Roman people without cause: he now had a great
opportunity of forging an alliance of friendship which would
be more powerful than war; and, despite his confidence in
his resources, he had a duty not to exchange certainty for
uncertainty: every war was taken up easily but it ceased only
with the greatest difficulty; start and finish did not lie in the
power of the same person; even some coward could begin it,
but it was laid aside only when the victors wanted. Accordingly,
Bocchus should give thought to himself and his kingdom and

not involve his flourishing situation with the ruinous plight of
Jugurtha. The king's words in response were calm enough: he   2
desired peace, but he pitied the fortunes of Jugurtha; if the
latter were given the same opportunity as himself, everything
would be agreeable. In reply the commander sent messengers   3
to counter Bocchus' demands; he on his side gave partial approval, rejected others. In this way, with the frequent sending
and re-sending of messengers by each man, time passed; and,
in accordance with Metellus' wish, the war dragged on in
abeyance.

But Marius, as we said above, had been made consul at the   84
most eager desire of the plebs, and, after the people had ordered
Numidia as the province for him, that was the time when he
regularly and defiantly hounded the nobility, to which he was
already hostile: he sometimes lashed them individually, sometimes collectively, he said repeatedly that he had seized the
consulship from them like spoils from the conquered, and other
things in addition which constituted bragging on his own behalf
and for them was a cause of pain. Meanwhile his priorities were   2
what was necessary for the war, and he demanded reinforcements for the legions, he summoned auxiliary help from the
peoples and kings,[115] and, besides this, he mustered all the most
courageous men from Latium and the allies (most known to
him for their soldiering, a few by reputation), and by canvassing
he compelled men whose service was completed to set off with
him. And the senate, though opposed to him, did not dare to   3
refuse him concerning any of these activities; in fact, decreeing
reinforcements had even delighted them, because soldiering was
not thought to please the plebs and Marius would lose either
his requirements for the war or the public's enthusiasm. But
that was a vain hope: so great was the desire of accompanying
Marius which had overwhelmed the majority. Each man's pri-   4
vate interpretation was that *he* would become wealthy from
plunder and would return home victorious, and other things of
this type; and Marius had stirred them up not a little by a
speech of his own. For, after everything which he had demanded   5
had been decreed and he wanted to enlist his soldiers, he called
a meeting of the people to encourage them and at the same time

(as he was accustomed to do) to harass the nobility. Then he spoke in this way:

85   'I know, Citizens, that it is not with the same qualities that the majority seeks command from you and, after acquiring it, exercises it: at first they are industrious, supplicatory, restrained; then they live a life of apathy and haughtiness. But

2   my view is different from theirs: for, just as the commonwealth as a whole is of more value than the consulship or praetorship, so it ought to be managed with greater care than these latter

3   two are sought. And I am not deceived by the magnitude of the business which, thanks to your very great kindness,[116] I am undertaking. To prepare for war and at the same time to spare the treasury; to compel into soldiering those whom one would not wish to aggrieve; to care for everything at home and abroad; and to do these things amidst the resentful, the obstructive

4   and the factious – that, Citizens, is harder than you think. In addition, if *others* fail, the old nobility, the courageous deeds of the ancestors, the wealth of relatives and in-laws, the many dependants – all these are present in support; but in *my* case all my hopes rest in myself, and it is necessary to safeguard them by prowess and blamelessness: other things lack the strength.

5   'This too I understand, Citizens, that the faces of all are turned towards me, that the fair-minded and good favour me (for my good deeds are reckoned to the credit of the commonwealth), but that the nobility is looking for a chance to attack.

6   Hence I must strive all the more keenly to ensure that you do

7   not become their captives and that their efforts are vain. From boyhood to this point in my life my existence has been such

8   that I regard all toil and danger as normal: it is not my intention, Citizens, to abandon after the receipt of my reward what I did

9   freely before your kindness to me. Those whose ambition has led them to feign probity find it difficult to control themselves in power; but, in my case, who have spent all my life in the best practices, good deeds have now become second nature through habit.

10   'You have ordered me to wage war with Jugurtha, a matter which the nobility has taken very hard. I beseech you, reflect in your hearts whether it would be better to make a change and

to send one from that gang of the nobility on this or some other business, someone with an old pedigree and many ancestral images[117] and no active service – the inevitable result being, of course, that his complete ignorance would make him tremble at so great a task and he would lose no time in taking on one of the people to advise him of his duty. Hence, it has often 11 happened that the one whom you have ordered to command seeks another commander for himself. And I know of men, 12 Citizens, who began to read both their ancestors' records and the military principles of the Greeks only after their election to the consulship – preposterous individuals,[118] in as much as action is posterior to election in time but precedes it in terms of reality and experience. Now compare their haughtiness, Citi- 13 zens, with myself as a new man: the things which they are accustomed to hear or read, I have either seen or done person- ally; their learning comes from literature, mine from soldiering. Now consider whether deeds or words are worth more. They 14 are contemptuous of my newness, I of their apathy; I am impugned for my status, they for their misdeeds – although I 15 consider that there is one nature common to everyone but that it is the most courageous who are the real aristocrats; and, if 16 one could ask of the fathers of Albinus or Bestia whether they preferred me or them as their offspring, what do you believe they would reply except that they wanted the best children possible? If they are right to despise me, let them do the same 17 for their own ancestors, in whose case, as in mine, nobility derived from prowess. They begrudge me my honorific office:[119] 18 so let them begrudge my toil, my blamelessness, even my dangers, because it was through these that I received it. But 19 men corrupted by haughtiness live their life just as if they were contemptuous of your honours; yet they seek them just as if they lived honourably. Assuredly they are deceived when they 20 have equal expectations of those very different things, the plea- sure of apathy and prowess's rewards. And even when they 21 speak in front of you or in the senate, they spend most of their speech in extolling their ancestors: by recalling their courageous deeds, they think they become more distinguished. But the 22 opposite is the case: the greater the distinction of *those* men's

23 lives, the more outrageous the lethargy of *these*. And that is of course how things are: ancestral glory is like a light for posterity, whose good or evil deeds it does not allow to remain
24 hidden. In this particular matter, Citizens, I confess my deficiency; but – what is much more distinguished – it is my
25 very own deeds of which I am able to speak. Now see how unfair they are: what they appropriate for themselves on the basis of another's prowess they do not grant to me on the basis of my own, evidently because I do not have ancestral images and because mine is a new nobility, which at least it is better to have won than to have inherited and corrupted.

26 'I am not unaware that, if they wished now to respond to me, there would be plenty of fluent and neat speech. But since, given your very great kindness to me, they lose no opportunity to maul both me and you with their insults, I decided not to stay silent, lest anyone should construe my reticence as a guilty
27 conscience. For in all honesty no speech can harm *me*, since truths inevitably provide a fine account, while falsehoods are
28 refuted by my life and behaviour. But, because the judgements which are accused are *yours*, you who have assigned to me the highest honour and the supreme action, reflect over and over
29 again whether you should be regretting them. I cannot, for the sake of your trust in me, point to the images or triumphs or consulships of my ancestors, but, if the occasion were to demand it, I can point to spears, the banner, shield-bosses and other military gifts, and, besides these, scars on the front of my
30 body. These are my images, these my nobility – not left by inheritance, as theirs are to them, but what I have achieved after very many toils and dangers.

31 'My words are not neat; but I place little value on that. Prowess itself is its own adequate evidence. It is they who need
32 artifice, to cover up in speech their shameful deeds. And I never learned Greek: there was little pleasure in learning it because it
33 had brought no benefit to its teachers in terms of prowess. But I am well taught in what is best by far for the commonwealth: striking the enemy, keeping guard, dreading nothing except a shameful reputation, tolerating winter and summer alike, resting on the ground, enduring want and toil at the same time.

These are the principles on which I shall encourage the soldiers; 34
and I shall neither treat them meanly but myself wealthily nor
make their toil my glory. This is command which is useful and 35
citizen-like. (For, when you live a life of safety and softness but
control your army by reprisals, that is being a master,[120] not a
commander.) It was by doing these and other such things that 36
your ancestors brought prestige both to themselves and to the
commonwealth. Relying on them, while itself dissimilar in 37
behaviour, the nobility is contemptuous of us who are their
rivals, and it seeks honours from you not on the basis of merit
but as if owed. But these haughtiest of men are far off course. 38
Their ancestors left them all they could – riches, images, a
distinguished memory of themselves; but they did not leave
them prowess, and nor could they: that alone is neither given
nor received as a gift. They say that I am coarse and of unculti- 39
vated behaviour because I have little knowledge of furnishing
a dinner-party and do not have an actor or consider my cook
of more value than my bailiff.[121] It gives me pleasure to make 40
this confession, Citizens: for I learned from my parent and other
upright men that women are suited to refinements, men to toil,
and that all good men should have more glory than riches: that
arms, not furniture, are a source of dignity.

  'So let them always do what gratifies them, what they con- 41
sider dear: love-affairs and drink. Let them spend their old age
where they had their adolescence, in dinner-parties, devoted to
their stomachs and the most shameful part of their bodies. Let
them leave sweat, dust and other such things to us, to whom
they are more agreeable than banquets. But no! When those 42
most shameful of men have disgraced themselves with their
outrages, they proceed to seize the rewards of the good. The 43
highly unjust result is that luxury and apathy – the worst of
qualities – are no obstacle to those who cultivate them but are
a disaster for their blameless commonwealth.

  'Because I have replied to them to the extent demanded 44
by my own behaviour, not by their outrages, I shall say a
few words about the commonwealth. First of all, be of good 45
heart concerning Numidia, Citizens. You have removed everything which has hitherto safeguarded Jugurtha – avarice,

46   inexperience and haughtiness.[122] Next, the army there is know-
     ledgeable of the locality – though, as Hercules is my witness,
     more committed than fortunate! A large part of it has been
47   reduced by the avarice or rashness of its leaders. Therefore,
     exert yourselves alongside me, you who are of military age, and
     serve the commonwealth, and let none be seized by dread aris-
     ing from the calamity of others or the commanders' haughti-
     ness. I will be with you personally in battle or in the column as
     both counsellor and partner in danger, and in every situation I
48   shall treat myself and you alike. And of course, with the gods'
     help, everything is ripe: victory, plunder, praise. If those results
     were uncertain or far off, nevertheless all good men ought to
49   come to the aid of the commonwealth: no one becomes immor-
     tal through cowardly apathy, nor did any parent wish that his
     children would be eternal, but rather that they should live their
50   lives as good and honourable men. I would say more, Citizens,
     if words bestowed prowess on the fearful; as for the committed,
     I think enough has been said.'

86   After making a speech of this type, Marius saw that the spirits
     of the plebs were stirred and he quickly loaded the ships with
     supplies, pay, arms and other utilities; he ordered his legate A.
2   Manlius to set off with them. Meanwhile he himself enlisted
     soldiers, not according to ancestral custom or from the classes
     but as the urge took each man, most of them assessed for their
3   person alone.[123] (Some people recalled that that was done from
     a lack of good men, others because of the consul's ingratiation,
     since they were the category by which he had been feted and
     elevated, and, for a man seeking power, the neediest are also
     the most advantageous, in that their own possessions are not
     dear to them – indeed they have none – and everything that
4   pays seems honourable.) So Marius, setting off for Africa with
     a rather greater number than had been decreed, arrived at
5   Utica within a few days. The army was handed over to him by
     P. Rutilius, the legate: for Metellus had fled from seeing Marius,
     lest he should set eyes on what his emotions had been unable
     to tolerate as news.

87   Filling up the legions and auxiliary cohorts,[124] the consul set
     off into territory that was fertile and laden with plunder, giving

everything captured there to the soldiers; then he attacked strongholds and towns poorly defended by nature and men, and conducted many – albeit insignificant – battles in different places. Meanwhile his new soldiers participated in the fighting 2 without dread; they saw that escapers were seized or slaughtered; that the most courageous were the safest; that it was by arms that freedom, fatherland, parents and everything else were protected, and glory and riches won. So in a short time new 3 men and veterans merged, and the prowess of them all became equal. As for the kings, when they learned about Marius' 4 arrival, they split up and left for difficult areas. That had been the decision of Jugurtha, who hoped that the enemy would soon spread out and be able to be attacked, and that, once their dread had been removed, the Romans, like most other people, would act with more laxity and licence.

Metellus meanwhile, having set off for Rome, was received 88 contrary to his expectations with heartfelt delight – dear to fathers and plebs alike, now that their resentment had passed away.

As for Marius, energetically and prudently he gave equal 2 attention to the circumstances of his own men and of the enemy, he found out the good points of each or the opposite, he reconnoitred the kings' routes, he anticipated their plans and ambushes and he allowed nothing to be slack on his side or safe on theirs. Having often attacked both the Gaetulians and 3 Jugurtha as they drove plunder from our allies, he had routed them on the march and actually stripped the king of his arms not far from the town of Cirta. But, after he realized that these 4 achievements contributed only to glory and not to finishing the war, he decided to surround individually those cities which in terms of men or position were most advantageous in the enemy's favour and contrary to his own: in this way Jugurtha would either be divested of his garrisons, if he did nothing, or would compete in battle. For Bocchus had been sending mes- 5 sages to him frequently: he wanted the friendship of the Roman people; Marius should not fear any hostile move from him. But 6 whether that was pretence in order to make an unexpected (and hence more serious) onslaught, or whether his volatile

temperament led him habitually to alternate peace and war, has
89 not been adequately ascertained. Nevertheless the consul, as he
had decided, approached fortified towns and strongholds and
partly by force, sometimes by dread or the prospect of rewards,
2   he turned them from the enemy. At first his objectives were
only modest, since he thought that Jugurtha, to safeguard his
3   people, would fall into his grasp; but, when he learned that
the man was far away and concentrating on other activities,
it seemed the time to attack greater and harder targets.

4   There was amongst the mighty deserts a great and thriving
town by the name of Capsa, whose founder was recalled as
having been Libyan Hercules. Its citizens were immune from
paying tax to Jugurtha and kept under only light command,
and for those reasons were considered very loyal; and they were
protected against enemies not only by their walls, arms and
men but also, and much more, by the harshness of the locality.
5   For, apart from the vicinity of the town, everything else was
desolate, uncultivated, devoid of water and infested with
snakes, whose violence, like that of all wild creatures, is more
active for the lack of food; in addition, the very nature of
snakes, already deadly, is inflamed more by thirst than by
6   anything else. A very great desire of taking possession of the
town had overwhelmed Marius, both on account of its useful-
ness in the war and because the exploit seemed hard and
Metellus with great glory had taken the town of Thala, which
was not differently situated and protected except for the fact
that at Thala there were several springs not far from the walls,
whereas the people of Capsa had the use of only one source of
running water (and that within the town), otherwise rainwater.
7   This was borne all the more easily there (as in the whole of
Africa which was uncultivated and far from the sea) because
the Numidians for the most part fed on milk and wild-animal
flesh and did not demand salt or other stimulants of the palette:
8   food for them was to counteract hunger and thirst, not a matter
of lust or luxury.

90   Therefore the consul, having reconnoitred everything, was (I
believe) relying on the gods: for against such great difficulties
he was not able to make adequate provision by planning (indeed

he even had the trial of a lack of grain, because the Numidians are more enthusiastic about fodder for their livestock than about ploughland and on the king's order they had accumulated in fortified areas whatever had grown, while the land was arid and empty of crops at that time, since it was the very end of the summer season); nevertheless, given the possibilities of the situation, he was adequately provident in what he furnished. He assigned to the auxiliary cavalry the task of driving along 2 all the livestock which had constituted the previous days' plunder; he ordered the legate A. Manlius with the unencumbered cohorts to go to the town of Lares, where he had placed the pay and supplies; and he said that after a few days he himself would arrive there for plundering. Having thus concealed his 3 project, he made for the River Tanais.

Each day on the journey he distributed the livestock to the 91 army by centuries[125] and by squadrons equally, and he took care that leather bags should be made from their skins: he thus mitigated the lack of grain and at the same time, though no one knew it, procured items which would soon be of use. Then, on the sixth day, when they arrived at the river, the very important function of the bags was realized.[126] Having made a camp which 2 was only lightly protected, he ordered the soldiers to take some food and be ready to leave exactly at sunset, and, disposing of all their packs, to load themselves and the baggage-animals with only water. Then, when it seemed to be time, he left the 3 camp and bivouacked when they had marched the entire night; he did the same on the next, and then, on the third, considerably before sunrise, he arrived at a hillocky area not more than two miles' distance from Capsa, and there he waited with all his forces as secretly as he could.

When the day began and the Numidians, in no dread of 4 enemy action, left the town in numbers, he suddenly ordered all the cavalry and with them the fastest infantry to make for Capsa at speed and to besiege the gates; then he himself followed quickly in concentrated fashion and did not allow the soldiers to plunder. When the townsfolk realized, the trepidation of their circumstances, their great dread, the unexpectedness of their misfortune and, in addition, the fact that some 5

of their citizens outside the walls were in the enemy's power –
6 all these compelled them to surrender. Nevertheless, the town
was burned, the adult Numidians killed, all others sold and
7 plunder divided amongst the soldiers. That action against the
code of warfare was taken not through avarice or some crime
of the consul's but because the place was advantageous to
Jugurtha and difficult for us to approach, and its people were
of a fickle and untrustworthy type, previously controlled neither
by kindness nor by dread.

92   After Marius had achieved such a result without any detriment to his men, he began – though already great and distinguished – to be considered still greater and more distinguished.
2 All his ill-advised decisions were interpreted as prowess; the
soldiers, kept under only moderate discipline and now wealthy
too, praised him to the skies; the Numidians feared him as more
than mortal; in short, everyone – allies and enemies – believed
either that he had a divine[127] mind or that everything was
3 presaged for him with the gods' assent. But the consul, now
that the affair had turned out well, made for other towns: a
few he took against Numidian resistance, more he destroyed
by fire after they had been abandoned owing to the woes of the
people of Capsa. Everywhere had its fill of grief and slaughter.
4 Finally, after taking possession of many areas (with his army
unbloodied in the majority of cases), he embarked on another
task, not of the same harshness as that associated with the
5 people of Capsa but just as difficult. Not far from the River
Muluccha (which separated the kingdoms of Jugurtha and
Bocchus), and surrounded by otherwise level ground, there was
a rocky mountain, sufficiently extensive for a modest stronghold and rising to an immense height, leaving only one very
6 narrow approach. This was the place which Marius intended
to take with the utmost force, because the king's treasures were
there. But the success of the process owed more to chance than
to planning.
7   The fort had enough men and arms, a large quantity of grain
and a source of water; the place was unfavourable for mounds
and towers and other machines; the route taken by the stronghold's inhabitants was quite narrow and sheer on both sides.

Penthouses were brought up in vain there and with great risk, 8
for, whenever they advanced a little, they were destroyed by
fire or stones. The soldiers could neither stand properly in front 9
of the works because of the unevenness of the place nor manage
within the penthouses without risk: all the best fell or were
injured; the dread of the others increased. Marius used up many 93
days and much effort anxiously debating with himself whether
to abandon the project, because it was fruitless, or to wait upon
fortune, which he had often enjoyed so successfully. When he 2
had been reflecting on this in turmoil for many days and nights,
by chance a certain Ligurian, a troop soldier from the auxiliary
cohorts who had left the camp to fetch water, noticed that, not
far from the side of the stronghold which was facing away from
the fighters, there were snails crawling amongst the rocks. He
reached out for one and then another and then more, and in
his enthusiasm for collecting them he gradually emerged almost
at the top of the mountain. When he realized that he was all 3
alone there, the desire for a difficult challenge (as is the way of
the human temperament) overwhelmed his thoughts. And by 4
chance amongst the rocks in that place a great oak tree had
taken root, at first horizontal a little way, then bending and
reaching a great height (as nature directs all vegetation). Supporting himself alternately by its branches and on protruding
rocks, the Ligurian arrived at the level area of the stronghold,
because all the Numidians who were there were concentrating
on the fighters. After reconnoitring everything which he thought 5
would be of use later, he returned the same way – not carelessly,
as he had climbed up, but testing and inspecting everything.
And so he went quickly to Marius, told him what he had done, 6
urged him to make an attempt on the stronghold from the
direction he had climbed up himself, and guaranteed to lead
the dangerous expedition.

Marius sent, along with the Ligurian, some of those present 7
to investigate his assertions; they each reported the exploit
difficult or easy according to their temperaments. Nevertheless,
the consul's interest was roused a little: so from the number of 8
trumpet-players and horn-players he chose five of the quickest
and with them four centurions as protection, and he ordered

them all to obey the Ligurian and settled on the next day for
94 their action. When it seemed time according to his instructions,
the man made his way to the place with everything prepared
and arranged. But those who were to climb up, informed in
advance by their leader, had changed their arms and equipment:
they had their heads and feet bare, so that their view and climb
amongst the rocks might be easier; on their backs were swords
and shields, but the latter were Numidian ones of hide, both
because of their weight and so that they would make less noise
2   if struck. As he went ahead, therefore, the Ligurian fastened
nooses to the rocks and any old protruding roots so that the
soldiers might haul themselves up and climb more easily; sometimes he gave a helping hand to those who were afraid because
of the unusualness of the route; when the ascent was a little
rougher, he sent them up one by one, unarmed, in front of him,
then followed himself with their arms; as for the parts which
seemed doubtful to attempt, he made a point of testing them
himself, and, by climbing up and down the same route quite
frequently and then immediately standing aside, he instilled
3   boldness in the rest. So, after a considerable period of great
tiredness, they eventually reached the stronghold, deserted in
that area because everyone, as on other days, was facing the
enemy.

Marius learned from messengers what the Ligurian had done,
and, although he had kept the Numidians concentrating on the
battle the entire day, that was the moment that he encouraged
his soldiers and he himself emerged from the penthouses and,
after the forming of a shell,[128] came up closer and at the same
time tried to terrorize the enemy from long range with launchers
4   and archers and slingers. But the Numidians, having often
overturned and burned the Romans' penthouses previously, did
not safeguard themselves by means of the walls of the stronghold but spent their time[129] in front of the wall, insulting the
Romans, accusing Marius of derangement, threatening our soldiers with servitude to Jugurtha and being generally defiant in
5   their success. In the meantime, while everyone – Roman and
enemy – was concentrating on the battle and the struggle was
proceeding with great force on both sides, for glory and empire

on the one hand and on the other for salvation, suddenly trumpets sounded in the rear. At first it was the women and boys who had come out to watch who fled, then those nearest the wall and finally everyone, armed and unarmed. When that 6 happened, the Romans pressed all the more keenly, routing and only injuring the majority; but then they were advancing over the bodies of the slaughtered, competing to make for the wall in their hunger for glory and not a single one at all delaying for plunder. Thus Marius' rashness was rectified by chance and 7 found glory instead of blame.

While that affair was in progress, however, the quaestor 95 L. Sulla arrived at the camp with the large force of cavalry which he had been left at Rome to muster from Latium and the allies. Since there has been occasion for us to mention this great 2 man, it has seemed appropriate to talk about his nature and life-style in a few words: we are not going to talk about Sulla's circumstances anywhere else, and L. Sisenna, the best and most diligent narrator[130] of all those who have talked of his circumstances, seems to me to have spoken with too little freedom of speech.

Sulla, then, was a noble of a patrician clan, his family now 3 almost eclipsed owing to the apathy of his ancestors,[131] equally erudite in Greek and Latin literature, great-hearted, desirous of pleasure but of glory still more desirous; he was a man of luxurious inactivity, yet pleasure never kept him from his activities; [. . .][132] except that on the question of a wife his behaviour could have been more honourable;[133] he was fluent, astute, and easy in friendship; he had an incredible depth of ingenuity for feigning activities and concealing them; he was a lavisher of many things and especially of money. Most fortunate[134] of all 4 men before his victory in the civil war,[135] his good luck never exceeded his industry, and many debated whether his courage or his fortune was the greater. As for what he did afterwards, I consider it uncertain whether there is more shame or distaste in discussing it.

Sulla, then, as was said above, arrived at Marius' camp in 96 Africa with cavalry, and, though previously callow and ignorant of warfare, became in a short time the shrewdest of all.

2   In addition, he addressed the soldiers benevolently, he did
    kindnesses to many who asked and to others of his own accord,
    and he unwillingly accepted the same – but returned them more
    quickly than any financial loan; he personally reclaimed nothing
    from anyone but rather worked on it that those indebted to
3   him should be as numerous as possible. He exchanged banter
    and business with the humblest; he was regularly present at the
    works,[136] in the column and for the watches, nor in the mean-
    while (the customary effect of crooked ambition) did he damage
    the reputation of the consul or any good man,[137] ensuring only
    that no one excelled him in counsel or muscle, while out-
4   stripping many. By such actions and qualities he soon became
    extremely dear to Marius and the soldiers.

97   But Jugurtha, after he had lost the town of Capsa and other
    useful protected places and a lot of money, sent messengers to
    Bocchus that he should bring forces to Numidia as early as
2   possible: the time for doing battle was at hand. But, when he
    heard that the man was hesitating and uncertainly debating the
    reasons for war and peace, he again (as before) bribed those
    closest to him with gifts and guaranteed the Moor himself a
    third of Numidia if either the Romans were driven out of Africa
3   or the war were concluded with his own territory intact. Lured
    by this prize, Bocchus came to Jugurtha with substantial
    numbers.
        After the armies of both had thus joined, they attacked
    Marius (who was already setting off for winter quarters) with
    only a tenth of the day remaining, deeming that the impending
    night would be a protection for them if they were conquered
    and, if they themselves conquered, of no hindrance, because
    they were knowledgeable of the area, whereas each eventuality
4   would be more difficult for the Romans in the darkness. It was
    therefore at the same moment as the consul learned from many
    about the enemy's arrival that the enemy was actually present;
    and before the army was able to deploy or to collect the packs
    or, in short, to receive any signal or command, our men were
    charged by the Moorish and Gaetulian cavalry, not in line
    nor any battle-like fashion but in hordes which had bunched
5   together by chance. Trembling in unexpected dread and yet still

mindful of their prowess, they all either seized arms or kept the enemy from those in the act of seizing; some mounted their horses and confronted the enemy; the fight came to resemble banditry rather than a battle: without standards, without ranks, cavalry and infantry were mixed up; one man would yield, another be butchered, many be surrounded from the rear as they fought against their opponents very bitterly; neither prowess nor arms offered sufficient protection, because the enemy were superior in numbers and had poured round on all sides.

Finally the Romans – veterans and therefore knowledgeable of warfare – formed circles wherever place or chance had brought some of them together, and in this way, both protected and arranged on all sides, they withstood the enemy's violence. Nor in that very bitter action was Marius terrified or more 98 downcast than previously, but with his squadron – which he had assembled from the most courageous men rather than his closest friends – he roved everywhere, sometimes helping his own men who were in trouble, sometimes attacking the enemy wherever the densest groups stood fast: it was by muscle that he aided his soldiers, since in the general confusion he could not issue commands.

Already the day had been spent and the barbarians still did 2 not slacken but, deeming that night was on their side, as their kings had instructed, they pressed more keenly. Then Marius 3 produced a plan from the various possibilities and, so that his men should have a place to retreat, he occupied two hills near to each other, of which one, insufficiently spacious for a camp, had a large source of water, while the other was advantageous to his purpose because, being largely high and sheer, it required little protection. He ordered Sulla with the cavalry to spend the 4 night at the water, while he himself gradually collected in one place his scattered soldiers (the enemy's confusion was no less) and then led them all at full pace to the hill. So the kings, 5 constrained by the difficulty of the place, were deterred from the battle, and yet they did not allow their men to go away too far but, surrounding each hill in numbers, sprawled out and bivouacked. Then, having made numerous fires, the barbarians 6 spent most of the night after their own fashion, rejoicing, leaping about and making noisy cries; and their leaders too, defiant because they had not fled, acted like victors.

7
99   All this was easy for the Romans to see from higher ground through the darkness and was a great encouragement. Very much reassured by the inexperience of the enemy, Marius ordered as great a silence as possible to be observed and not even the trumpets to sound, as was usual at each watch. Then, when dawn came and the now tired enemy had been overtaken by sleep a short while before, he suddenly ordered the watchmen and likewise the cohorts', squadrons' and legions' trumpet-players all to sound their trumpets simultaneously, and the

2   soldiers to raise a shout and burst through the gate. The Moors and Gaetulians, suddenly roused by the unfamiliar and dreadful sound, could neither flee nor seize arms nor do anything or

3   make any provision at all: in the noise and shouting, with no one coming to help and our men pressing, a sort of derangement had overcome them all amidst the commotion, alarm and terror. Finally they were all routed and put to flight; very many arms and military standards were captured; and more were killed in that battle than in all its predecessors: for their flight was hampered by sleep and their unaccustomed dread.

100   Then Marius, as he had started to do, set off for winter quarters: for reasons of supply he had decided to spend the time in seaside towns. He did not become lethargic or overbearing because of his victory, but marched in a rectangular column as

2   if in sight of the enemy. Sulla was with the cavalry on the far right; on the left with the slingers and archers A. Manlius was in charge, as also of the cohorts of Ligurians besides; as first and last he had placed the tribunes with the unencumbered

3   maniples. Deserters, expendable and very knowledgeable of the region, reconnoitred the enemy's route. At the same time, the consul made provision for everything as if no one had been assigned to it; he was at everyone's side, praising and criticizing

4   those who deserved it: personally armed and concentrating, he compelled the same in the soldiers. He protected the camp in the same way as he marched: he sent cohorts from the legions to be on the lookout at the gates,[138] auxiliary cavalry in front of the camp; besides this, he placed others in fortifications on

top of the rampart and went round the watches in person, not distrusting that what he had commanded would happen, but so that the soldiers would willingly accept toil shared with their commander. And indeed Marius at that and other times in the Jugurthine War controlled his army by appealing to their sense of decency rather than to penalties. Many said that this was due to ingratiation, others that he had been used to harshness from boyhood and that what the rest call suffering he had regarded as pleasure. And yet the commonwealth was served as well and properly as under the most savage of commands.

Finally, on the fourth day, not far from the town of Cirta, the scouts quickly showed themselves on all sides simultaneously, meaning the presence of the enemy. But, because they were returning from different directions, one from one quarter and another from another and yet all indicating the same thing, the consul was uncertain how to draw up his line and, without changing its order, he waited where he was, prepared for anything. There was thus frustration for the hopes of Jugurtha, who had divided his forces into four, deeming that, of them all, at least some would have an even chance of coming upon the enemy from the rear. Meanwhile Sulla, with whom the enemy had made contact first, encouraged his men squadron by squadron and, with the horses packed as densely as possible, he and others attacked the Moors; the rest remained in position, protecting their bodies from javelins thrown from long range and butchering anyone who came to grips. While the cavalry was battling in that fashion, Bocchus attacked the end of the Romans' line with the infantry which his son Volux had brought and had not taken part in the earlier fighting through delays on the march. At that time Marius was busy at the front, because that was where Jugurtha was with a large number of men. But then the Numidian, learning of Bocchus' arrival, secretly diverted to his infantry with a few others. Thereupon in Latin – he had learned to speak it at Numantia[139] – he shouted out that our men were fighting in vain and that a little earlier he had killed Marius with his own hand. At the same time he displayed his sword smeared with gore, which he had bloodied in the fighting as he slaughtered our infantry fairly energetically.

7   When the soldiers heard this, they were terrified more by the frightfulness of the deed than the reliability of the message, and at the same time the barbarians' spirits were lifted and they
8   advanced more keenly against the stunned Romans. And the latter were now not far from fleeing when Sulla, returning from crushing those against whom he had gone, charged the Moors
9   from the flank. Bocchus immediately turned away. As for Jugurtha, during the time when his desire was to support his men and to hold on to the victory which he had now almost achieved, he was surrounded by cavalry and, with everyone slaughtered right and left, took evasive action amongst the enemies' weapons
10 and burst out alone. And meanwhile Marius, having put the cavalry to flight, hurried up to help those of his men who he
11 had heard were now being driven back. Finally, the enemy were now routed on all sides. At that moment it was a dreadful spectacle across the open plains: pursuit and flight, slaughter and capture; horses and men struck down; and many of the wounded could neither flee nor remain still but sometimes struggled up only to collapse at once. In the end everywhere was strewn with weapons, arms and corpses as far as the eye could see; and, amidst it all, the ground stained with blood.

102 After that point the consul was now victor without a doubt, and he arrived at the town of Cirta, his original destination
2   when he had set out. Five days after the barbarians had fought unsuccessfully a second time, legates from Bocchus came there asking Marius, in the words of the king, to send to him his two most loyal men: he wished to speak with them about his own and the Roman people's interest. Marius at once ordered
3   L. Sulla and A. Manlius to go. Although they were going in response to a summons, it was nevertheless decided to say some words in the king's presence, in order either to influence his mood, if it was antagonistic, or to fire it more strongly, if
4   desirous of peace. And so Sulla, to whose fluency (though not age) Manlius conceded, spoke a few words of this type:
5   'King Bocchus, it is a great delight to us that the gods advised a man such as yourself eventually to prefer peace to war and not to defile your fine self by mixing with that worst of all men, Jugurtha, and simultaneously to remove from us the bitter

necessity of pursuing you in your error no less than that greatest
of criminals. In addition, from the very beginning of their com-   6
manding an empire it seemed better to the Roman people to
find friends rather than slaves and they deemed it safer to be in
command of the willing rather than the enforced. To you, no   7
friendship is more advantageous than ours, first because we are
far away, affording the least chance of offence but the same
goodwill as if we were neighbours; second, because we have
subjects in abundance, but neither we nor anyone at all ever
had enough friends. Would that this had been your decision   8
from the start: in that case you would have received from the
Roman people many more favours up to the present time than
you have suffered misfortunes. But, because most human affairs   9
are directed by Fortune, who evidently decided that you should
experience our strength as well as our goodwill, now, since she
is allowing it, hurry to proceed exactly as you have begun. You   10
have many opportunities to compensate for your mistakes more
easily by duty. Finally, take it to heart that the Roman people   11
has never been outdone in kindnesses; as for its effectiveness in
war, you know that yourself.'

In response Bocchus spoke placidly and generously, including   12
a few words in defence of his misdeed: he had taken up arms
in no hostile spirit, he said, but to safeguard his kingdom; he   13
could not have allowed Marius to devastate the part of Numidia
from which he had expelled Jugurtha by force and which had
become his by the prerogative of war; besides, when he had
sent legates to Rome previously, he had been rejected as a
friend; yet he would overlook the past and, if Marius allowed   14
it, he would now send legates to the senate.

Then, when that possibility had been granted, the barbarian's   15
mind was influenced by friends whom Jugurtha, having learned
of Sulla's and Manlius' delegation and dreading what was being
planned, had bribed with gifts. Marius meanwhile, having   103
settled his army in winter camp, set off with the unencumbered
cohorts and some of the cavalry for a lonely region to besiege
a royal tower where Jugurtha had installed all his deserters as
a garrison. Then Bocchus conversely – either by reflecting on   2
what had happened to him in the two battles or advised by

other friends whom Jugurtha had left unbribed – chose from
all his possible connections five whose loyalty was known and
3   whose talents were highly effective. He ordered them to go as
legates to Marius and then, if he agreed, to Rome, and he
allowed them the freedom to conduct negotiations and to con-
4   clude the war in whatever manner. They quickly set off for the
Romans' winter quarters but then, surrounded and despoiled
by Gaetulian bandits on the way, fled in an undignified panic
to Sulla, whom the consul, when setting off on his expedition,
5   had left as propraetor. He did not treat them like enemy liars,
as they deserved, but considerately and generously – for which
reason the barbarians deemed both that the Romans' reputation
for avarice was false and that on account of his munificence to
6   them Sulla was a friend. For even then lavishness was unknown
to many: no one was thought munificent without the corres-
7   ponding intention; all gifts were ascribed to generosity. So they
revealed to the quaestor Bocchus' instructions; at the same time
they asked him to help them as their supporter and counsellor;
and in a speech they extolled the resources, loyalty and greatness of their king, and other things which they believed either
useful or indicative of goodwill. Then, after Sulla had guaranteed them everything, they waited where they were for about
forty days, being taught how to speak in front of Marius and
in front of the senate similarly.

104   After Marius had concluded the business on which he had
been concentrating, he returned to Cirta and was informed of
the arrival of the legates; he ordered them and Sulla to come
from Tucca, the praetor L. Bellienus likewise from Utica, and
in addition everyone of the senatorial order anywhere, and with
2   them he reviewed the instructions of Bocchus. The legates were
empowered to go to Rome, and in the meantime a truce was
asked of the consul. This met with the agreement of Sulla and
the majority; but more defiant proposals came from a few,
evidently ignorant of human affairs, which, fleeting and volatile
3   as they are, are always changing to the opposite. As for the
Moors, with all their requests met, three set off for Rome with
Cn. Octavius Ruso, who as quaestor had transported pay to
Africa, and two returned to the king. From them Bocchus was

glad to hear their news in general and in particular the generosity and enthusiasm of Sulla. And at Rome, after his legates had   4
asked for pardon on the grounds that the king had made a
mistake and had fallen to the crime of Jugurtha, their request
for a treaty of friendship was responded to in this way: 'The   5
senate and the Roman people is usually mindful of kindness
and injury; but it grants indulgence to Bocchus for his misdeed
because he repents. A treaty of friendship will be given when
he deserves it.'

When Bocchus learned of this, he asked Marius by letter to   105
send Sulla to him so that at his discretion thought might be
given to their common business. The man was sent with a guard   2
of cavalry and Balearic slingers; besides these there went archers
and a Paelignian cohort[140] with skirmishing arms for the sake
of speed on the journey (and affording them no less protection
than other arms against the enemies' weapons, because they
too are light). Finally, on the fifth day of the journey, Volux,   3
Bocchus' son, suddenly showed himself on the open plains with
no more than a thousand cavalry, whose careless and sprawling
advance convinced Sulla and all the others that its number was
greater than the reality and produced in them the dread of an
enemy. So each man prepared himself, tested his arms and   4
weapons, and concentrated; there was a certain degree of fear,
but greater was the hope to be expected from conquerors
against those whom they had often conquered. Meanwhile the   5
cavalry sent ahead to reconnoitre reported that all was quiet
(as it was). Volux on his arrival addressed the quaestor, saying   106
that he had been sent by his father Bocchus to meet them and
to be their guard as well. Thereafter on that day and the next
they marched together without dread.

After, when the camp had been sited and the day had turned   2
to evening, the Moor with an ambiguous expression suddenly
ran panicking to Sulla and said that he had learned from scouts
that Jugurtha was not far off; at the same time he asked and
urged Sulla to flee with him secretly during the night. But the   3
other, with his defiant spirit, said that he had no fear of a
Numidian who had been routed so often: he had ample confidence in his men's prowess; even if certain ruin was at hand, he

would remain rather than, in betrayal of those whom he was leading, save by shameful flight a life which was unpredictable

4 and perhaps soon destined to pass away through illness. Nevertheless, warned by Volux to set off during the night, he approved the plan and immediately ordered the soldiers to finish eating and to stay in camp, and as many fires as possible to be lit, and then to leave in silence at the first watch.

5 With everyone tired from their night-time march, Sulla was already measuring out camp at sunrise when Moorish cavalry reported that Jugurtha had bivouacked at a distance of roughly

6 two miles in front of them. When they heard this, a mighty dread overcame our men: they believed they had been betrayed by Volux and tricked into an ambush; and there were some who said that there must be requital with muscle and that so

107 great a crime on his part must not be left unavenged. Although Sulla thought the same, he nevertheless kept the Moor from harm. He urged his men to be courageous in spirit: often before, a committed few had fought well against a host; the less they spared themselves in battle, the safer they would be, nor did it become one who had arms in his hands to seek the help of his unarmed feet and at the moment of greatest dread to turn

2 towards the enemy a body which was naked and blind.[141] Then, attesting that Jupiter the Greatest should be present to testify to the crime and treachery of Bocchus, he ordered Volux to

3 leave the camp for acting in a hostile fashion. Tearfully the other begged him not to believe that: none of this had been brought about through cunning but rather through the craftiness of Jugurtha, to whose scouting activities his route had

4 become known; but, because Jugurtha did not have large numbers and his hopes and resources depended upon his own father,[142] he believed that the man would dare nothing openly

5 when he himself – the son – was present to testify to it. Therefore the best thing to do, he said, seemed to be to pass openly through the middle of their camp: he would go alone with Sulla, either sending the Moorish cavalry ahead or leaving them where

6 they were. In view of the situation, the matter was approved; they set out at once, and, because they came upon Jugurtha unexpectedly, they passed through unscathed while he wavered

and hesitated. Then within a few days they reached their   7
intended destination.[143]

It was there that a certain Numidian by the name of Aspar   108
was conducting regular and friendly relations with Bocchus:
Jugurtha, after he had heard that Sulla had been summoned,
had sent him ahead as an advocate and to spy secretly on
Bocchus' plans. Besides him there was Dabar, the son of Massu-
grada, from the clan of Masinissa but inferior on his mother's
side (her father had been born to a concubine), who because of
the many good features of his temperament was dear to the
Moor and well liked by him. Since on many previous occasions   2
Bocchus had experienced the latter's loyalty to the Romans, he
sent him at once to Sulla to report that he was prepared to do
what the Roman people wanted: Sulla should choose the day,
place and time for a dialogue and should have no fear of
Jugurtha's legate:[144] his own relations with Jugurtha were kept
completely intact, he said, so that their common cause[145] could
be conducted with greater freedom: there had been no other
way of taking precautions against ambush. (But *I* discover that   3
Bocchus, from Punic loyalty[146] rather than for the reasons which
he expressed, strung along both the Romans and the Numidian
with the hope of peace; that he was accustomed regularly to
turn over in his mind the question whether to hand Jugurtha
to the Romans or Sulla to Jugurtha; and that his inclination
persuaded him against us but his dread in our favour.)

Sulla replied that he would say a few words in front of Aspar   109
but the rest secretly, with no one or as few possible present; at
the same time he explained what the reply to himself should
be. After they had assembled as he had wished, he said that he   2
had come on a mission from the consul to find out from him[147]
whether he intended peace or war. Thereupon the king, as he   3
had been instructed, ordered him to return ten days later: he
had still made no decision yet, but on that day would respond.
Thereafter both withdrew to their camps. But, when the night   4
was much advanced, Sulla was summoned secretly by Bocchus:
only loyal interpreters were called upon by each side, and
besides them there was Dabar as intermediary, an upright man
and to the liking of both. And immediately the king began thus:

110   'Never did I deem it would be the case that, as the greatest
        king in this land and of all those that I know, I should owe
2   thanks to a private individual. And, as Hercules is my witness,
        before knowing you, Sulla, it was I who brought help to the
        many who asked and to others of my own accord, since I
3   needed nothing myself. Such a demotion usually causes pain in
        everyone else, but I am delighted: let my loss at this late stage
        be the price of your friendship, than which I hold nothing
4   dearer in my heart. You have only to test it: take and use my
        arms, men, money – in short, whatever your spirit pleases –
        and as long as you live may you never think that thanks has
        been returned to you: as far as I am concerned, it will always
5   be untouched.[148] In a word, you will want for nothing, provided
        I know about it: according to my reckoning, it is less outrageous
        for a king to be outdone by arms than in munificence.

6   'Yet listen to a few words about your commonwealth, for
        the care of which you have been sent here. I neither made war
        on the Roman people nor ever wanted it made, but I safe-
7   guarded my territory by arms against armed men. Yet that I
8   overlook, because it pleases you thus. Wage with Jugurtha the
        war that you want. I shall not go beyond the River Muluccha,
        which was between me and Micipsa, nor shall I allow Jugurtha
        to enter. In addition, if you ask for anything worthy of both
        me and your people, you will not depart rejected.'

111   In response Sulla spoke briefly and modestly on his own
        behalf but at some length concerning the peace and their
        common interests. Finally he revealed to the king that, because
        the senate and the Roman people had proved more effective at
        arms, they would not consider his guarantees as thanks: he
        would have to do something which seemed to be in their inter-
        ests rather than his own. And such an opportunity was indeed
        readily available, because he had control over Jugurtha, and, if
        he handed him over to the Romans, he would be owed a very
        great deal: friendship, treaty, the part of Numidia which he
        now sought – all these would then come to him automatically.
2   At first the king demurred: relations, in-laws, a treaty had
        passed between them; in addition, he dreaded that, by showing
        a loyalty that was only fleeting, he might alienate the hearts of

his compatriots, for whom Jugurtha was dear and the Romans resented. But finally, having been prevailed upon more often, he softened and promised that he would do everything in accordance with Sulla's wishes. As for feigning the peace for which the Numidian – exhausted by war – was hungry, they made what seemed a useful arrangement. Having settled upon their cunning in this way, they parted. 3 4

On the next day the king called Aspar, Jugurtha's legate, and said that through the agency of Dabar he knew from Sulla that the war could be laid aside under certain conditions: could he therefore find out the opinion of his king. Delightedly the man set off for Jugurtha's camp; then, fully informed by the latter, he sped on his way and returned to Bocchus after eight days and reported that, while Jugurtha desired to do everything that was being commanded, he had little confidence in Marius: often before, a peace agreed with Roman commanders had proved fruitless; but, if Bocchus wanted the interests of both of them to be consulted and a certified peace, he should do his best to ensure that they all convened for a dialogue as if concerning peace, and should there hand Sulla over to himself:[149] when he had such a man in his power, that would be the time for a treaty to be made on the order of senate or people! A noble individual in the power of the enemy not through his own cowardly apathy but for the sake of the commonwealth would not be abandoned. 112 2 3

Turning these things over privately for a long time, the Moor at length gave his promise, but whether his hesitation was due to cunning or was real we have not adequately discovered. For the most part the intentions of kings are as volatile as they are severe, and often self-contradictory. Afterwards, a time and place having been agreed for their convening for the dialogue concerning peace, Bocchus called on Sulla and Jugurtha's legate in turn, treated them generously, and gave the same guarantees to both. They for their part were equally delighted and filled with good hope. 113 2

But that night, which was the one before the day decided for the dialogue, it is said that the Moor, having summoned his friends and – on changing his intention – immediately dismissed 3 them,[150] conducted a long debate with himself, his expression and eyes as variable as his mind; but one may be sure that, despite his silence, the secrets of his heart were thereby revealed.

4 Nevertheless, he at last ordered Sulla to be summoned and in accordance with the latter's wishes he laid an ambush for the
5 Numidian. Then, when day came and it was reported to him that Jugurtha was not far away, with a few friends and our quaestor[151] as if the meeting had an honorific purpose he pro-
6 ceeded to a hillock very easily seen by the ambushers. The Numidian with his many connections (unarmed, as had been agreed) advanced to the same place and at a given signal was immediately ambushed by simultaneous attacks from all sides.
7 Everyone else was butchered; Jugurtha was handed in chains to Sulla and escorted by him to Marius.

114 During the same time there was an unsuccessful fight against
2 the Gauls by our leaders Q. Caepio and Cn. Mallius.[152] At that, all Italy trembled in dread; and the Romans both then and down to the time within our recollection have held that, while all else is straightforward for their prowess, their struggles with
3 the Gauls are for salvation, not for glory. But, after it was reported that the war in Numidia was concluded and that Jugurtha was being led to Rome in chains, Marius was elected consul in his absence and Gaul was decreed as his province, and on the Kalends of January[153] he triumphed as consul with
4 great glory. And at that time the hopes and resources of the community rested in him.

HISTORIES

Introductory Note

A power struggle between Marius and Sulla in the early 8os resulted in Sulla's eventually winning the contested command against Mithridates VI, king of Pontus in Asia Minor. After Sulla departed for the east, however, Marius took violent possession of the city of Rome; and, although he himself died in 86, it was inevitable that his followers would be confronted by Sulla when the latter returned victorious in 83. The confrontation precipitated open civil war. Sulla, after emerging as the winner in the following year, instituted the proscriptions as a means of purging the state of his enemies: the victims were condemned to death without trial, their property was confiscated and, since their names were published on a list, they were at the mercy of anyone who sought the rewards offered for killing them. Sulla's personal position was confirmed when he was appointed dictator in 82; and he used his powers to strengthen (and increase the membership of) the senate and to weaken the tribunate. Sulla relinquished the dictatorship in 81 and was elected consul for the following year; but in 79 he retired from public life and died early in 78, the year in which Sallust's *Histories* begin.

The consuls of 78 were Q. Lutatius Catulus, a long-standing supporter of Sulla, and M. Aemilius Lepidus, a Marian who had prospered from the proscriptions and to whom Sallust, in the first long fragment to survive from the *Histories*, gives a speech (1.55 = 48). The mutual hostility of these two men soon erupted into conflict. Lepidus championed the cause of those who, especially in Etruria, had been evicted from their land by Sulla so that it could be settled by his own supporters; when

Lepidus was summoned back to Rome by the senate in 77, he marched on the city. As a result of the intervention of the senior senator, L. Marcius Philippus (1.77 = 67), the senate empowered Catulus and Pompey, at this period a rising star, to suppress Lepidus' revolt. Pompey's reward for his successful participation in this venture was to be sent to Spain, where another anti-Sullan renegade, Q. Sertorius (1.88 = 77), was proving too much for the proconsul there, Q. Metellus Pius (2.70 = 59).

From this point the history of the Roman republic is inseparable from the career of Pompey the Great (as he would become known). Late in 75 he wrote to the senate from Spain, complaining of a lack of support and funding (2.98 = 82), a theme already alluded to by the consul, C. Cotta, in his 'state of the nation' speech to the people (2.47 = 44); and in 74 Sertorius entered upon an alliance with the irrepressible Mithridates VI. Pompey nevertheless persevered and in 73, when at home he was already being regarded as the man likely to restore to the tribunes the powers which Sulla had taken away from them (or so it was alleged by Licinius Macer in the speech given to him at 3.48 = 34), his tactics were such that Sertorius was eventually assassinated by some of his own supporters. This left Mithridates to be dealt with. His third war against Rome had started in the previous year, and soon the king was looking round for allies (4.69 = 67). In due course he would be defeated by Pompey, who in 61 celebrated a triumph for his victory. But these events are beyond the scope of the extant *Histories*.

BOOK 1

1 (1) The affairs of the Roman people, as conducted in the consulship of M. Lepidus and Q. Catulus and thereafter, on campaign and at home, are here compiled.[1]

3 (5) In so great a body of most learned men, we[2] ...

4 (3) The most articulate man of Roman stock dispatched in a few words[3] ...

6 (7) Nor has a different side in the civil wars shifted me from the truth.

7 (8) The first dissensions befell us through a flaw in the human character, which always acts in an impatient and indomitable manner in the struggle for freedom or glory or domination.

8 (2) For from the beginning of the City to the Macedonian war with Perseus[4] ...

11 (9–10) The Roman cause, in respect of empire, was at its strongest in the consulship of Ser. Sulpicius and M. Marcellus, when the whole of Gaul this side of the Rhine between Our Sea and the Ocean (except where marshes made for impassability) had been subjugated.[5] On the other hand, it acted in accordance with the best morals and greatest harmony in the period between the second and last Carthaginian war[6] [...][7] But disharmony, avarice, ambition and all the other ills customarily arising from success experienced their greatest increase after the razing of Carthage.[8] For the injustices of the stronger and the plebs' resultant secessions from the fathers,[9] as well as other dissensions, were endemic right from the beginning, and after the expulsion of the kings the principles of fairness and restraint lasted only until dread of Tarquinius and the critical war with Etruria[10] were put aside. Thereafter the fathers harassed the

plebs with commands fit only for slaves, made decisions in a kingly fashion about execution and flogging,[11] evicted people from the land, and, with everyone else disenfranchised, lived in sole command. Overwhelmed by these savageries and especially by debt (since with the constant warfare they were enduring taxation and campaigning simultaneously), the plebs armed themselves and occupied the Sacred Mount and the Aventine[12] and thereupon acquired for themselves tribunes of the plebs and other rights. On each side the end of disharmony and struggle was the Second Punic War.[13]

12 (12) When at last the dread of Carthage was removed and the way was clear to engage in conflict, there arose numerous disturbances, rebellions and, lastly, civil wars, in as much as a powerful few, to whom many had yielded to gain their good-will, aspired to domination under the honourable names of fathers and plebs;[14] and citizens were not called 'good' or 'bad' on account of their services to the commonwealth (the corruption being universal) but whoever was wealthiest and gained greater strength from injustice was regarded as good because he defended the present situation.

16 (13) From that time our ancestors' morals did not drop gradually, as before, but like a torrent: young men were so corrupted by luxuriousness and avarice that it is rightly said that theirs was a generation which could neither hold private assets itself nor allow others to do so.

55 (48) Speech of Lepidus, the consul, to the Roman people[15]

1   'Your clemency and probity, Citizens, for which you are the greatest and distinguished amongst all other peoples, cause me considerable fear in the face of the tyranny of L. Sulla. By giving too little credence to the behaviour in others which you yourselves regard as unspeakable, you may be trapped, especially since all his hopes rest upon crime and treachery and he does not think himself safe unless he is worse and more

infamous than your dread of him, so that, once you are his
captives, your wretchedness will deprive you of your concern
for freedom. Alternatively, if you take precautions, you may
be preoccupied more by safeguarding against danger than by
revenge. As for his retainers, men of the greatest names and   2
benefiting from the best of ancestral examples, I cannot wonder
at them enough: the price they pay for their dominion over you
is their own servitude, and they prefer each of these, with its
accompanying injustice, to living as free men in accordance
with the ideals of justice. Ah, the so distinguished progeny of   3
the Bruti and Aemilii and Lutatii,[16] born to overthrow what
their ancestors procured through prowess! For what else was   4
it that we protected from Pyrrhus,[17] Hannibal, Philip and
Antiochus[18] except our freedom and each person's individual
abode and our refusal to obey anyone but the laws? And all   5
these things, seized as if from foreigners, are now in the possession of that warped Romulus,[19] who, not satisfied with the
disasters to so many armies and consuls and other leaders
whom the fortune of war had consumed, is more cruel at the
very moment when success turns most men from anger towards
compassion. Indeed, alone of all in the memory of the human   6
race, he devised punishments for those to come afterwards, so
that injustice would be their more certain lot than life;[20] and
with the utmost crookedness the monstrosity of his criminality
has kept him safe all the while that the dread of a harsher
slavery has frightened you from reclaiming your freedom.

  'It is action and confrontation that are required, Citizens, to 7
prevent your spoils becoming theirs, not postponement nor
relying on prayer for help – unless perchance you hope that
Sulla is already feeling disgust and shame at his tyranny and
will risk greater danger by relinquishing his criminal gains. But 8
he has reached the point where he regards nothing as glorious
unless it is safe, and all means of retaining his domination as
honourable. Hence that calm and that tranquillity with free-   9
dom[21] – things which many virtuous men pursued in preference
to toil with honours – are no more: this is the time for servitude 10
or for commanding, for experiencing dread or for inflicting it.
What more is there? What human things survive, what divine   11

things are unpolluted? The Roman people, a short while ago
the controller of nations, is now stripped of its command, of
glory and of justice, and, incapable of action and despised, is
12   left with not even the sustenance fit for slaves. A great force of
allies and from Latium is being kept by one man from the
citizenship given to them by you for their many exceptional
deeds,[22] and a few retainers have occupied the ancestral abodes
13   of the innocent plebs as a reward for their crimes. The laws,
the courts, the treasury, the provinces, the kings are in the
hands of one man, as is, in short, jurisdiction over the execution
14   and life of citizens; at the same time you have seen human
15   sacrifices and tombs stained with citizens' blood. Is anything
else left to men besides breaking the cycle of injustice or dying
with manly prowess? For nature has fixed the same end for all,
even those girded with a sword, and no one awaits the ultimate
necessity without some daring deed, unless he is of a womanly
disposition.

16   'Yet it is I who am rebellious, says Sulla, when I complain
about the prizes for disruption; and desirous of war, when I
17   claim back the rights of peace – evidently because there is no
other way in which you will be secure and sufficiently safe in
your commanding position unless Vettius from Picenum and
the secretary Cornelius[23] squander what others have fairly
acquired, unless you all approve the proscription of innocents
for the sake of their riches, the torture of illustrious men, the
City emptied by exile and slaughter, the goods of our wretched
18   citizens sold off or given away like Cimbrian plunder.[24] But it
is me he charges with possessions taken from the goods of the
proscribed; yet the very greatest of his own crimes is that neither
I nor anyone at all was sufficiently safe if we acted correctly.
And the things which I then bought in fear on payment of the
price I am nevertheless restoring to their rightful owners,[25] and
19   it is not my policy to allow any plundering of our citizens. Let
the symptoms of frenzy which we have endured be enough –
Roman armies coming to grips with one another and arms
directed away from foreigners upon ourselves. Let there be an
end to all the crimes and insults, of which Sulla is so unrepentant

that he both counts his deeds as glory and, if he could, would
do them more greedily.

'I am no longer afraid of what you think about him but of   20
how daring you are, lest, as each waits for a different leader,
we first become captives, not of his resources (which are useless
and corrupt), but of your own lethargy, which permits him to
proceed with his seizures and to seem as fortunate as he is
daring.[26] For – apart from his defiled retainers – who wants the   21
same as he, or who does not want everything changed apart
from victory? The soldiers, no doubt, whose blood has procured
riches for Tarula and Scirtus, those worst of slaves![27] Or those
to whom, in the undertaking of magistracies, Fufidius[28] was
preferred, that shameful serving woman, a disgrace to every
honorific office! And so it is that the greatest confidence is   22
generated in me by the victorious army through whose wounds
and toils nothing was achieved apart from a tyrant. Unless   23
perchance they marched out to overthrow the tribunician
power, which their ancestors established by force of arms, and
to rob themselves of the laws and the courts – for an exceptional
reward, since, banished to marshes and woods, they knew only
insult and resentment, and prizes in the hands of the few.

'Why therefore does he progress with such a great column[29]   24
and confidence? Because successful circumstances are, amaz-
ingly, a screen for vice (but, if they are undermined, he will be
as despised as he was feared); or else to display harmony and
peace, the names which he has bestowed on his crime and his
parricide.[30] And he says that the commonwealth and the end of
the war depend upon the plebs' remaining expelled from their
land – the bitterest form of citizen plunder – and upon his
having in his hands what once belonged to the Roman people:
justice and judgement in all matters. If these are what you   25
understand by "peace" and "consensus", give your approval
to the greatest disruptions ever to destroy the commonwealth,
agree to the laws he has imposed, welcome tranquillity with
servitude, and hand down to posterity an example for ensnaring
the commonwealth for the price of its own blood! As for me,   26
although this highest of commands has brought me enough

in terms of my ancestors' reputation, of status and even of
protection, it was nevertheless not my intention to make a
personal fortune, and a dangerous freedom seemed preferable
27 to a calm servitude. If you approve of this, Citizens, lend your
support and, with the best help of the divinities, follow the
lead and initiative of M. Aemilius, the consul, to recover your
freedom!'

77 (67) Speech of Philippus[31] in the senate

1 'My particular wish, conscript fathers, would be for the
commonwealth to be calm or, in times of danger, to be defended
by all its readiest men, and, finally, for crooked projects to be
a source of harm to their advocates. But, on the contrary,
everything is disrupted by rebellion – and on the part of those
who ought rather to have prevented it; lastly, what the worst
and stupidest have decreed is required to be done by the good
2 and the wise. For, although you resent war and arms, nevertheless, because they please Lepidus, they are required to be taken
up – unless perchance it is someone's intention to proffer peace
3 and then to endure war. By the good gods who still protect this
City despite our neglecting all concern for them, M. Aemilius,
the ultimate in outrageous individuals, a man about whom one
cannot decide whether he is more evil or more cowardly, has
an army for the suppression of freedom and, from being an
object of contempt, has made himself dreaded! But, as for you,
muttering and faltering with words and the prophecies of seers
you desire peace more than you defend it,[32] and you do not
understand that the mildness of your decrees deprives you of
4 your dignity and him of his dread – and rightly, since he
acquired the consulship as a result of his seizures and a province
with its army on account of his rebelliousness. What would he
have taken on account of good deeds, when you have granted
5 such prizes to his crimes? It will of course be said that his favour
was won by those who right up to the last decreed legates,
peace, harmony and other things of this kind. No! Despised
and regarded as unworthy of the commonwealth, those men

are considered to be his plunder because the dread which leads them to reclaim peace is that which had lost them possession of it.

'For my part, from the first moment when I saw Etruria[33] swearing allegiance, the proscribed being summoned and the commonwealth being ravaged by bribery, I thought that haste was required and with a few others I followed the counsels of Catulus.[34] But those who kept extolling the good deeds of the Aemilian family and kept saying that the Roman people had increased its greatness by being forgiving and that Lepidus even then had made no progress (when he had taken up arms privately for the suppression of freedom) – such people perverted public policy because each of them sought resources or patronage for themselves. Yet at that time Lepidus was only a bandit with camp-followers and a few knife-men, none of whom would exchange his life for a day's wage; but now he is a proconsul with the power of command (which was not bought but was given by you) and with legates still legally obeying him, and on him converge the most corrupt men of all ranks, burning with need and desires, goaded by consciousness of their crimes, for whom calm lies in rebellion and in peace disruption. These people seed commotion from commotion, war from war – once it was the retainers of Saturninus, afterwards those of Sulpicius, then of Marius and Damasippus,[35] now of Lepidus. In addition to this, Etruria and all the remnants of war are alerted, the Spains are in armed turmoil, and Mithridates,[36] on the flank of those taxpayers of ours by whom we are still sustained, is looking out for a day for war: in fact, apart from a suitable leader, nothing is missing for the undermining of the empire. So I beg and beseech you, conscript fathers, to pay attention and not to allow the licence for crime to spread by contact, like some frenzy, to the unaffected. For, when it is the wicked whom the prizes follow, it is not easy for anyone to be gratuitously good.

'Or are you waiting until he moves up his army again and assaults the City with steel and flame? That is much closer from the situation in which he is now than is the distance from peace and harmony to the civil wars which he has taken up against

6

7

8

9

10

everything divine and human – and not in answer to some
injustice which he or (as he pretends) his followers have suf-
11 fered, but to undermine the laws and freedom. For in his mind
he is driven and ravaged by desire and by the dread of being
harmed: devoid of a policy, restless, attempting one thing after
another, he dreads tranquillity but hates war; he sees the need
for the absence of luxuriousness and licence and in the mean-
12 while takes full advantage of your lethargy. I do not have
sufficient judgement as to whether I should call it dread or
cowardice or madness, when each of you seems to want no
more contact with such evil than with a thunderbolt yet seems
not even to try to prevent it.

13   'I beseech you, reflect how the nature of things has been
reversed: formerly, public wickedness was organized secretly,
assistance openly, and for that reason the good easily forestalled
the wicked; but now peace and harmony are disrupted openly
and defended secretly. Those who are pleased by this are in
14 arms, while you are in dread. What are you waiting for, unless
perchance you are ashamed and annoyed at doing right? Or
have Lepidus' instructions influenced your minds? He says he
is pleased that each person's property is being returned, and yet
he holds on to that of others; that the codes of warfare are being
revoked, when he himself uses armed force; that citizenship is
being confirmed for those from whom he says that it has not
been taken away; and that for the sake of harmony there is
the restoration of the tribunician power, from which all the
15 disharmony has been kindled. You are the most wicked and
shameless of all men![37] Are the citizens' destitution and grief a
concern to you, who have nothing of your own except what
has been procured by arms or through injustice? Your aim is a
second consulship, as if you have returned the first; you seek
harmony through war, by which its procurement is disrupted.
To us you are a traitor, to them[38] disloyal, the enemy of all
good men. How unashamed you are in the face both of men
and of gods, whom you have violated with your word or by
16 perjury! Since you are as you are, I urge you to keep to your
opinion and to retain your arms and, being restless yourself,
not to detain us in anxiety by postponing your rebellions. You

are one whom neither the provinces nor the laws nor the household gods tolerate as a citizen: proceed along the path you have begun, so that as quickly as possible you may find your deserts.

'But as for you, conscript fathers, for how long by your delaying will you endure[39] an unsafe commonwealth and attempt only verbal fighting? Levies have been held against you, money has been extorted publicly and privately, garrisons have been brought back and installed, laws are commanded at whim – while in the meantime you arrange legates and decrees. As Hercules is my witness, the more greedily you seek peace, the more bitter the war will be, since he realizes[40] that he has been sustained by dread rather than by fairness or goodness. For whoever claims to reject disruption and the slaughter of citizens, and on that account keeps you unarmed despite Lepidus' being armed, is proposing that you should rather endure the sufferings of the conquered although you have the ability to inflict them: as a result such a person is urging him to accept peace from you and you to accept war from him. If these circumstances please you, if so great a paralysis has overwhelmed your minds that, forgetting the crimes of Cinna (on whose return to the City the glory of the senate perished),[41] you are going to entrust yourselves and your spouses and your children to Lepidus, what need is there of decrees, of Catulus' help? He and other good men are concerned for the commonwealth in vain. Act as you will, arrange for yourselves the patronage of Cethegus[42] and other traitors who desire to resume the seizures and burnings and once again to arm units against the household gods. But, if freedom and the truth please you more, issue decrees worthy of your name and reinforce the mood of courageous men. A new army is at hand and, in addition, colonies of veteran soldiers, all the nobility, the best leaders. Fortune follows better men; soon all that has been assembled as a result of our lethargy will dissipate.

'For that reason I propose as follows: that, because M. Lepidus has assembled an army on his personal initiative and along with the worst elements and enemies of the commonwealth is leading it against the City contrary to the authority of this

17

18

19

20

21

22

order, Ap. Claudius the interrex along with Q. Catulus the proconsul and the others who have the power of command should act as defenders of the City and should do their utmost to prevent the commonwealth from suffering any damage.'[43]

88 (77) He was a man of great glory when a tribune of the soldiers in Spain under T. Didius' command, and of great use in the Marsic War in the acquisition of soldiers and arms;[44] and yet the many things achieved by his leadership and muscle remain uncelebrated, first because of his ignobility, then because of writers' jealousy,[45] although during his lifetime he exhibited them in his appearance by numerous frontal scars and a gouged out eye. In fact he took the greatest delight in his physical disfigurement and was not worried by its manifestations, because his retention of the rest was more glorious.

BOOK 2

47 (44) Speech of C. Cotta,[46] the consul, to the Roman people

After a few days Cotta, having changed his clothing[47] and in great sorrow because instead of the desired goodwill of the plebs [. . .],[48] spoke in this manner in an assembly of the people:

1   'Citizens, many are the dangers that I have experienced at home and on campaign, many the adversities, some of which I bore, others I repelled with the help of the gods and my own prowess. Through all of them there was never any lack of thought in my action or, in my decisions, of hard work. Failure and success used to change my resources but not my mind.

2   But in the present wretched circumstances, on the contrary, everything including Fortune has deserted me. In addition to this, old age (a burden in itself) doubles my concern, since, with my life already passed, in my wretched state it is not possible

3   for me to hope even for an honourable death. For, if I am your parricide[49] and, though born a second time,[50] now consider my household gods and my fatherland and the highest command to be cheap, what torture is adequate for me when alive, what

punishment when dead? By my crime I have exceeded all the reprisals said to exist amongst the inhabitants of the underworld.

'From my earliest adolescence I have lived my life, both as a 4 private citizen and in my magistracies, in your sight. Those who wanted had the advantage of my tongue, my advice, my money; and I never employed any crafty fluency or my talent in order to do evil. Despite my great hunger for personal favour, I undertook the greatest antagonisms on behalf of the commonwealth; both it[51] and I were overcome by them, and, when I needed another's help and was expecting only more troubles, you, Citizens, gave me back my fatherland and household gods along with a rank of great dignity. In return for these good 5 deeds I would scarcely seem sufficiently grateful if to each of you individually I yielded up my spirit, which I cannot do: life and death belong by right to nature; if one lives without disgrace amongst one's fellow citizens, with fame and fortune intact, that is something given and received as a gift.

'You have made us consuls, Citizens, when the common- 6 wealth is greatly hampered at home and at war. The commanders in Spain are demanding pay, soldiers, arms and grain, and their circumstances are compelling because, with the defection of the allies and Sertorius' flight through the mountains,[52] they are able neither to compete hand to hand nor to make any useful preparations. Armies are being supported in Asia and 7 Cilicia on account of the excessive power of Mithridates; Macedonia is full of enemies, as are the coasts of Italy and the provinces, while in the meantime taxes, small and unreliable in wartime, scarcely maintain a part of our costs: hence the fleet which protected our supplies is smaller on its voyages than before. If these circumstances have been brought on by our 8 misconduct or lethargy, act as your anger dictates, exact your reprisal; but, if it is our common fortune which is bleaker, why are you making a start which is unworthy of you and of us and of the commonwealth?

'And as for myself, whose age is nearer to death, I do not 9 seek to avert the latter if it removes some disadvantage from you; and it would not be more honourable for me soon to end

my life owing to my physical constitution rather than on behalf
10 of your salvation. Look! Here I am in front of you – C. Cotta,
consul, and I am doing what our ancestors often did in bleak
wars: I promise and dedicate myself on behalf of the common-
11 wealth.[53] Consider to whom you will entrust it thereafter: for
no good man will want an honour of this kind, since he will be
required to render an account of hazard and the sea and a war
12 waged by others, or else die a shameful death. Only keep in
mind that I was not slain for any crime or avarice but that I
willingly gave up my spirit as a gift in return for the greatest
13 benefits. For your own sake, Citizens, and for that of your
ancestors' glory, endure adversity and look after the interests
14 of the commonwealth. Many a care is attached to the highest
command, many mighty toils, which it is pointless to decline
and seek the affluence of peace, since all the provinces, kingdoms, seas and lands are bleak or exhausted with war.'

70 (59) But Metellus, returning to Further Spain after a year,[54]
was viewed with great glory by all those, in gender both men
and women, who converged on him from every side through
the streets and dwellings. Whenever the quaestor C. Urbinus
and others, knowing his wishes, invited him to dinner, their
concern for him exceeded Roman conventions and even those
of mortal men, their houses furnished with tapestries and
emblems, and stages constructed for the display of the actors;
at the same time the ground was sprinkled with saffron, and
other things resembling a celebrated temple. In addition, as he
was sitting, a net would lower an image of Victory and, to the
accompaniment of noise from a thunder machine, would place
it on his head as a crown; and, as he was arriving, he was
supplicated with incense like a god. An embroidered toga usually constituted his dress as he reclined, while the dishes were
of the choicest – and not only from across the whole province,
but several varieties of bird and wild beast, previously
unknown, came over the seas from Mauretania. By these means
he had detracted from his glory to a certain extent, especially
in the eyes of the elderly and upright men who regarded those
things as haughty, grave and unworthy of the Roman empire.

87 (69) Then, with the signal given abruptly (it being already the second watch), they commenced the fight simultaneously from both sides[55] – in the great commotion at first throwing their weapons uncertainly from a distance in the darkness of night, but after, when the Romans were deliberately not responding with weapons or shouting, they deemed that they had been stunned by fear or that their fortification had been abandoned, and they hurried greedily into the ditches and from there – the swiftest types – across the rampart. But it was then that those standing above them finally threw rocks, weapons and stakes and, at close quarters, dislodged with blows or shield-bosses many who had emerged near them. At this sudden source of fear, some were pierced through at the rampart, some toppled onto their own weapons and the ditches became half filled as many of them crashed down there; the rest found safe flight owing to the uncertainty of night-time and a dread of ambush. Then, after a few days, surrender was enforced by the lack of water, the town was burned and its occupants sold; and, as a result of that terrifying development, legates soon came from Isaura Nova begging for peace, and they promised hostages and that they would carry out orders. Therefore Servilius,[56] knowing the enemy's defiant nature and that it was not weariness of war but sudden fear which persuaded them of peace, approached their walls as soon as possible with all his forces lest they change their minds about the dispatch,[57] while in the meantime demonstrating mildness to the legates and that the surrender would be arranged more easily with everyone present. In addition to this he kept his soldiers from ravaging the land and from all damage; the townsfolk provided grain and supplies in accordance with their[58] wishes; and, to prevent their being suspicious of him, he had sited his camp on flat ground. Then a hundred hostages were provided in accordance with the command and, when deserters and all arms and launchers were demanded, the younger men – at first concertedly and then depending on the circumstance of each one – caused a commotion across the whole city with the loudest of shouting and asserted that, while they had breath, they would not give

up arms or allies. But those of an unwarlike age, to whom the power of the Romans was well known from of old, desired peace; yet, conscious of the damage which had been done,[59] they dreaded that, despite the surrender of arms, they would nevertheless soon suffer the ultimate fate of victims. Amidst this trepidation, as everyone in a commotion consulted together, Servilius, deeming that surrender would be pointless without the pressure of dread, unexpectedly occupied a mountain from which the town of Isaura[60] was in the range of weapons and which was sacred to the Great Mother.[61] (There was a belief that the goddess from whose name it derived dined there on fixed days and that sounds could be heard . . .)

98 (82) Letter of Cn. Pompeius[62] to the senate

1   'If it had been *against* you and our fatherland and our house-hold gods that I had undertaken so many toils and dangers on those occasions from my early adolescence when, under my leadership, the most criminal enemies were routed and salvation was obtained for you, your decisions against me in my absence would have been no more severe than your actions hitherto, conscript fathers. After I was flung into the savagest of wars – despite my age – with the most deserving of armies, you have done your best to destroy me by hunger, the most wretched

2   death of all. Was it with this expectation that the Roman people sent its children to war? Are these the prizes for wounds and for blood spilled so often on account of the commonwealth? Exhausted by writing and by sending legates, I have used up all my private resources and hopes, while in the meantime you have scarcely given a single year's expenditure over three years.

3   By the immortal gods, do you reckon that I am a personification of the treasury or that I can keep an army without grain and pay?

4   'I acknowledge that I set off for this war with more enthusi-asm than thought, in as much as, having received from you only a nominal command, within forty days I assembled an army and removed from the Alps into Spain an enemy already working at the neck of Italy; and through them[63] I opened up a

route different from Hannibal's and more favourable to us. I 5
captured Gaul, the Pyrenees, Lacetania and the Indigetes,[64] and
with new soldiers – and many too few of them – I withstood
the first attack of the victorious Sertorius and I passed a winter
in camp amongst the most savage of enemies, not in towns or
for the sake of ingratiating myself. Why then should I itemize 6
the battles or winter campaigns, the towns razed or captured,
when the reality is more effective than words? The capture of
the enemy camp at Sucro, the battle at the River Turia, the
destruction of the enemy leader C. Herennius along with the
city of Valentia[65] and his army – all these distinctions are well
known to you. For which, grateful fathers, you respond with
destitution and hunger.

'Thus the condition of my army is the same as the enemy's: 7
neither receives pay; each, if victorious, is able to enter Italy. It 8
is this to which I warn and beseech you to pay attention, and
not to compel me by need to look after my own private interests.
The part of Nearer Spain which is not held by the enemy has 9
been devastated to the point of annihilation by us or by Sertorius – apart from the maritime communities, which too are an
expense and a burden for us. Gaul sustained Metellus' army
last year with pay and grain, and now it can scarcely survive
itself because of poor crops. As for me, I have used up not only
my private assets but also my credit. You are left. If you do not 10
come to our aid, my reluctant prediction is that the army – and
with it the whole war in Spain – will transfer to Italy.'

This letter was read out in the senate at the beginning of the
following year;[66] but the consuls arranged between themselves
the provinces decreed to them by the fathers: Cotta had Nearer
Gaul, Octavius Cilicia.[67] The next consuls, L. Lucullus and M.
Cotta,[68] were severely stunned by Pompeius' letter and messengers, and, both because of the critical situation and fearing that
the return of the army to Italy would bring them neither praise
nor esteem, they then used every means to arrange for pay and
reinforcements, with special efforts being made by the nobility,
many of whom were already then giving tongue to their defiance
and matched their speech with their deeds.[69]

BOOK 3

48 (34) Speech of Macer,[70] tribune of the plebs, to the plebs

1 'If, Citizens, you thought too little about the difference between the rights left to you by your ancestors and the present servitude contrived by Sulla, I would have had to use many words in speaking to you and you would have had to be taught the injustices for which, and the number of occasions on which, the plebs conducted an armed secession from the fathers,[71] and the way in which they contrived for tribunes of the plebs 2 to be the defenders of all their rights. As it is, however, it is left to me only to encourage and to be first in going down the road 3 where I think freedom must be grasped. And it does not escape me that I am embarking alone – powerless and with the empty semblance of a magistracy[72] – on dislodging the highly resourceful nobility from its mastery, and that a faction of the guilty 4 lives much more safely than does the guiltless man alone. But apart from the good hope which I have derived from you and which has conquered my dread, I have decided that reverses in a struggle for freedom have more influence with a courageous man than not to have struggled at all.

5   'And yet all the others, though created to represent your rights, for reasons either of favour or hope or reward have turned the whole power of their command against you, and they consider it better to commit wrong for payment than to 6 do right for nothing. And so all of them have already yielded to the mastery of a few who on a military pretext have taken over the armies, kingdoms and provinces and hold a citadel constructed out of your spoils, while in the meantime, in the manner of cattle, you present yourselves as a crowd to individuals to be possessed and enjoyed, stripped of everything which your ancestors left you – except that by your votes you are designating masters for yourselves as once you did 7 guardians. And so everyone has yielded to their side, but soon, if you recover what is yours, the majority will move in your

direction: it is a rare person who has the spirit to defend what pleases him; the others all belong to the stronger.

'Do you have doubt whether there can be any obstruction to 8 your unanimous progress, when they were so afraid of your laxity and lethargy? Unless perchance it was for other reasons than dread that C. Cotta, a consul from the very centre of the faction, restored to the tribunes of the plebs certain of their rights.[73] And, although L. Sicinius, who was the first who dared to speak about the tribunician power, had been stopped to the accompaniment only of your mutterings, nevertheless, before you wearied of this injustice, they dreaded your resentment at it.[74] This is something at which I cannot sufficiently wonder, Citizens: for you understood that your hopes had been in vain. With the death of Sulla, who had imposed on you a criminal 9 slavery, you believed that your troubles were at an end; but there rose up, far more savage, Catulus.[75] Commotion inter- 10 vened in the consulship of Brutus and Mamercus; then C. Curio was your master right up to the extermination of the blameless tribune.[76] As for Lucullus, you saw the animosity with which 11 he moved against L. Quintius last year.[77] How great, finally, is the disruption now stirred up against me! But of course they were driven to no purpose if they intended to end their mastery before you your servitude – especially since in the present civil war, despite other things being said, the struggle on both sides[78] was for mastery over you. And so, while the other consequences 12 of licence or hatred or avarice flared up merely for a time, there persisted only one thing which was sought on both sides – and snatched away for the future was the tribunician might, the weapon procured by your ancestors for freedom. It is this to 13 which I warn and beseech you to pay attention, and not to change the names of things in the light of your cowardice, calling servitude "tranquillity". Enjoyment of that itself,[79] if outrage overcomes truth and honour, is not a possibility: it would have been, if you had been completely passive; but, as it is, they are now paying attention, and, because every injustice is safer for its gravity,[80] they will hold you in a tighter grip if you are not victorious.

14   ' "What, therefore, do you propose?" one of you might inter-
ject. First of all, that you abandon the conduct which you are
presently pursuing of an energetic tongue and cowardly heart,
15   with no thought of freedom outside the place of assembly. Then
– and I am not summoning you to those manly tasks by which
your ancestors procured tribunes of the plebs, afterwards a
patrician magistracy, and votes free from the patricians' influence – since all power lies with you, Citizens, and you have at
least the ability to execute or not execute on your own behalf
the orders which you now endure on behalf of others, are you
16   waiting for Jupiter or some other god to be your counsellor? By
carrying out those great commands of the consuls and decrees of
the fathers, Citizens, you are ratifying them, and of your own
accord you are hurrying to abet and aid their licence with
17   regard to you. Nor am I urging you to avenge injustices, but
rather that you should desire respite from them; and it is not
through any wish for disharmony (as they charge) but for an
end to it that I am reclaiming things according to the law of
nations,[81] and, if they tenaciously retain those things, it will not
be arms or secession that I propose but that you provide no
18   more of your own blood. Let them exercise and hold their
commands in their own way; let them seek their triumphs; let
them and their ancestral images[82] pursue Mithridates, Sertorius
and the remnants of the exiles; but let the danger and toil escape
19   those who are given no share in the fruits – unless perchance
the compensation for your services is that sudden grain law, in
which they reckoned everyone's freedom at five measures,[83]
which is of course worth no more than the sustenance in a
prison. For, just as one's death there is prevented by this
meagreness but one's strength languishes, so such a small
amount does not release you from family concerns and deludes
20   anyone's apathy with the slenderest of hopes. Yet, no matter
how generous the amount, it was being presented as the reward
for your servitude, and what kind of paralysis is constituted by
being deceived and by owing a spontaneous debt of gratitude
21   for the unjust treatment of your own property? You must
beware of guile: for there is no other way in which they will
prevail over everyone or try to do so. Thus they devise palli-

atives at the same time as they defer you till the arrival of Cn. Pompeius, the very man whom they lifted onto their shoulders[84] in their fear of him but whom they soon mauled when their dread was removed. Nor are they ashamed, those "defenders 22 of freedom" as they call themselves, that without one man so many of them neither dare to redress injustice nor are able to defend justice. To me, at least, it is sufficiently proved that 23 Pompeius, a young man of such glory, prefers to be chief with your blessing rather than their ally in mastery and that he above all will be the initiator[85] of the tribunician power. But 24 previously, Citizens, you as individuals had your protection in numbers, not in one man collectively; nor was any single mortal able to give or take such things away from you.

'And so enough words have been said: for it is not ignorance 25 which brings things to a halt but you have been seized by 26 some kind of paralysis whereby you are not moved by glory or outrage and you have exchanged everything for your present cowardice, deeming that you have ample freedom, no doubt because you are spared flogging and you can go about here and there – the presents of your rich masters. And yet these same 27 things are not enjoyed by rustics, but they are slaughtered amidst the antagonisms of the powerful and are given as gifts to magistrates in the provinces. Thus the fighting and conquering 28 benefit only a few; the plebs, whatever happens, are like the conquered and will be more so every day, at least if those men are more concerned to retain their mastery than you are to reclaim your freedom.'

BOOK 4

69 (67) Letter of Mithridates[86]

'King Mithridates to King Arsaces: greetings. All who in times 1 of their own success are begged to join an alliance in war ought to reflect whether it is possible for them to live in peace at that moment and, next, whether what is being sought is sufficiently just, safe and glorious, or unfitting. In your own case, if it were 2 possible for you to enjoy everlasting peace, if your enemies were not strategically placed criminals, and you were not to have exceptional fame if you overwhelmed the Romans, then I would not dare to seek an alliance with you and would hope

3 in vain to merge my misfortunes with your prosperity. And as for those things which seem to give you pause – anger at Tigranes for the recent war[87] and my own scarcely favourable circumstances – if you are only prepared to assess them prop-

4 erly, they will constitute very great encouragement. The former, being beholden to you, will welcome whatever kind of alliance you want, while in my case Fortune, despite seizing so much away from me, has given me the power to make good recommendations, and – something which appeals to those who flourish – despite not being at my strongest, I am providing an example whereby you can arrange your affairs better.

5 'The Romans have only a single reason – and that too a long-standing one – for making war on all nations, peoples and kings: a profound desire for empire and for riches. That was why they first took up war with Philip, king of the Macedonians,[88] with whom they pretended friendship while they

6 were under pressure from the Carthaginians. When Antiochus came to his aid, they guilefully diverted him by the concession of Asia, and later, when Philip was broken, Antiochus was despoiled of all land this side of the Taurus and ten thousand

7 talents.[89] Next it was Perseus, Philip's son, whom, after many varied struggles, they received into their trust before the Samothracian gods,[90] but then, astute devisers of treachery that they are, they killed him by sleeplessness[91] because they had entered

8 an agreement to grant him his life. Eumenes, whose friendship they proudly parade, they initially betrayed to Antiochus as the price of peace; after, treating him as the guardian of captured land, by expenses and insults they transformed him from king into the most wretched of slaves, and, on the pretence of an unjust will, they led his son Aristonicus in triumph like an enemy because he had sought to retrieve his father's kingdom; and they

9 themselves occupied Asia.[92] Finally they snatched Bithynia on the death of Nicomedes, although Nysa, whom he had called his queen, had undoubtedly had a son as an offspring.[93]

'Why should I call upon my own case? Though separated 10
from their empire on all sides by kingdoms and tetrarchies, it
was because of a rumour that I was rich and would not be
enslaved that they assailed me by means of a war with Nicomedes,[94] though I was not unaware of their crime and had
previously invoked, as witnesses to what happened, the Cretans
(the only free people at all at that period) and King Ptolemy.[95]
Avenging these injustices, I drove Nicomedes from Bithynia 11
and recovered Asia (the spoils of King Antiochus) and I removed
from Greece the burden of servitude. Archelaus,[96] the ultimate 12
in slaves, hampered my projects by betraying my army. And
those who were kept from fighting by cowardice or by a twisted
astuteness (so that they should remain safe at the cost of my
labours) are paying the most bitter penalties – Ptolemy postponing war from day to day but only for a price,[97] the Cretans
attacked once and now unlikely to have an end to it except in
being razed.[98] I realized that on account of their internal dis- 13
orders battle had been deferred rather than peace granted,
and – despite the facts that Tigranes disagreed (he belatedly
approves of my words), that you were far distant, and that
everyone else was beholden to them – I nevertheless started war
again and routed Marcus Cotta, the Roman leader, on land at
Chalcedon and by sea I stripped him of a very fine fleet.[99] While 14
I was delayed in a siege at Cyzicus[100] with a large army, the
grain failed, with no one round about making any effort at
support; at the same time, winter kept us off the sea. Trying
therefore to return to my ancestral kingdom under no compulsion from the enemy, because of shipwreck at Parium and
Heraclea[101] I lost the best of my soldiers along with their fleets.
After the reconstitution of my army at Cabera[102] and various 15
battles between me and Lucullus, scarcity once again afflicted
us both. For him a nearby refuge was the kingdom of Ariobarzanes,[103] which was untouched by the war; I, surrounded by
wastes, withdrew into Armenia; and the Romans followed, not
me, but their habit of overthrowing all monarchies, and,
because they prevented a large number from fighting in a
narrow place, they now parade Tigranes' carelessness as a
victory.[104]

16   'Now, I beseech you, reflect whether you think that our being
overwhelmed will make you stronger in resisting or will bring
an end to the war. I know, of course, that you have great
resources of men, arms and gold; and for that reason you are
being targeted by us for an alliance and by them for plunder.
Yet my plan – while Tigranes' kingdom is still intact, and since
my soldiers are experienced in war – is to finish off the war far
from home with little labour through our own bodily efforts,
because we can neither conquer nor be conquered without
17   endangering you. Or are you unaware that the Romans turned
their arms in this direction only after the Ocean had put an end
to their progress westwards, and that from their very inception
they have possessed nothing except what they have seized –
home, spouses, lands, empire? That they were formerly migrants
without fatherland or parents, founded to be a plague[105] upon
the globe, who are prevented by nothing human or divine from
looting and destroying allies and friends, peoples distant and
nearby, needy or powerful, and from regarding everything
which is not subservient – especially monarchies – as their
18   enemy? Only a few want freedom, the majority want masters
who are just; we are suspect, as rivals and, at the right time,
19   future avengers. As for yourself, who possess Seleucea,[106] greatest of cities, and the kingdom of Persis with its fabled riches,
what can you expect from them except guile at present and
20   afterwards war? The Romans keep their arms directed at everyone, the sharpest against those who, when conquered, afford
the greatest spoils; it is by daring and deceiving, and by seeding
21   wars from wars, that they have become great: by these means
they will annihilate everything – or they will fall if (and this is
not difficult) you and we, respectively from Mesopotamia and
Armenia, encircle an army without grain and without help but,
thanks to fortune or our own deficiencies, still unscathed.
22   You will be attended by the reputation that, having set out to
23   help great kings, you crushed the world's bandits. That is what
I advise and urge you to do; do not prefer postponing your
destruction at the expense of ours to becoming the conqueror
in an alliance.'

Notes

Notes to *Catiline's War*

1. *Cyrus ... nations*: In the mid 6th century Cyrus the Great by a series of conquests became 'the first Persian king to bring together territories into an imperial framework' (*OCD*, p. 423). At roughly the same time the Spartans (Lacedaemonians) started to form what is known as the 'Peloponnesian League' of allied cities (*OCD*, pp. 1133–4), while in the early 5th century Athens established the Delian League, which in due course became indistinguishable from an Athenian empire (*OCD*, pp. 441–2).

2. *change in fortune*: I.e. for those in command, who, when their behaviour deteriorates, find themselves supplanted by someone else.

3. *finds*: The meanings of the Latin verb *quaerere*, which Sallust uses here, include 'seek', 'obtain as the result of one's efforts', 'acquire' (*OLD*).

4. *commonwealth*: *Res publica* is commonly translated as 'the commonwealth' or 'the state'.

5. *author*: Here used in the sense of 'performer', referring to the person who performs deeds, not to the person who writes about them (and who has just been mentioned). Sallust is deliberately using language which will suggest an equivalence between the roles of writer and performer.

6. *nor to spend my life ... slaves*: Others translate 'nor to spend my life concentrating on agriculture or hunting, servile tasks'; but the difficulty with the traditional interpretation is that agriculture and hunting were not regarded as 'servile tasks' by the Romans: indeed Cato the Elder, whom Sallust imitates frequently (and in this very sentence), famously wrote a work on agriculture.

7. *Sulla*: Dictator 82–81; see *Jug.* 95.

8. *Rome ... unrestricted*: There were two principal legends

concerning the foundation of Rome: that the city was founded
by Aeneas and other survivors of the Trojan War (*OCD*,
pp. 22–3) and that it was founded by Romulus and Remus
(*OCD*, p. 1335). At some point the two stories were combined
and made consistent with each other. Sallust's phrase 'on my
understanding' indicates his awareness of other traditions besides
the one he adopts here. The story of Aeneas is the subject of
Virgil's epic, the *Aeneid*. 'Aborigines' was a name given to pre-
Roman inhabitants of Italy.

9.   *fathers*: Sallust is referring to members of the senate, 'fathers'
being an alternative term for 'senators'.

10.   *haughty domineering*: A reference to the last king of Rome,
Tarquinius Superbus or 'Tarquin the Haughty' (traditionally
534–510).

11.   *annual commands and paired commanders*: The consulship; the
traditional date of its establishment is 509.

12.   *greatly talented writers*: Presumably referring to Thucydides,
Xenophon, Demosthenes and Isocrates, the most famous
Athenian prose writers.

13.   *punishment ... contrary to command*: For an example, see
52.30.

14.   *Carthage ... eradicated*: Sallust regarded the destruction of
Carthage in 146 as a turning-point in Roman history: see especially *Jug.* 41.2–3 and *Hist.* 1.12.

15.   *desire for money ... then for empire*: Contradicted by 11.1,
where avarice takes second place to ambition. There is thus a
strong possibility that in the present sentence the words 'money'
and 'empire' have been wrongly transposed by a scribe who was
misled by the sequence 'For avarice ...' and 'Ambition
reduced ...' in 10.4 and 5. In other words, it is likely that Sallust's
original arrangement in 10.3–5 was chiastic (empire ... money
~ avarice ... ambition).

16.   *wicked ... beginning*: See *Jug.* 95.4 and note.

17.   *the army ... ancestral custom*: The reference is to the First
Mithridatic War, 88–85.

18.   *undermined ... the seas*: Latin authors frequently refer to the
remarkable seaside villas which were constructed by the wealthy
and which often incorporated parts of cliffs and the like: see
J. H. D'Arms, *Romans on the Bay of Naples* (1970).

19.   *slept ... anticipated them all*: I.e. they used appetizers and emet-
ics to provoke hunger and thirst, and resorted unnecessarily to
warm baths and sleep.

20. *Pompeius . . . distant lands*: Pompey the Great was in the east fighting Mithridates 66–63, not returning home till 62.

21. *high hopes of . . . consulship*: I.e. candidature in 64 for the consulship of 63.

22. *Kalends of June*: 1 June (64).

23. *Sura . . . Curius*: Lentulus Sura had been praetor in 74, consul in 71, and would hold a second praetorship in 63 (see 46.5); Autronius Paetus had been quaestor in 75, the same year as Cicero, and was consul designate for 65 but subsequently disqualified for bribery (see 18.2); Cassius Longinus had been praetor along with Cicero in 66. Servius, father of the two Sullas, was brother of the dictator Sulla (5.6). L. Calpurnius Bestia was tribune of the plebs in 62; Q. Curius (on whose key role see 23.1–4, 26.3, 28.2) had perhaps been quaestor in 71. No details are known of the careers of Cethegus, the two Sullas (the P. Sulla described at 18.2 as a consul designate is a different person), Vargunteius, Annius Chilo or Porcius Laeca.

24. *Fulvius . . . Cornelius*: Little is known of these equestrians apart from their roles in the Catilinarian narrative.

25. *Crassus*: Consul in 70, censor in 65, and consul again in 55. See *OCD*, pp. 857–8.

26. *briefly*: The manuscripts have 'truthfully' (*uerissume*) but the grammarian Diomedes, quoting this sentence, reads 'briefly' (*breuissume*), and brevity seems to be Sallust's aim in this digression (see 19.6, 'about the earlier conspiracy enough has been said'). The subject of the digression is the so-called First Catilinarian Conspiracy, 'a peculiar fabrication' (Syme, *Sallust*, p. 87).

27. *consulship of . . . Tullus and . . . Lepidus*: I.e. 66.

28. *laws of canvassing*: Assumed to be the Lex Calpurnia of 67, whose punishments comprised a fine, expulsion from the senate and disqualification from holding office.

29. *consulship*: Evidently referring to the consular election held later in 66 to replace the two disqualified consuls designate.

30. *Piso*: In 66 Cn. Calpurnius Piso was elected quaestor for the following year (see 19.1). Though Sallust describes him as an 'adolescent', the term is somewhat flexible, since the minimum age for the quaestorship was twenty-seven.

31. *Nones of December*: 5 December (of 66).

32. *Kalends of January*: 1 January (of 65).

33. *fasces*: A bundle comprising rods and an axe, carried by lictors (see *Jug.* 12.3) and symbolizing magisterial (especially consular) office. See *OCD*, pp. 587–8.

34. *two Spains*: The two Spanish provinces (mentioned again at *Jug.*
     19.4; *Hist.* 1.77.8) were formed in 197 as Nearer Spain (see *Cat.*
     19.1, 21.3; *Hist.* 2.98.9) and Further Spain (*Hist.* 2.70). See
     OCD, pp. 1429–50.

35. *Nones of February*: 5 February (of 65).

36. *curia*: The senate house; mentioned again at 32.1, 43.3; *Jug.*
     15.2.

37. *praetorian power*: Provinces were normally governed by pro-
     magistrates, viz. ex-praetors or ex-consuls; when for some reason
     a less-qualified governor was in charge, as here, he was given
     the appropriate power during his term of office (see *OCD*,
     pp. 1248–9). Piso may well have been originally assigned to the
     province as subordinate to a governor who died before he could
     take up office.

38. *tetrarchs*: Minor eastern kings under Roman protection (see also
     Hist. 4.69.10).

39. *rejections*: At the electoral polls.

40. *For how long ... men?*: Sallust puts into Catiline's mouth a
     striking allusion to the first sentence with which Cicero attacked
     Catiline in his First Catilinarian speech on 8 November 63:
     'For how long, then, Catiline, will you exploit our endurance?'
     Likewise, Catiline's addressing his followers as 'most courageous
     of men' recalls Cicero's expression 'courageous men', used a little
     later of those whose outlook resembles Cicero's own (*In Cat.*
     1.2, 3).

41. *riches ... mountains*: See 13.1 and note.

42. *unable to achieve victory over their riches*: I.e. they have so much
     money that, no matter how much they spend, there is always
     enough left. Sallust's metaphors are drawn from warfare.

43. *fresh accounts*: I.e. the cancellation of all debt.

44. *Piso ... Mauretania*: For Piso see 18.4–5 and 19.1–5; P. Sittius
     was an equestrian and financier whom Sallust probably knew
     personally (they both had African connections).

45. *Antonius ... constraint*: C. Antonius Hybrida, uncle of Mark
     Antony, had been praetor along with Cicero in 66 and would be
     the latter's consular colleague in 63 (24.1). Catiline hoped that
     Antonius' being 'hampered' by financial constraints would secure
     his allegiance but he was detached from Catiline by Cicero (26.4),
     although he did not face his former ally in the decisive battle
     (59.4).

46. *said repeatedly that he was doing so*: Reading *dictitasse facere*
     instead of the transmitted *dictitare fecisse*.

47. *resentment . . . which arose later*: Though Cicero was regarded as a hero immediately after the suppression of the Catilinarian conspiracy, his role in the punishment of the conspirators was later used against him and in 58 he was forced into exile, from which he returned in the following year.

48. *the seas and the summits*: Proverbial for 'the whole world' or similar.

49. *new man*: See Introduction, note 6.

50. *Manlius . . . war*: Little is otherwise known of Manlius. Faesulae is modern-day Fiesole.

51. *Sempronia*: She reappears in the story only at 40.5, where the absence from Rome of her husband (D. Iunius Brutus, the consul of 77) is noted.

52. *for the next year*: I.e. for 62. The 'preparations' which Sallust mentions at the start of the sentence are those of 24.2–4 ('he prepared arms . . . kill them').

53. *settling the matter of his province*: The consuls of any given year would determine by lot or agreement which of them should govern the provinces assigned to them by the Lex Sempronia (see *Jug.* 27.3 and note). In the present case the allocated provinces were Cisalpine Gaul and Macedonia; Cicero renounced any claim to the latter, which was the richer, in favour of his colleague Antonius.

54. *Plain*: The Plain of Mars (Campus Martius), where the elections were held. See J. R. Patterson, *Political Life in the City of Rome* (2000).

55. *Septimius . . . Iulius*: Nothing else is known of them.

56. *there*: A reference to Laeca's house; the night was that of 6/7 November (Cicero, *Sull.* 52).

57. *Sullan colonies*: When Sulla returned from his eastern campaigns (11.5), he settled his veterans on land in Etruria and Campania, as well as other areas, evicting the previous occupants.

58. *should do their utmost . . . any damage*: The so-called *senatus consultum ultimum* (see also *Hist.* 1.77.22), whose language is represented slightly differently by different authors, was passed on 21 or 22 October. At 28.4 ('Meanwhile . . .') Sallust has reverted to a period before that described in the intervening paragraph (27.2–28.3).

59. *the sixth day before the Kalends of November*: 27 October (so too Cicero, *In Cat.* 1.7), the only specific date given by Sallust in the year 63.

60. *Rex . . . holding a triumph*: Q. Marcius Rex had been consul in

68 and proconsul of Cilicia the following year; Q. Metellus Creticus had been consul in 69 and proconsul in Crete and Achaea 68–65. Commanders holding *imperium* could not normally enter the City of Rome; a triumph could not be celebrated except by a commander holding *imperium*: hence those hoping to celebrate a triumph had to wait outside the City until permission was granted. Marcius Rex died without ever celebrating a triumph; Metellus Creticus had to wait till 62 for his.

61. *Rufus . . . Celer*: Pompeius Rufus became proconsul in Africa the following year; Q. Caecilius Metellus Celer became consul in 60.

62. *Paullus*: L. Aemilius Lepidus Paullus became consul in 50.

63. *Plautian Law*: Covering acts of violence against the state or individuals.

64. *written version*: Cicero's First Catilinarian, delivered on 8 November 63 (see Introduction, pp. xvi–xvii).

65. *patrician*: A member of one of Rome's oldest and most aristocratic families (*OCD*, pp. 1123–4).

66. *immigrant citizen . . . of Rome*: Though Cicero was born 60 miles from Rome in Arpinum, inhabitants of that town had enjoyed full rights as Roman citizens for over a hundred years.

67. *parricide*: The word is not restricted to a killer of one's father and is often used metaphorically (see e.g. *Cat.* 51.25, 52.31; *Hist.* 1.55.24, 2.47.3).

68. *extinguish . . . demolition*: A reference to the practice of demolishing buildings in order to stop the spread of a fire (see e.g. Tacitus, *Annals* 15.40.1).

69. *dead of night*: The night was that of 8/9 November: see Cicero, *In Cat.* 2.12 (delivered on 9 November but not mentioned by Sallust).

70. *lacking . . . in*: The translation has both 'lacking' and 'lacking in' (with 'lacking' to be understood in the latter case) because there is an equivalent variation in the Latin.

71. *praetor*: Matters involving debt came under the jurisdiction of the urban praetor (also 33.5).

72. *silver . . . debt*: A reference to the Lex Valeria of 86, named after L. Valerius Flaccus (*OCD*, p. 1578).

73. *secession from the fathers*: There were reputedly three 'secessions of the plebs' (in 494, 449 and 287), demonstrations of independence and discontent (*OCD*, p. 1376). Sallust here, as at *Hist.* 3.48.1, uses 'fathers' as a synonym for 'patricians' (for which see 31.7 note). See also *Jug.* 31.6, 31.17; *Hist.* 1.11, 3.48.1, 3.48.17.

74. *Massilia*: Modern-day Marseille.

75. *Catulus*: Consul in 78 (see *Hist.* 1.1). See also *Cat.* 49.1–2; *Hist.* 1.77.6, 3.48.9; *OCD*, p. 893.

76. *revolutionary scheme*: The adjective (Latin, *nouo*) is deliberately ambiguous between its literal and metaphorical meanings: it could refer equally to Catiline's going to Manlius' camp (cf. 32.1, 36.1) or into exile at Massilia (cf. 34.2).

77. *asked . . . your children*: The reference is obscure.

78. *Flaminius . . . Arretium*: Nothing else is known of Flaminius. Arretium is modern-day Arezzo.

79. *senate's decrees*: See 30.3–7 (especially 6) and 36.2–3 (especially 2).

80. *Sullan victory . . . same*: This seems primarily to refer to the fact that in 81 Sulla, after returning to Rome from the east, doubled the membership of the senate from 300 to 600 and enriched many of the new members by dubious means.

81. *whose right to freedom had been curtailed*: See *Hist.* 1.55.6 and note.

82. *consulship . . . Crassus*: In 70.

83. *Pompeius . . . wars*: Pompey was given commands against the pirates in 67 (by the Lex Gabinia) and against Mithridates in 66 (by the Lex Manilia).

84. *There were . . . executed*: With this sentence Sallust resumes the narrative of 36.5 before it was interrupted by the intervening digression. Neither of the Fulvii mentioned here is otherwise known.

85. *Umbrenus . . . Allobroges*: Umbrenus is not known outside the Catilinarian narrative. The Allobroges were a Celtic tribe from the province of Transalpine Gaul; their legates were in Rome to ask the senate for relief from the debt into which they had fallen as a result of Roman taxation.

86. *Sanga . . . relied*: A local community would often have a patron to represent its interests. Such relationships were hereditary: the otherwise unknown Sanga was presumably a descendant of Q. Fabius Maximus Allobrogicus, first conqueror of the Allobroges.

87. *Nearer and Further Gaul*: Alternative names for Cisalpine and Transalpine Gaul.

88. *C. Murena . . . legate*: C. Licinius Murena was temporarily standing in for his brother, L. Licinius Murena (consul 62), proconsul in Transalpine Gaul (whether 'Nearer Gaul' is a mistake of the author or of a scribe is unclear).

89. *Catiline . . . Faesulae*: One would expect Catiline to have arrived

at Manlius' camp at Faesulae long since (see 36.1–2), and his plan was to come *from* there to Rome (32.2, 43.2, 44.6); it is generally agreed that 'Faesulae' here is wrong, but whether the mistake is that of Sallust or a scribe is unclear.

90. *Volturcius*: Not known outside the Catilinarian narrative.

91. *written below*: The same letter is quoted, with slight differences in wording, by Cicero (*In Cat.* 3.12).

92. *praetors ... Pomptinus*: In the following year Valerius Flaccus became governor of the province of Asia, and Pomptinus of Transalpine Gaul in succession to Murena (see 42.3 note).

93. *Milvian Bridge*: Carrying the Flaminian Way north across the River Tiber.

94. *Caeparius*: Nothing else is known of him.

95. *had summoned*: Reading *aduocarat* for the transmitted *aduocat*.

96. *Sibylline books*: Collection of oracular texts held in the temple of Jupiter Capitolinus under the care of the priests known as quindecemvirs. See *OCD*, pp. 1400–1401.

97. *three Cornelii ... fated*: Cornelius was the gentile (family) name of Cinna, who was consul in four consecutive years (87–84), and of Sulla, who was dictator 82–81 (see 5.6 note), as well as of Lentulus himself.

98. *burning of the Capitol*: In 83 (see Cicero, *In Cat.* 3.9).

99. *Lentulus Spinther ... senator*: Lentulus Spinther was consul in 57; Cornificius had been praetor in or before 66; C. Caesar is Julius Caesar, the five-times consul and dictator; for Crassus see 17.7 note; Terentius is otherwise unknown.

100. *conspiracy revealed*: Seemingly an oblique allusion to Cicero's Third Catilinarian speech, delivered before the people on 3 December.

101. *Tarquinius*: Otherwise unknown. The 'day' to which Sallust refers was 4 December (see previous note).

102. *Piso*: Consul in 67, becoming governor in Transalpine and Cisalpine Gaul until 65. This paragraph about hostility to Caesar interrupts the main narrative of the conspiracy, to which Sallust returns at 50.1 ('While this was going on . . .').

103. *attacked ... Transpadane*: Earlier in 63 Piso had been prosecuted by Caesar for extortion during his governorship of Gaul and defended by Cicero. The term translated here as 'reprisal' (*supplicium*) is sometimes short for 'ultimate reprisal' (*summum supplicium*), meaning execution (see 51.39). Execution is certainly meant at 50.4 and 52.36; here too the likely meaning is that

Caesar had accused Piso of an unwarranted execution. 'Transpadane' refers to the area of Cisalpine Gaul north of the River Po
or to someone living there.

104. *pontificate . . . Caesar*: The election to the office of high priest
(*pontifex maximus*) had taken place in 64 or earlier in 63 when
Caesar was thirty-seven and Catulus about twenty years older.
The latter was also a senior consular (78), as was the other
unsuccessful candidate, Servilius Isauricus (79).

105. *a motion . . . custody*: This was the famous debate of 5 December
at which Cicero delivered his Fourth Catilinarian speech; Sallust
omits all reference to this, but instead puts lengthy speeches into
the mouths of Caesar (51) and Cato (52.2–36).

106. *Silanus*: Consul in 62.

107. *reprisal*: I.e. execution.

108. *Furius*: Not previously mentioned and not known outside the
Catilinarian narrative (see Cicero, *In Cat.* 3.14).

109. *he had said*: Retaining the manuscripts' *dixerat*. This reading
suggests that the section of text which I have bracketed is in
parenthesis, referring to an earlier debate and not to the famous
debate of 5 December, which, having been introduced at 50.3, is
returned to at 50.5. The OCT accepts the emendation *dixit* ('he
said'), evidently on the assumption that the debate of 5 December
is being referred to throughout.

110. *Nero*: Ti. Claudius Nero was grandfather of the future emperor
Tiberius.

111. *conscript fathers*: A traditional way of referring to senators.

112. *Macedonian War . . . Perseus*: The Third Macedonian War,
171–168. See *Hist.* 4.69.7 and note.

113. *Rhodians . . . Roman people*: The people of Rhodes had helped
Rome in the war against Antiochus III (see *Hist.* 4.69.6 and note)
and had been rewarded by extensive territories in Asia Minor.

114. *all the Punic Wars*: There were three Punic Wars: 264–241,
218–201 and 149–146.

115. *Porcian Law*: Three Porcian laws were passed between 195 and
181, limiting the punishment which a magistrate could inflict on
a Roman citizen. One of the laws may have been the work of the
Elder Cato.

116. *thirty men . . . commonwealth*: After the Spartans defeated the
Athenians in the Peloponnesian War (431–404), they imposed
on them the rule of the so-called Thirty Tyrants.

117. *Damasippus*: As praetor in 82 L. Iunius Brutus Damasippus

killed several prominent individuals on the orders of the consul, C. Marius (son of the famous Marius), and then was himself killed by Sulla after the battle of the Colline Gate.

118. *Samnites*: Inhabitants of Samnium, an area of central Italy (*OCD*, p. 1351).

119. *Cato*: Great-grandson of the famous Elder Cato (the Censor), he had been quaestor in 64 and was currently tribune-elect for 62.

120. *I propose . . . still armed*: The sentence is of course ironical.

121. *Torquatus . . . command*: This famous incident involved T. (not A.) Manlius Torquatus in the Latin War of 340 (not the Gallic War twenty years earlier). See also 9.4.

122. *twice*: The reference is uncertain.

123. *triumvirs*: Latin *tresviri capitales*, minor officials who oversaw executions.

124. *Nor . . . flight*: As it stands, this sentence is rather opaque. It has been much discussed and the text variously emended.

125. *Cimbrian War*: Marius defeated the invading Cimbri at Vercellae, in the Po valley, in 101; see also *Jug.* 114.

126. *Petreius*: Praetor at some point before the present year.

Notes to *The Jugurthine War*

1. *or its subjects*: Or perhaps 'or your parents'. The Latin word *parentes* can mean both.

2. *relinquishing . . . power of a few*: Sallust seems to be referring to those, like P. Servilius Isauricus (consul in 41), who held office as mere creatures of the Triumvirs (here described as the 'few'): see Syme, *Sallust*, pp. 216–18.

3. *seeking their favour . . . dinner-parties*: The reference is to bribing the lower classes in return for their electoral support.

4. *Maximus . . . prowess*: Q. Fabius Maximus Cunctator, the first of whose several consulships was in 233, was the famous opponent of Hannibal; P. Scipio could be either of those mentioned below (5.4, 7.4). The ancestral images to which Sallust here refers were wax face masks (see next note): they were kept in cupboards in the atrium of a house and brought out for funerals, when they would be worn by individuals impersonating the ancestors. Other forms of ancestral image were painted portraits (illustrating a family tree) and busts of various kinds: see H. I. Flower, *Aristocratic Masks and Aristocratic Power in Roman Culture* (1996).

5. *it is not that wax nor . . . power in it*: The implied contrast is

between the wax of which ancestral images were moulded and the wax tablets on which would be written the historical texts to which Sallust is about to refer.

6. *new men*: See Introduction, note 6. Such 'newness' (85.14) recurs frequently in *Jug.*: 8.1, 63.7, 65.5, 73.7, 85.13, 85.25.

7. *I ... turn*: For this meaning of *redeo* see D. H. Berry, *Cicero: Pro P. Sulla Oratio* (1996), p. 209.

8. *Second Punic War*: 218–201.

9. *P. Scipio ... prowess*: P. Cornelius Scipio Africanus, consul in 205 and 194.

10. *Syphax*: Chief of a Numidian tribe, the Masaesuli; after siding with the Carthaginians against the Romans, he was captured by the latter in 203 and died in captivity in Italy two years later (*OCD*, p. 1463).

11. *when during the Numantine War ... Roman people*: The reference is to 134, the penultimate year of the lengthy siege of Numantia (near modern-day Garray), a town in northern Spain.

12. *P. Scipio*: P. Cornelius Scipio Aemilianus, consul in 147 and 134, who later acquired the cognomen Numantinus.

13. *our men*: It is characteristic of Roman (but not of Greek) historians sometimes to refer to their own side as 'us', 'our men' etc. (see J. Marincola, *Authority and Tradition in Ancient Historiography* (1997), pp. 287–8).

14. *overcome resentment ... glory*: Normally resentment would be the *consequence* of glory (as at 55.3), but Jugurtha has successfully avoided it.

15. *lictor*: Lictors were officials who accompanied a magistrate at Rome (*OCD*, p. 860); Sallust has transferred the term to Numidia.

16. *keys ... delivered to Hiempsal*: I.e. at the end of each day.

17. *province*: I.e. the Roman province of Africa, founded after the destruction of Carthage in 146.

18. *Aemilius Scaurus*: Consul in 115.

19. *tainted freehandedness*: Retaining *polluta licentia* on the admittedly questionable assumption that the noun can be used *tout court* to refer to bribery. The participle too has been widely queried, and it is not clear whether the *licentia* is Jugurtha's (as translated) or that of his recipients.

20. *L. Opimius ... harshness*: L. Opimius was consul in 121. In the aftermath of the deaths of the radical Gaius Gracchus and his associate Flaccus (consul in 125), their supporters were evidently killed in large numbers.

21. *only Asia . . . in Europe*: The ancients divided the world into two
    or three vast areas: in the threefold division, Africa was an area
    to itself; on the other scheme, Africa was regarded as part of
    either Europe (as Sallust says) or Asia.

22. *As its boundaries . . . west*: Sallust refers to the Straits of Gibral-
    tar, separating 'Our Sea' (the Mediterranean; again at 18.4 and
    12 and *Hist.* 1.11) and 'Ocean' (here the Atlantic; cf. 18.5 and
    Hist. 1.11, 4.69.17), which in the ancient imagination was
    regarded as a great river encircling the whole world. See
    J. S. Romm, *The Edges of the Earth in Ancient Thought* (1992).

23. *Catabathmos*: A Greek formation, meaning 'a step down', and
    therefore etymologized by 'sloping'.

24. *King Hiempsal's*: Not the Hiempsal already mentioned (5.7, 9.4–
    12.6), who was Jugurtha's adoptive brother, but Hiempsal II,
    grandson of Mastanabal (5.6–7) and nephew of Jugurtha; he
    was father of Juba I, an ally of Pompey the Great.

25. *Nomads*: The Greek word for 'pasture' is *nomos*; *nomades* are
    those who move from pasture to pasture.

26. *each party relying on the other*: I.e. the Persians and the Gaet-
    ulians.

27. *going with the sea's current*: I.e. from east to west, according to an
    ancient belief that the Mediterranean flowed out into the Ocean.

28. *Cyrene . . . Thera*: Cyrene is modern-day Shahat (*OCD*,
    pp. 421–2) and Thera is Santorini (*OCD*, p. 1507).

29. *Syrtes . . . empire*: In fact the order of these places from east to
    west is the Greater Syrtis (modern-day Gulf of Sidra or Sirte),
    the Altars of the Philaeni (for them see 79.2–10), Leptis Magna
    (Lebda in Libya), the Lesser Syrtis (Gulf of Gabès, Tunisia),
    something 'one would hardly gather from Sallust's description'
    (Summers).

30. *the Spains*: For the two Spanish provinces see *Cat.* 18.5 note.

31. *held most recently*: I.e. before the Third Punic War (149–146).

32. *Mauri*: Henceforth the translation will refer to these people as
    'Moors'.

33. *crowd of civilians*: Literally, 'of men wearing the toga', i.e. from
    Italy (see 26.2).

34. *both for themselves and for them*: I.e. both for the Romans and
    for the two warring parties.

35. *kind*: I.e. favourable to Jugurtha.

36. *law of nations*: *Ius gentium* is defined as 'A universally recognized
    code or rule of behaviour between nations or individuals' (*OLD
    ius* 8a). See also *Jug.* 35.7; *Hist.* 3.48.17.

37. *kindnesses*: To Jugurtha.
38. *same supporters of the king*: See 13.7–9, 15.2, 16.1.
39. *province*: Viz. Africa (see 13.4 note), of which Utica was the capital.
40. *Italians ... defenced*: See 21.2. The translation 'defenced' is to be explained by the fact that Sallust has used a much rarer verb (*defensare*) than the normal 'defend' (*defendere*); so too at 60.3 (and 97.5, where a different translation is required).
41. *armed men*: Reading *armatis*; other manuscripts have *armatus* ('and any armed businessmen that were encountered').
42. *Sempronian Law ... next consuls*: The Lex Sempronia of Gaius Gracchus (123) laid down that, before the elections, two provinces (or 'spheres of duty') should be assigned to the upcoming consuls; after the elections, the actual assignment of the provinces between the consuls was determined by lot or agreement (see *Cat.* 26.4). The year being discussed here is 111.
43. *after killing Hiempsal*: See 13.6.
44. *and resentment*: Reading *inuidias*; other manuscripts have *insidias* ('and ambush').
45. *grain ... truce was being observed*: Military convention dictated that the Romans had the right to demand grain from the Numidians since the latter had requested a truce; but 'openly' suggests that secret negotiations were already in progress between the consul and Jugurtha.
46. *on a collective basis*: The phrase (*per saturam*) was apparently applied technically to a law subsumed amongst other laws: here the council members' opinions seem to have been sought on all aspects of the surrender simultaneously rather than item by item.
47. *a faction*: I.e. the nobility.
48. *secession*: See *Cat.* 33.3 and *Jug.* 31.17 notes.
49. *Ti. Gracchus ... was slain*: Elder brother of Gaius (16.2 note) and killed in 133.
50. *slaughter ... Fulvius*: See 16.2 note.
51. *paid tax to a few nobles*: See *Cat.* 20.7.
52. *they have transferred ... apathy*: I.e. they ought to feel dread themselves because of their criminal behaviour, but the citizens, because of their apathy, feel it instead.
53. *kindnesses*: A way of referring to the electoral process, whereby the people were regarded as doing a kindness to those whom they elected to office.
54. *Aventine in armed secession*: For the three 'secessions of the plebs' see *Cat.* 33.3 note; whether the Aventine Hill in Rome was

the destination of more than one of them is disputed. See *OCD*,
p. 1376.

55. *if you do not . . . in future*: Others translate 'if they do not extort
from you the licence so to act in future'.

56. *L. Cassius*: L. Cassius Longinus, who became consul in 107.

57. *everything . . . mentioned above*: Especially at 29.3–6.

58. *reprisal*: Execution. See *Cat.* 49.2 note.

59. *him over there*: Memmius is perhaps to be imagined as pointing
towards Jugurtha.

60. *in the year after Bestia*: I.e. 110. Sp. Postumius Albinus' colleague
was in fact M. Minucius Rufus; it was the latter's brother whose
first name was Quintus.

61. *in the earlier proceedings*: Presumably a reference to Bomilcar's
first appearance in court (at 35.7).

62. *propraetor*: Here, as at 37.3 and 103.4, the term refers to an
officer (*legatus*) left in charge of the army in the commander's
absence.

63. *in the month of January*: The date (109) conflicts with 43.1,
where the consuls of 109 are described as still 'designate' and the
aftermath of Aulus' forthcoming rout is therefore attributed to
the year 110. Some scholars thus delete 'in the month of January'
here as a scribal gloss on 'the harshness of winter'.

64. *legate*: Used here to mean 'deputy' (which is what Aulus was:
36.4), though Sallust uses the same word in another of its senses,
'delegates' or 'ambassadors', immediately below.

65. *denes*: A dene is a defile, often wooded.

66. *squadrons*: Latin *turmae*, mentioned quite frequently from now
on, are cavalry units.

67. *those of the Latin name*: At this period, inhabitants of Latium
(the area south of Rome), who enjoyed a diminished form of
Roman citizenship known as the 'Latin right': see *OCD*,
pp. 790–91.

68. *tribune of the plebs*: His tribunate was in 109.

69. *They*: Presumably the nobles.

70. *Bestia's legate*: See 28.4.

71. *the destruction of Carthage*: In 146.

72. *more harsh and bitter*: I.e. than the adverse circumstances themselves.

73. *Ti. and C. Gracchus . . . other wars*: The maternal grandfather
of the Gracchi was P. Cornelius Scipio Africanus (5.4); their
father had enjoyed military success in Spain and Sardinia (180–
177).

74. *hope of sharing*: Presumably power.

75. *Tiberius . . . Flaccus*: Ti. Gracchus was killed during his tribunate in 133; C. Gracchus had been, or was, a member of the commission overseeing the foundation of a colony on the site of Carthage, when he and M. Fulvius Flaccus were killed in 121. See also 16.2.

76. *it is preferable . . . immoral one*: Whether the Latin is to be translated thus and, if so, what the meaning is, are matters of dispute.

77. *treaty . . . foul*: Sallust here puns on the Latin words for 'treaty' (*foedus*) and 'foul' (also *foedus*).

78. *consuls designate*: Q. Caecilius Metellus and M. Iunius Silanus were consuls in 109 and hence were designate in 110. Their description here therefore conflicts with the earlier statement that Aulus' rout occurred in or shortly after January of 109 (37.3 and note).

79. *kings*: I.e. kings friendly to Rome.

80. *delay to the elections*: See 37.1–2.

81. *on sideways routes*: Presumably Sallust means longer (and hence more testing) routes than the more direct alternatives.

82. *mapalia*: See 18.8.

83. *grain*: See 29.4 note.

84. *C. Marius*: See 63.1–7 on this famous figure.

85. *Numidia . . . division*: See 16.2 and 5.

86. *mountain . . . parallel course*: The distance between the parallel courses of river and mountain has been impugned as absurdly wide, and, since numerals are notoriously prone to corruption in manuscripts, *iii* or *vii* have been suggested instead of *xx*.

87. *middle of it*: Sallust seems to mean the middle of the mountain, though some think that he means the middle of the area between the mountain and river.

88. *sideways route*: The reference seems to be to 48.3. Scholars are not agreed whether Sallust's phrase *transuorso itinere* means 'sideways to the mountain' or 'sideways to Metellus' line of march'. The former, adopted here, seems better suited to the general context (Sallust's accounts, below, of Metellus' route and his troop deployment); but such phrases as *transuorso itinere* are normally used of persons (e.g. 45.2), and there seems to be no parallel for *iter* used of a hill or mountain.

89. *he himself . . . his men*: Whether this is the correct rendering of a very strange sentence is unclear.

90. *maniples*: A maniple was 'a unit of infantry in the Roman army,

consisting of two centuries, a third of a cohort' (*OLD* 3a): i.e. a total of 120 men. See also *OCD*, p. 918.

91. *At first Metellus ... drawn it up*: Sallust's account of Metellus' manoeuvres is very difficult to understand. Metellus first transforms his marching column (49.5) into a battle-line (49.6). If we assume that his army is being described in the terms of the late second century BC, the strange phrase 'threefold support' will probably refer to the traditional battle-line consisting of the three ranks of *hastati*, *principes* and *triarii*. Since Jugurtha's men were evidently stretched out along the hill on the right flank of the Romans' marching column, Metellus' rearrangement will have resulted in his triple line facing right. However, since Metellus' object was to reach and cross the plain, he must have ordered his men, while remaining in battle formation, to turn left and to resume their march in its original direction. As a result, the Roman vanguard ends up 'sideways on' (49.6) and, when the army resumes its march, the left wing becomes the vanguard (50.2). Confusingly, the word translated as 'vanguard' at 49.6 (*principium*) is normally the collective noun for the *principes*, who, despite their name, fought in the second line. Even more confusingly, we are told that Marius was in charge of the *postprincipia* (50.2), which, despite its name, also denotes the second line (*OLD* 2); and that Metellus ended up among the *principes* (50.2). Since it seems absurd for Sallust to refer so frequently to the second line, it is assumed that he is using *principium* and *principes* to refer to the front line.

His apparent misuse of technical military terms raises a further question. During the late second and early first centuries BC, the Roman army abandoned the maniple as a unit and adopted the cohort instead. The present battle is often said to be the last in which maniples were deployed (cf. 49.6), but whether Sallust, like Tacitus many years later, was using the term anachronistically is uncertain. Indeed, since the technical name for the later cohort formation was the 'triple line' (*triplex acies*), Sallust's reference to 'the line as a threefold support' may indicate that some of his terminology here is that of his own day. For these issues see J. E. Lendon, *Soldiers and Ghosts: A History of Battle in Classical Antiquity* (2005), pp. 427–8.

92. *P. Rutilius*: P. Rutilius Rufus, consul in 105, wrote an autobiography which Sallust is thought to have used for his account of the Muthul battle.

93. *they*: The Romans.

94. *where he had been sent ahead*: The area near the river: see 50.1.
95. *but the land ... plundering. He led ... the rest*: These two sentences are in the opposite order in the manuscripts but the resulting sense is poor. Their transposition effects a slight improvement and is adopted in the OCT.
96. *project*: For which see 54.6 and 55.4–7.
97. *yet they ... for too long*: Or perhaps, 'nor would the Numidians have been able to resist for too long' (the Latin can mean either). The remainder of this paragraph too is problematic. It is assumed here that the 'combination of infantry and cavalry' is Roman and that the 'almost defeated enemy' are the Numidians; but numerous interpreters have it the other way round.
98. *former ... latter*: The infantry are 'the former' and the cavalry are 'the latter'.
99. *In this way ... enemy*: The exact meaning of this sentence is uncertain: 'waiting' renders *expeditis*, which is assumed to be dative and to mean literally 'prepared' or 'ready', but the word may be ablative and may refer to light-armed troops.
100. *the winter ... province*: Winter of 109–108. The 'province' is of course Africa (13.4 note).
101. *Bomilcar ... betrayal*: See 35.4–9 for Bomilcar's great friendship with Jugurtha and his vicissitudes at Rome.
102. *in the same place as a cadet of his father's*: Literally, 'in the same tent with his father'. Q. Metellus Pius could not have been expected to reach the consulship before 86 and did not in fact reach it until 80, almost thirty years later.
103. *Gauda ... diminished responsibility*: Gauda was Jugurtha's half-brother (see 5.7). A secondary heir would inherit if the first heir(s) failed to take up an inheritance for one reason or another.
104. *terms*: I.e. terms agreed with the conspirators.
105. *turpitude*: Sallust here plays on Turpilius' name.
106. *for he was a citizen from Latium*: The meaning and significance of these words are controversial. *Roman* citizens were not supposed to be beaten and killed, but it is not clear whether Sallust means 'he was a <Roman> citizen, from Latium', for example, or 'he was a citizen with only Latin rights' (for which see 39.2 note). R. Seager tentatively suggests reading *ex Lati<n>o*, 'only from/after being a Latin', the man's change of status explaining Metellus' contempt for him.
107. *abandoned in dread*: See 62.1–9.
108. *as the situation demanded*: The Latin says *uti res posceret, ex tempore* ('as the situation demanded, in accordance with the

needs of the moment'), which seems redundant. The latter phrase
has been deleted as a gloss.

109. *magistrates*: Tribunes.

110. *a new man . . . consulship*: Marius' election in 108 to the consulship of 107 was the first of a new man since that of P. Rupilius,
consul in 132. Marius' colleague was to be L. Cassius Longinus
(see 32.1 note).

111. *edge of Africa*: The eastern edge: see 19.3 and note.

112. *sweeping*: The etymology is Greek: the verb *syrein* means 'to
sweep along' and is virtually synonymous with the Latin *trahere*,
which Sallust uses here.

113. *Bocchus' daughter . . . married Jugurtha*: Or perhaps 'Jugurtha's
daughter had married Bocchus' (the manuscripts are divided).

114. *Perseus*: See *Hist.* 4.69.7 and note.

115. *peoples and kings*: I.e. those of friendly foreign nations.

116. *your . . . kindness*: See 31.16 note.

117. *ancestral images*: See 4.5 and note. (They are mentioned again
at 85.25, 29, 30, 38.)

118. *preposterous*: Literally, 'pre-posterous' means 'back to front':
Sallust explains the word in what follows, as the translation
attempts to show.

119. *honorific office*: Marius' consulship.

120. *being a master*: I.e. of slaves.

121. *furnishing a dinner-party . . . bailiff*: The historian Livy, writing
during the principate of Augustus (31 BC–AD 14), said that
luxurious living was imported to Rome in 187 with the triumph-
ant return of Roman troops from Asia Minor:

> It was then that lute-girls and female harpists and other delights of
> convivial entertainment [assumed to include actors] became the
> accompaniments of banquets; and banquets themselves began to be
> produced with greater care and expense. It was then that cooks, to
> the ancients the cheapest of menials in both estimation and use,
> began to be at a premium, and what had been a service activity
> began to be considered an art. (39.6.8–9)

122. *avarice, inexperience and haughtiness*: 'The nouns refer respectively to Bestia, Aulus Albinus and Metellus' (Summers).

123. *for their person alone*: There were at this period five 'classes',
which were based on property qualifications and comprised all
those liable for military service. Here Sallust refers to the
humblest in society who did not belong to a class but were

recorded by the state simply because they existed ('for their person alone'). Recruiting them for military service was not 'ancestral custom'.

124. *filling up . . . cohorts*: See *Cat.* 56.2.

125. *centuries*: 'A military unit of (nominally) 100 soldiers' (*OLD* 1).

126. *the very important function . . . realized*: Others render 'a very great quantity of bags had been produced'.

127. *divine*: Latin *diuinus* can mean 'second-sighted', 'foresighted', as well as 'divine'.

128. *shell*: The term (Latin *testudo*) is used either of a wooden screen to protect those engaged in siege operations or of a tightly packed group of soldiers holding their shields above themselves to form a shell-like covering.

129. *spent their time*: Deleting *dies noctisque* ('day and night').

130. *Sisenna . . . narrator*: L. Cornelius Sisenna, praetor in 78, wrote an account of the Social and Civil Wars (OCD, pp. 399–400). See also Introduction, p. xxv.

131. *apathy of his ancestors*: I.e. they had not been politically active.

132. *[. . .]*: Some words (e.g. 'he was respectful towards his intimates') seem to be missing from the text at this point.

133. *except . . . honourable*: Sallust's meaning is not at all clear, but Sulla's enthusiasm for 'other men's wives' appears to be referred to in *Hist.* (1.60, cf. 61). Sulla had five wives in all.

134. *Most fortunate*: Latin *felicissumo* alludes to the cognomen 'Felix' ('Fortunate') which Sulla acquired (see also *Hist.* 1.55.20).

135. *victory in the civil war*: In 82, when he defeated the younger Marius (son of the man in *Jug.*). See also *Cat.* 51.32 note. Sulla was regarded as the classic example of a man whose career fell into two parts, 'good' and 'bad' (as Sallust himself proceeds to say), the latter explained by the notorious proscriptions. See also *Cat.* 11.4.

136. *works*: I.e. earthworks, such as those involved in building ramparts.

137. *any good man*: A striking contrast with Marius himself (see 64.5, 84.1).

138. *gates*: Reading Lipsius' *portas* for the transmitted *porta*.

139. *at Numantia*: See 7.1–7.

140. *Balearic slingers . . . Paelignian cohort*: The inhabitants of the Balearic islands were famous for their skill in the use of slings. The Paeligni were a people of central Italy.

141. *to turn . . . naked and blind*: I.e. to show their backs to the enemy.

142. *his own father*: I.e. Volux' father, Bocchus.
143. *intended destination*: Viz. Bocchus' headquarters (see 105.1).
144. *Jugurtha's legate*: I.e. Aspar.
145. *common cause*: Of Bocchus and Sulla.
146. *Punic loyalty*: A byword at Rome for treachery.
147. *him*: I.e. Bocchus.
148. *it will always be untouched*: Gratitude is being imagined as an amount of money: no matter how much Sulla removes, Bocchus will always regard the amount as never having been touched.
149. *to himself*: I.e. to Jugurtha.
150. *immediately dismissed them*: Omitting *ceteris* (with some manuscripts).
151. *our quaestor*: I.e. Sulla.
152. *unsuccessful fight . . . Cn. Mallius*: The battle against the Cimbri took place at Arausio (modern-day Orange in France) on 6 October 105. Cn. Mallius Maximus was consul in that year, Q. Servilius Caepio consul in 106.
153. *Kalends of January*: 1 January (104).

Notes to *Histories*

1. *The affairs . . . here compiled*: Literally, 'I have compiled the affairs of the Roman people . . .' The year specified is 78.
2. *we*: Authorial plural, referring to Sallust himself.
3. *articulate man . . . few words*: The reference is to Cato the Elder (234–149), author of the *Origines* (the first historical work to be written in Latin), whose influence on Sallust was often mentioned in antiquity (see Introduction, p. xxvii).
4. *Macedonian war with Perseus*: The Third Macedonian War (171–168); Perseus was king of Macedon 179–168 (see 4.69.7 and note). There are variant readings, *primordio* and *principio*, for the word translated here as 'beginning': the former is used also by Livy in his preface (1), the latter by Tacitus in one of his (*Annals* 1.1.1).
5. *Gaul . . . had been subjugated*: The reference is to 51 and Julius Caesar's conquest of Gaul. For 'Our Sea' and the 'Ocean' (here the North Sea/English Channel) see *Jug.* 17.4 note.
6. *period between . . . Carthaginian war*: I.e. between 201 and 149.
7. *[. . .]*: The lacuna is thought to have contained a reference to the Roman fear of Carthage (the so-called *metus hostilis*, 'dread of the enemy': see *Cat.* 10.1; *Jug.* 41.2–3; *Hist.* 1.12).
8. *razing of Carthage*: In 146, when the Third Punic War ended.

9. *plebs' resultant secessions . . . fathers*: For the 'secessions of the plebs' see *Cat.* 33.3 note; there is another reference in the penultimate sentence of this fragment, where the plebs' two destinations are mentioned.

10. *Tarquinius . . . Etruria*: After the expulsion of Tarquinius Superbus in 510 (*Cat.* 6.7 note), Rome's last king joined forces with various communities in Etruria in an attempt at regaining power.

11. *about execution and flogging*: Literally, 'about life and hide [*or* back]'.

12. *Sacred Mount . . . Aventine*: The Sacred Mount, a hill northeast of Rome, and the Aventine, the southernmost hill of Rome.

13. *Second Punic War*: 218–201.

14. *names of fathers and plebs*: See *Cat.* 38.3.

15. *Lepidus . . . consul, to the Roman people*: M. Aemilius Lepidus was consul in 78. His speech is an attack on Sulla, who, despite having resigned his dictatorship by the end of 81 at the latest, is oddly represented as still in power (see Introduction, pp. xxvi–vii).

16. *progeny of the Bruti . . . Aemilii . . . Lutatii*: D. Iunius Brutus (consul 77), Mam. Aemilius Lepidus Livianus (consul 77) and Q. Lutatius Catulus (consular colleague, and enemy, of the speaker).

17. *Pyrrhus*: King of Epirus, fought against Rome 280–275.

18. *Philip and Antiochus*: See 4.69.5–6 and notes.

19. *Romulus*: In legend the founder and first king of Rome (traditionally 753–715), with whom Sulla is being ironically compared.

20. *injustice . . . more certain lot than life*: Sulla had ordained that the children of the proscribed were ineligible to hold office (see also *Cat.* 37.9).

21. *tranquillity with freedom*: A pre-echo of a phrase and concept (*otium cum dignitate*, 'tranquillity with dignity') which Cicero stressed in the mid-50s (*On behalf of Sestius* 98, *On the Orator* 1.1, *Letters to Friends* 1.9.21). See also section 25 below.

22. *citizenship . . . deeds*: Citizenship had been extended to the allies by various laws of 90 and 89 but the formalities of enrolment had not been carried out. When he landed in Italy, Sulla made an agreement to respect their rights and he seems to have kept his word, though he too did nothing to bring the process to completion (the new citizens were not finally enrolled until the census of 70). It is not clear whether Lepidus is making a tendentious reference to Sulla's omission or whether he is alluding to the dispossessed who had been on the wrong side in the civil war.

23. *Vettius ... Cornelius*: L. Vettius was an equestrian follower of Sulla and a man of dubious loyalties (*OCD*, p. 1593); Cornelius, a slave freed by Sulla, later became quaestor in 44 (Cicero, *De Officiis* 2.29).

24. *Cimbrian plunder*: See *Cat.* 59.3 and note.

25. *And the things ... rightful owners*: Both the text and meaning of this sentence are disputed.

26. *fortunate ... daring*: Reading *audeat* (Laetus' emendation of the transmitted *audeas*). With 'fortunate' Lepidus seems to be alluding to Sulla's cognomen Felix, 'Fortunate': see also *Jug.* 95.4.

27. *worst of slaves*: Nothing else is known of them.

28. *Fufidius*: Praetor in 81 and governor of Further Spain in 80.

29. *great column*: Of followers.

30. *parricide*: See *Cat.* 31.8 note.

31. *Philippus*: L. Marcius Philippus (consul in 91 and a supporter of Sulla) was now, in 77, leader of the senate (*princeps senatus*: cf. *Jug.* 25.4). His speech 'answers' that of Lepidus (*Hist.* 1.55 = 48), who was now leader of an armed revolt.

32. *muttering ... you defend it*: The precise meaning of this sentence is unclear.

33. *Etruria*: Area to the northwest of Rome and a base of Lepidus' support.

34. *Catulus*: Q. Lutatius Catulus, consul in 78 (*Hist.* 1.1): see 3.48.9, *Cat.* 34.3 and elsewhere.

35. *Saturninus ... Damasippus*: L. Appuleius Saturninus was tribune in 103 and 100, P. Sulpicius was tribune in 88 (see *OCD*, pp. 130–31 and 1455 respectively); for the younger Marius and L. Iunius Brutus Damasippus see *Cat.* 51.32 and note.

36. *Mithridates*: Mithridates VI, king of Pontus (see further 4.69).

37. *You are the most wicked ... of all men!*: From here to the end of the paragraph Philippus addresses Lepidus directly.

38. *them*: Philippus means Lepidus' own supporters.

39. *for how long ... endure*: A pre-echo of the famous opening of Cicero's First Catilinarian speech (see *Cat.* 20.9 and note).

40. *he realizes*: Reading *intellegat* (Steup's emendation of the transmitted *intelleget*).

41. *Cinna ... perished*: In 87, the year of his consulship, L. Cornelius Cinna was driven out of Rome but later marched on the city and took his revenge by killing some of the leading men who were his enemies (here described as 'the glory of the senate').

42. *Cethegus*: P. Cornelius Cethegus had been a supporter of Sulla

and was a powerful figure of the time. The relationship (if any) between him and the Catilinarian conspirator C. Cornelius Cethegus (*Cat.* 17.3 etc.) is unknown.

43. *do their utmost ... damage*: Philippus is proposing the *senatus consultum ultimum* (see *Cat.* 29.2 and note). Ap. Claudius Pulcher had been consul in 79; for the emergency office of interrex see *OCD*, pp. 761–2.

44. *He was ... arms*: The reference is to Q. Sertorius, praetor in 83 and now leader of a revolt in Spain; for both him and T. Didius (consul 98) see *OCD*, pp. 1393 and 466 respectively. The 'Marsic War' is the Social War (91–87).

45. *writers' jealousy*: Cf. *Cat.* 3.2.

46. *C. Cotta*: C. Aurelius Cotta was consul in 75 and a distinguished orator.

47. *changed his clothing*: A sign of mourning or dire straits.

48. *[...]*: The text is corrupt and no satisfactory emendation has been proposed.

49. *parricide*: See *Cat.* 31.8 note.

50. *born a second time*: Cotta had gone into exile as a result of the Lex Varia of 90; this is a reference to his return in 82.

51. *both it*: I.e. the commonwealth.

52. *Sertorius' flight through the mountains*: Sertorius was famous for his adoption of guerrilla tactics.

53. *I promise ... commonwealth*: Cotta is referring to the practice of *deuotio* or self-sacrifice (*OCD*, p. 460), saying that he will offer no resistance if the plebs should turn on him and kill him. As an example of the level of violence at this time see *Hist.* 2.45: 'as both consuls by chance were escorting Q. Metellus, a praetorian candidate who afterwards had the designation "Creticus", down the Sacred Way, with a great commotion the plebs attacked them and, as they fled, pursued them to Octavius' house ...'

54. *Metellus ... after a year*: Q. Caecilius Metellus Pius, already mentioned at *Jug.* 64.4, had been consul in 80 with Sulla; he was subsequently sent to fight Sertorius in Spain. The present fragment is set in 74.

55. *fight ... from both sides*: The enemy forces (the Isaurians, in Asia Minor) are evidently divided into two. (The year is 75.)

56. *Servilius*: P. Servilius Vatia, consul in 79, later acquired the *cognomen* 'Isauricus' for his successes in this campaign.

57. *dispatch*: I.e. of the hostages.

58. *their*: I.e. the soldiers'. Cf. *Jug.* 29.4 note.

59.   *had been done*: By the besieged.

60.   *the town of Isaura*: Reading *in Isauram oppidum* for *in fugam oppidi*.

61.   *Great Mother*: The goddess Cybele.

62.   *Cn. Pompeius*: In 77 Pompey had been sent to Spain to help Q. Metellus Pius (see 2.70 note) in the fight against Sertorius. The present letter, which is of course Sallust's own composition, is from the narrative of 75.

63.   *them*: I.e. the Alps.

64.   *Lacetania ... Indigetes*: Respectively a district and a people in northeast Spain.

65.   *Sucro ... Valentia*: Valentia is modern-day Valencia, and the Turia is the river which runs through it; it is not clear whether Sucro is also a river (modern Júcar, which flows into the Mediterranean just south of Valencia) or, as translated, the homonymous town. Gaius Herennius, tribune in 80, was a supporter of Sertorius.

66.   *following year*: I.e. 74.

67.   *Cotta ... Cilicia*: The consuls of 75 were C. Aurelius Cotta (see 2.47 note) and L. Octavius. Cilicia was a province in southern Asia Minor.

68.   *Lucullus ... Cotta*: L. Licinius Lucullus, famous as a gourmet, went on to become a famous general; M. Aurelius Cotta was brother of the consul of 75 (for whom see previous note).

69.   *matched their speech with their deeds*: The text is uncertain.

70.   *Macer*: C. Licinius Macer was tribune of the plebs in 73; he was also a historian, whose work has survived only in fragments.

71.   *secession from the fathers*: For this (again at section 17) see *Hist.* 1.11 and *Cat.* 33.3 note.

72.   *empty semblance of a magistracy*: Sulla had deprived the tribunes of their power.

73.   *restored ... rights*: A reference to the Lex Aurelia on tribunician power of 75, the year of Cotta's consulship (see 2.47).

74.   *L. Sicinius ... it*: A reference to the year 76 (see note 76 below); Sicinius' first name is given as Gnaeus at Cicero, *Brutus* 216.

75.   *Catulus*: Consul in 78 (see 1.1 and 1.77.6 note).

76.   *Brutus ... blameless tribune*: D. Iunius Brutus (cf. 1.55.3) and Mam. Aemilius Lepidus Livianus were consuls in 77; as consul in 76, C. Scribonius Curio opposed and evidently eliminated Sicinius, the 'blameless tribune'.

77.   *last year*: L. Licinius Lucullus was consul in 74 (see 2.98), the year in which L. Quintius was tribune.

78. *both sides*: For the phrase here and in the following sentence see 1.12 and note.

79. *that itself*: The reference is to the misnamed 'tranquillity', just mentioned.

80. *injustice is safer for its gravity*: Cf. *Jug.* 31.14: 'the worst of evil-doers are the safest'.

81. *the law of nations*: See *Jug.* 22.4 note.

82. *ancestral images*: See *Jug.* 4.5 and note.

83. *grain law ... at five measures*: In 73 the consuls M. Terentius Varro Lucullus and C. Cassius Longinus passed a law distributing five measures of grain a month to the urban plebs.

84. *lifted onto their shoulders*: The metaphor is derived from carrying someone aloft in a litter.

85. *initiator*: In the sense of Pompey's being a proposer of the restoration of the tribunes' power. This did indeed happen in 70, the year of his consulship (see *Cat.* 38.1), but whether he was already committed to this step in 73 is unclear.

86. *Mithridates*: the king of Pontus urges Phraates III of Parthia (Arsaces is a dynastic name) to join him in the fight against Rome (the Third Mithridatic War). The year is probably 69.

87. *Tigranes ... war*: Tigranes I, king of Armenia, had been expanding his kingdom at Parthia's expense.

88. *war ... Macedonians*: The Second Macedonian War against Philip V was 200–197.

89. *Antiochus ... talents*: Antiochus III, king of Syria, was defeated twice by Rome in 191–190.

90. *Samothracian gods*: After the Third Macedonian War, Perseus sought asylum at a temple on the island of Samothrace, where he engaged in a formal surrender to the Romans.

91. *sleeplessness*: For the story of sleep deprivation see Plutarch, *Aemilius Paulus* 37.2.

92. *Eumenes ... Asia*: Eumenes II, king of Pergamum, died *c.* 160 and was succeeded by Attalus III, who bequeathed the kingdom to Rome in his will (133). Aristonicus, an illegitimate son of Eumenes, seized control of the kingdom but was defeated by Rome (130–129). Pergamum became the Roman province of Asia.

93. *Bithynia ... offspring*: The kingdom of Bithynia in northwest Asia Minor was bequeathed by its last king, Nicomedes IV Philopator, to Rome on his death in 75 or 74 (*OCD*, pp. 244–5, 1043).

94. *war with Nicomedes*: The First Mithridatic War (88–85).

95. *Ptolemy*: Ptolemy VIII of Egypt.
96. *Archelaus*: A general of Mithridates who deserted to Rome (83).
97. *Ptolemy . . . price*: Ptolemy XI spent over twenty years (81–59) trying to formalize a friendship with Rome.
98. *Cretans . . . razed*: The first attack on Crete was in 74; further attacks in 69–67 resulted in its becoming a Roman province.
99. *started war . . . fleet*: The Third Mithridatic War started in 74, the year when M. Cotta was consul (see 2.98.10). Chalcedon is a city on the Asian side of the Bosporus, opposite Byzantium.
100. *Cyzicus*: City on the southern shore of the Propontis (modern-day Sea of Marmara). See *OCD*, pp. 423–4.
101. *Parium . . . Heraclea*: Parium (modern-day Kemer) was also on the southern shore of the Propontis, near the entrance to the Hellespont; Heraclea was on the southern shore of the Black Sea (*OCD*, pp. 1113 and 684).
102. *Cabera*: A stronghold of Mithridates in the kingdom of Pontus and in 72 the site of a battle won by the Roman commander Lucullus.
103. *kingdom of Ariobarzanes*: Cappadocia.
104. *withdrew . . . victory*: A reference to operations near Tigranocerta (modern-day Silvan) in Armenia in 69.
105. *plague*: Reading *pesti* (R. H. Martin) for the transmitted *peste* or *pestem*.
106. *Seleucea*: City on the River Tigris, originally founded by King Seleucus I in the late fourth century, became one of the great cities of the Hellenistic world. It was conquered by Parthia in 141 (*OCD*, p. 1380).

Maps

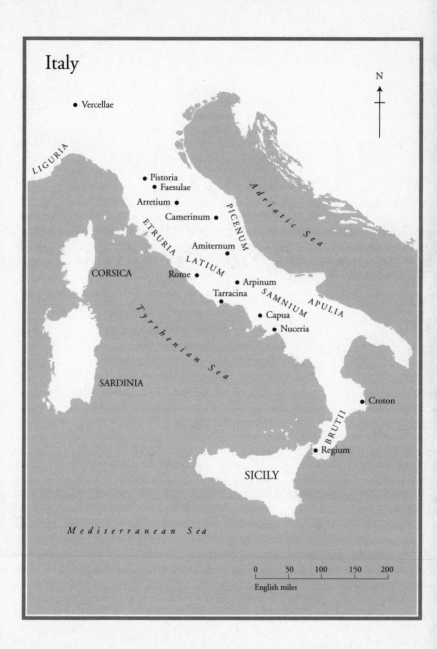

Italy

N

Vercellae

LIGURIA

Pistoria
Faesulae
Arretium
Camerinum

PICENUM

Adriatic Sea

ETRURIA

Amiternum

LATIUM

CORSICA

Rome
Tarracina
Arpinum

SAMNIUM

APULIA

Capua
Nuceria

Tyrrhenian Sea

SARDINIA

Croton

BRUTII

Regium

SICILY

Mediterranean Sea

0   50   100   150   200

English miles

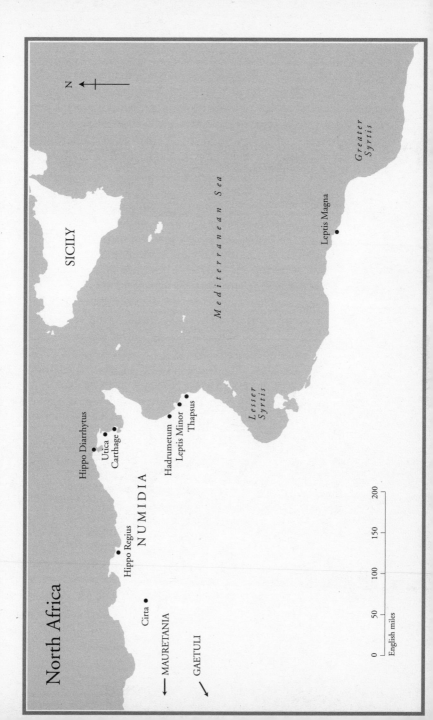

North Africa

SICILY

Mediterranean Sea

Greater Syrtis

Leptis Magna

Lesser Syrtis

Hippo Diarrhytus
Utica
Carthage

Hadrumetum
Leptis Minor
Thapsus

N U M I D I A

Hippo Regius

Cirta

MAURETANIA

GAETULI

N

| | | | | |
0   50   100   150   200
English miles

Index of Names, Peoples and Places

Notes. Romans are generally, but not always, listed by their family names (thus 'Tullius Cicero, Marcus' rather than 'Cicero'); cos. = consul; pr. = praetor; qu. = quaestor; tr. pl. = tribune of the plebs. All dates are BC unless stated otherwise.

PENGUIN CLASSICS

THE CAMPAIGNS OF ALEXANDER
ARRIAN

'His passion was for glory only, and in that he was insatiable'

Although written over four hundred years after Alexander's death, Arrian's *Campaigns of Alexander* is the most reliable account of the man and his achievements we have. Arrian's own experience as a military commander gave him unique insights into the life of the world's greatest conqueror. He tells of Alexander's violent suppression of the Theban rebellion, his total defeat of Persia, and his campaigns through Egypt, India and Babylon – establishing new cities and destroying others in his path. While Alexander emerges from this record as an unparalleled and charismatic leader, Arrian succeeds brilliantly in creating an objective and fully rounded portrait of a man of boundless ambition, who was exposed to the temptations of power and worshipped as a god in his own lifetime.

Aubrey de Sélincourt's vivid translation is accompanied by J. R. Hamilton's introduction, which discusses Arrian's life and times, his synthesis of other classical sources and the composition of Alexander's army. This edition also includes maps, a list for further reading and a detailed index.

Translated by Aubrey de Sélincourt
Revised, with a new introduction and notes by J. R. Hamilton

PENGUIN CLASSICS

THE CONQUEST OF GAUL
CAESAR

'The enemy were overpowered and took to flight.
The Romans pursued as far as their strength enabled them to run'

Between 58 and 50 BC Julius Caesar conquered most of the area now covered by France, Belgium and Switzerland, and invaded Britain twice, and *The Conquest of Gaul* is his record of these campaigns. Caesar's narrative offers insights into his military strategy and paints a fascinating picture of his encounters with the inhabitants of Gaul and Britain, as well as lively portraits of the rebel leader Vercingetorix and other Gallic chieftains. *The Conquest of Gaul* can also be read as a piece of political propaganda, as Caesar sets down his version of events for the Roman public, knowing he faces civil war on his return to Rome.

Revised and updated by Jane Gardner, S. A. Handford's translation brings Caesar's lucid and exciting account to life for modern readers. This volume includes a glossary of persons and places, maps, appendices and suggestions for further reading.

Translated by S. A. Handford
Revised with a new introduction by Jane F. Gardner

PENGUIN CLASSICS

THE ANNALS OF IMPERIAL ROME
TACITUS

'Nero was already corrupted by every lust, natural and unnatural'

The Annals of Imperial Rome recount the major historical events from the years
shortly before the death of Augustus to the death of Nero in AD 68. With clarity
and vivid intensity Tacitus describes the reign of terror under the corrupt Tiberius,
the great fire of Rome during the time of Nero and the wars, poisonings, scandals,
conspiracies and murders that were part of imperial life. Despite his claim that
the *Annals* were written objectively, Tacitus' account is sharply critical of the
emperors' excesses and fearful for the future of imperial Rome, while also filled
with a longing for its past glories.

Michael Grant's fine translation captures the moral tone, astringent wit and stylish
vigour of the original. His introduction discusses the life and works of Tacitus and
the historical context of the *Annals*. This edition also contains a key to place names
and technical terms, maps, tables and suggestions for further reading.

Translated with an introduction by Michael Grant

PENGUIN CLASSICS

THE AGRICOLA *AND* THE GERMANIA
TACITUS

> 'Happy indeed were you, Agricola,
> not only in your glorious life but in your timely death'

The Agricola is both a portrait of Julius Agricola – the most famous governor of Roman Britain and Tacitus' well-loved and respected father-in-law – and the first detailed account of Britain that has come down to us. It offers fascinating descriptions of the geography, climate and peoples of the country, and a succinct account of the early stages of the Roman occupation, nearly fatally undermined by Boudicca's revolt in AD 61 but consolidated by campaigns that took Agricola as far as Anglesey and northern Scotland. The warlike German tribes are the focus of Tacitus' attention in *The Germania*, which, like *The Agricola*, often compares the behaviour of 'barbarian' peoples favourably with the decadence and corruption of Imperial Rome.

Harold Mattingly's translation brings Tacitus' extravagant imagination and incisive wit vividly to life. In his introduction, he examines Tacitus' life and literary career, the governorship of Agricola, and the political background of Rome's rapidly expanding Empire. This edition also includes a select bibliography, and maps of Roman Britain and Germany.

Translated with an introduction by H. Mattingly
Translation revised by S. A. Handford

PENGUIN CLASSICS

METAMORPHOSES
OVID

'Her soft white bosom was ringed in a layer of bark,
her hair was turned into foliage, her arms into branches'

Ovid's sensuous and witty poem brings together a dazzling array of mythological tales, ingeniously linked by the idea of transformation – often as a result of love or lust – where men and women find themselves magically changed into new and sometimes extraordinary beings. Beginning with the creation of the world and ending with the deification of Augustus, Ovid interweaves many of the best-known myths and legends of ancient Greece and Rome, including the stories of Daedalus and Icarus, Pyramus and Thisbe, Pygmalion, Perseus and Andromeda, and the Fall of Troy. Erudite but light-hearted, dramatic and yet playful, the *Metamorphoses* has influenced writers and artists throughout the centuries from Shakespeare and Titian to Picasso and Ted Hughes.

This lively, accessible new translation by David Raeburn is in hexameter verse form, which brilliantly captures the energy and spontaneity of the original. The edition contains an introduction discussing the life and work of Ovid as well as a preface to each book, explanatory notes and an index of people, gods and places.

A new verse translation by David Raeburn with an introduction by Denis Feeney

PENGUIN CLASSICS

THE LETTERS OF THE YOUNGER PLINY

'Of course these details are not important enough for history ...
you have only yourself to blame for asking for them'

A prominent lawyer and administrator, Pliny (*c.* AD 61–113) was also a prolific
letter-writer, who numbered among his correspondents such eminent figures as
Tacitus, Suetonius and the Emperor Trajan, as well as a wide circle of friends and
family. His lively and very personal letters address an astonishing range of topics,
from a deeply moving account of his uncle's death in the eruption that engulfed
Pompeii and observations on the early Christians – 'a desperate sort of cult carried
to extravagant lengths' – to descriptions of everyday life in Rome, with its scandals
and court cases, and of his own life in the country. Providing a series of fascinating
views of imperial Rome, his letters also offer one of the fullest self-portraits to
survive from classical times.

Betty Radice's definitive edition was the first complete modern translation
of Pliny's letters. In her introduction, she examines the shrewd, tolerant and
occasionally pompous man who emerges from these.

Translated with an introduction by Betty Radice

THE STORY OF PENGUIN CLASSICS

Before 1946 ... 'Classics' are mainly the domain of academics and students; readable editions for everyone else are almost unheard of. This all changes when a little-known classicist, E. V. Rieu, presents Penguin founder Allen Lane with the translation of Homer's *Odyssey* that he has been working on in his spare time.

1946 Penguin Classics debuts with *The Odyssey*, which promptly sells three million copies. Suddenly, classics are no longer for the privileged few.

1950s Rieu, now series editor, turns to professional writers for the best modern, readable translations, including Dorothy L. Sayers's *Inferno* and Robert Graves's unexpurgated *Twelve Caesars*.

1960s The Classics are given the distinctive black covers that have remained a constant throughout the life of the series. Rieu retires in 1964, hailing the Penguin Classics list as 'the greatest educative force of the twentieth century.'

1970s A new generation of translators swells the Penguin Classics ranks, introducing readers of English to classics of world literature from more than twenty languages. The list grows to encompass more history, philosophy, science, religion and politics.

1980s The Penguin American Library launches with titles such as *Uncle Tom's Cabin*, and joins forces with Penguin Classics to provide the most comprehensive library of world literature available from any paperback publisher.

1990s The launch of Penguin Audiobooks brings the classics to a listening audience for the first time, and in 1999 the worldwide launch of the Penguin Classics website extends their reach to the global online community.

The 21st Century Penguin Classics are completely redesigned for the first time in nearly twenty years. This world-famous series now consists of more than 1300 titles, making the widest range of the best books ever written available to millions – and constantly redefining what makes a 'classic'.

The Odyssey continues ...

The best books ever written

PENGUIN CLASSICS

SINCE 1946

Find out more at www.penguinclassics.com